Graceful Battle

Gary Confer

ISBN: 145059025X
ISBN-13: 9781450590259

ACKNOWLEDGMENTS

During our life's journey, we are sometimes the shepherd and sometimes the sheep. My life has been no exception although I recognize that I have spent much more time crawling on all fours in need of direction, rather than walking upright providing safety and guidance to others. It is the essence of the nurturing life; one hand to reach for help, the other to lend a hand—an unbroken chain that gets us all through life.

There are many who deserve my deepest and most heartfelt appreciation. Cristina Norcross—a friend, an accomplished poet, and my mentor in the craft and art of writing. Within this book is a poem she wrote for Lauri. Matthew and Megan—their hands, hearts, and minds helped shape the content and the character of this work. Cindy Davis—who provided an editorial eye and ear which compensated for my own insufficient literary senses.

While not recognized by actual names in this book, a multitude of family members and friends provided Lauri and me with a limitless amount of love and support during her graceful battle. Their sturdy backs and comforting souls continue to carry me along.

Finally, my eternal thanks to Lauri for teaching me that just as sure as a sunrise will be followed by a sunset, so too will a sunset be followed by a sunrise.

FORWARD

My wife, Lauri, died of pancreatic cancer on July 12, 2008. She was forty-eight years old. Time may heal all wounds, but it does so by leaving a scar, a visual and emotional reminder that we will never again be the same.

A common thread that runs through the fabric of humanity regardless of ethnic, social, religious, or any other characterization of diversity, is that at some time in life, we are all exposed to tragedy and loss. It is a universal commonality that neither recognizes nor respects any boundary, whether physical or psychological.

The only saving grace associated with loss is that it is unmistakably and intimately related to gain. You cannot feel the black hole depths of unimaginable despair, unless you have also risen to the pinnacle of happiness and delight. It is an undeniable truism that unless you know light, you would not fear the darkness. The comfort of warmth embraces your body and soul because you have experienced the isolation of the cold. This is why losing a loved one is so gut wrenchingly painful. The loss pulls at every thread of your being, striving to unravel the entire tapestry of your existence. You feel as though you can't go on because you have lost the consistency of matter that binds you together.

What stitches you back together over time is recognition and reflection on the gain, the good times you shared, and the joyful memories you created. By mentally resurrecting their smile, their soothing touch, the essence of their being, you use this positive and life giving energy to reconstruct and sustain your own life. You can see your loved one's spirit and form carried on by those who were closest to them. Maybe the mother and daughter shared the same emerald twinkle in their eyes. Maybe the father and son shared the same bold, chiseled jaw. It is these inherited or acquired gems that span the generations and allow us to re-experience a treasure from our past. It is either by the reality of ongoing life, or by the warmth and love we resurrect from memories, that we garner the strength to go on living. We don't heal by forgetting. We mend by remembering.

During our initial battle with her cancer, Lauri and I were convinced her life expectancy was measured in only a few short months. Being a physician gave me keen insight into the challenges we faced. This intimate knowledge was at times a blessing, and at times a curse. The realignment of one's priorities that follows such news is both partly instinctual and partly learned. During this adjustment, and in the face of little hope of successful medical intervention, I pondered what I could give Lauri at such a desperate and desolate time. There are many instances in life when mere mortal intervention is woefully insufficient to sustain us.

What Lauri lacked most of all was a secure future. My first thought was to attempt to give her one. College graduations, weddings, grandchildren, and so many other experiences were now shrouded in a cloud of uncertainty. During Lauri's darkest hours, we shared our hopes and dreams for life after death, a future free from terminal cancer. When earthly hope is beyond our grasp, heavenly thoughts become as permanent and optimistic as the lifelines on the palms of our own hands.

I composed the following pages with justifiable concern as they are filled with very personal and intimate details of our life and beliefs. All of the names, except Lauri's and mine, were changed to retain the anonymity and privacy of those who shared this journey with us. While our five children provided immeasurable support and comfort to Lauri and me during this most challenging of times in both our lives, I chose to protect their privacy by only including limited details of their involvement and few personal details about them. They were, and remain, the five most treasured individuals in my and Lauri's life.

The idea for this book was conceived while Lauri was alive. We had many discussions about life and the afterlife as these two issues represented daily contemplations for both of us. Lauri experienced some comfort from our spiritual reflections. It was her hope that others might benefit as well.

Lauri and I recognized that some individuals who read this book would themselves be struggling against cancer. Like Lauri, they might not have the stamina to read the entire story. Therefore, the most spiritual portion of the work, Chapter 43 through the end, can be read independent of the remainder of the book.

I wrote the majority of the book after Lauri's passing. It was my wish that it might lend some meaning to her death. Her life, as she lived it, needed no such help. I chose to make it personal because I wanted it to be authentic. This story, as a reflection of life as we all live it, is composed of part fact, part fiction, and part faith.

I was once told that it is no coincidence we are blessed with two hands. We are given one hand to receive gifts from others, and one hand to pass those gifts on. Lauri was a precious gift given to me. She enriched my life in ways that no words can ever do justice. This narrative is my gift of a future to her. It is an attempt to shed light on a time of darkness. It was Lauri's hope that others might glean the same comfort and peace that these words and beliefs brought to her. This book is her gift to you.

chapter 1

LAURI'S HEART LEAPT into her throat as a disjointed chorus of honking horns pierced the motionless serenity of the stagnant bumper-to-bumper traffic. Her commute north to New Hampshire, "God's Country", as Gary half jokingly referred to it, consisted of an inch by inch asphalt escape from Boston, the accelerator having as much utility as a hood ornament. Cars were locked in a molasses-based serpentine ballet that snaked for miles. Most often, lateral movements exceeded forward progress.

As her right hand searched the cavernous spaces of the center console for a compact disc, Lauri silently gave thanks that her fiancé wasn't traveling with her. While there were few circumstances that irritated Gary, being helplessly confined in rush hour gridlock pushed every one of his hot buttons. He would have opted for a sharp stick in the eye, a catastrophic career ending injury for a radiologist.

For Lauri, traffic, like most irritations in life, was accepted as an inconvenience without embracing the frustration. Lauri had a Teflon attitude. As she pulled out a compact disc, the frosty breeze from the air conditioner made her shiver. The unblemished surface of her exposed forearm became roughened with a field of blossoming goosebumps as she slid the shining metal disc into the slot. She pushed the play button, cranked the knob to the right, and then let her hand fall to the temperature controls. *Music full blast, air conditioning off.*

Lauri engaged the window control, allowing the outside warmth to buffer the interior coolness. The air, tainted with exhaust fumes, muted the pleasant aroma of the vanilla air freshener. As she looked to her left, Lauri witnessed the breathtaking and familiar skyline of Boston in the side mirror. Her life, her entire life, was connected to this city: born there, fished the waters of the harbor with her father (always allowing her dad to bait the hook), shopped the stores for hours with her mother and friends, danced away the night in clubs during her youth, and spent her entire adult life working there. The city was full of memories, all good. In the near future, Lauri's relationship with the city would involve an intimacy with the elite medical facilities that she could have never dreamed of.

A beautiful day. Others were less thrilled. At ninety-five degrees and ninety percent humidity, the thickness of the air required a focused effort to inhale and exhale. Lauri considered this weather to be a gift, a glorious relief from the frigid northeastern winters. For her, summer was an all too brief pause on the calendar. If only she could suspend the orbit of the Earth around the sun at its current location, her life would be perfect. Not too much to ask for, she thought, as she motored up Route 3, leaving her lifelong residence in Massachusetts for a new life in New Hampshire. The irony was not lost in her mind. She never imagined leaving the Bay State, and she was literally stunned to be heading north rather than south. While Florida would have been a more appropriate destination for her body with its attraction for warmth and sunshine, superior needs beckoned. Her heart quite literally drove her north to the Granite State.

Paige, Lauri's youngest, and Jack, Gary's last born, had both completed the rite of passage from adolescence to early adulthood; they graduated from high school. Lauri stressed over the decision to uproot her family and move north. Like most parents, the wants and needs of her children were the primary compass that directed most of life's decisions. She and Gary had committed to each other in many ways over the past five years of long distance dating, but their greatest and most unalterable conviction was to respect and accept their mutual and primary attachment to their offspring. It was summer, just beyond the weeks of graduation, and now the two parents were embracing their own rite of passage as they moved in together. In six months they would be tying the knot and making the most cherished New Year's resolution of all to each other.

The melding of the two families was not seamless, but the basic fabric was strong with years of stitched together triumph and tribulation behind them. They selected Nashua as the physical location to germinate their new, intertwined family roots, as it was equidistant to Lauri's employment in downtown Boston and Gary's hospital radiology practice. With each parent working full-time and commuting an hour each way, coupled with five spirited children between 18 and 23 years of age, dull moments would be a rare but welcome occurrence.

Lauri joyously sang her favorite Christmas song as she had mistakenly loaded a seasonally inappropriate compact disc into the car's sound system. She loved the holidays. It was sheer joy to echo the festive tunes without the more typical chaotic meteorological trappings.

Despite the moistening heat and crushing fatigue from the one-hour ride home, Lauri was smiling. She was thankful for her new life, and hey, in another half orbit around the sun, it would be Christmas.

"Hey Baby, I'm home," Lauri called out, as she stepped into the foyer. The greeting resonated off of the marble floor and up the flight of stairs to the main level of the three and a half story condo she now shared with Gary. He had worked a 24-hour call shift at the hospital which ended at 7 a.m. that morning. He returned home after Lauri had already begun her morning commute to Boston. They were in the earliest phase of adjusting to cohabitation; a lifestyle neither had embraced for over seven years.

Gary's form came into gradual view as he crossed the hardwood floor and stopped at the top of stairs. He grinned, spying his new housemate bending over to release her overstuffed leather attaché weighted down with the day's toil. Her willowy frame allowed Lauri to flex down and recoil with ease, causing her mid-length, tastefully styled blonde hair to first cascade forward and than fall back, revealing the smooth curves of a tranquil face. The light entering from the leaded glass sidelights and the arched window above the front door silhouetted her enticing form. Rays of sunshine rained down from above through the large skylight and reflected off her crystal blue eyes.

As when they first met, Gary was slightly stunned by her not so subtle beauty. "Hey Baby," he said. "How was your day?"

"Really good." Lauri's tone lacked genuine enthusiasm. "A drink would be nice."

Gary recognized her ingrained habit of forcing the glass to be half full. He knew she was fatigued from the extended commute, one of the sacrifices made for love. "Will martinis do the trick? Ready in two shakes, not stirs. Meet me on the deck."

Lauri smiled up at her fiancé who was barefoot, in Bermuda shorts, and wearing a white tee shirt with CANCUN stenciled across the chest. His broad muscular shoulders slightly stretched the fabric. Unfortunately, the extra fifteen pounds centered at the gut level did the same. He had a typical, mid-life, former jock body. He was on the cusp of male pattern baldness with distinguished, as Lauri called it, graying brown hair at the temples. With the gradual loss of top cover, he chose to have Lauri cut his hair shorter and shorter, rather than attempt to disguise the baring of his scalp. Lauri felt he had mature, rugged, good looks.

"Okay. That sounds great," Lauri said, as a true calmness settled in. Her relationship with Gary had smoothed all of the sharp corners in her life. His presence had a way of absorbing many of her burdens. She was home, in their home, and life really was good. "Any news from the kids?" Lauri's rejuvenated intonation shifted from drawn to maternally inquisitive.

"No." Gary's reply was somewhat muffled as he turned and headed to the kitchen to combine the vodka, citrus liquor and ice using the preferred method of a famous British secret agent.

Lauri climbed the multiple flights of stairs from the entry to the top floor master bedroom and reflected on how busy the new household would be this summer. Nick R, 23 years of age and

Lauri's oldest, had recently graduated from college and would be living with them, working and saving money with hope of acquiring his own place very soon. Nick C, 20 years old and Gary's oldest, would be splitting his residence between his parents' homes, spending the weekdays with his dad and Lauri, as it was a shorter commute to Boston for his summer internship in the financial district. Lauri chuckled to herself, recalling the ongoing confusion caused by them each choosing to name their first child Nicholas. Who would have known that two decades later they would be blending a second family with two boys of the same name? They were careful to refer to them as Nick R or Nick C.

Ben, Lauri's 20-year-old, middle child, would be off to Martha's Vineyard in a couple of weeks to work as a traffic officer, padding his résumé for future employment in the law enforcement field. Jack, 18 years old and Gary's youngest, had a local summer job prior to beginning college. He stayed in tune with his high school musician buddies with hope of landing a gig or two. Paige, eighteen, the baby of Lauri's children and the lone female of the brood, would soon be off to her counselor position at an all girls' summer camp, the envy of her four "brothers." For her, it was a welcome relief from the overbearing attention of the male dominated family. Full belly laughs and heart straining challenges were sure to be plentiful for this soon-to-be second marriage entourage.

"You're looking more comfortable," Gary said, as Lauri stepped onto the deck.

"Oh, I thought you'd like this skimpy little thing." Lauri cast a coy smile at her new roommate and slid down into the stretch fabric patio chair, lifting up her shaken, not stirred, martini. "Thanks." She sipped the cool, soothing liquid, anticipating its calming effect. "I may need another." Lauri crossed her long, slender legs, and began rocking her right leg to and fro. "How was your call?"

"Routine. Lots of trauma cases through the ER. Best thing is that it's over." Gary's post-call day off was always a welcome drudgery. It was a great opportunity to check off items from the errand list, but as a consequence of prolonged sleep deprivation, he wandered around in a fog, a fugue of the mental, not musical variety.

Gary rarely recounted his work demands at home as all it seemed to do was accentuate a bad experience without any beneficial relief. He made of point of going into detail if there was some instructive value for the kids, such as an alcohol-related accident with severe or fatal injuries. His commanding rendition of the heartbreaking emotional and gory physical details both figuratively, and literally, drove the point home. By design, his dramatic, and at times melodramatic, display was enough to nauseate and frighten the listener. He believed that parenting at times required scaring your children into awareness, and hopefully into compliance.

Gary had moved into the four-bedroom condo on the fifteenth fairway eighteen months earlier. The expansive and sun drenched spaces were a necessity for the volume of familial traffic. Lauri thrust her heart and soul into the dwelling. The tender loving touch of her decorating instincts was obvious to any visitor. Gary didn't understand the necessity of having such a vibrant mixture of colors and textures. It took him months to adjust to the deep velvet red walls in the kitchen and dining room. However, it was certainly a benefit not to be able to discern spaghetti sauce splatter against the initially disturbing marinara-like background. He thought it might be prudent to purchase some shirts in that particular shade.

The interior was admirably complemented by Lauri's assortment of blooming plants outside the home. The corners of the lower porch were accented with two large ceramic planters overflowing with an assortment of flowering plants and greens. The two upper decks, one off of the living room and the other on the third floor off the master bedroom, were adorned with metal flower baskets hung along the edge of the railing. They perpetually blossomed from May to October, much to the pleasure of the golfers as they struggled from the 15th tee to green. Friends' and neighbors' comments that the multi-level façade facing the course was reminiscent of a Tuscan villa in summer brought intense pride and pleasure to Lauri.

She gazed eastward over the deck railing and the scent of freshly cut grass filled the air. "I love this place. I fell in love with the view and knew we would spend hours sitting out here. Don't you just love it?"

"I do." Gary turned toward Lauri as he stood in front of the grill sweating. "Now, those are two words that have gotten a lot of guys into trouble."

Lauri crinkled her nose, rocked her head from side to side, and flashed a playful tight-lipped grin at him. "If you think it's hot now, just wait."

Gary chuckled as he closed the lid on the grill. He stepped toward Lauri, bending over and tenderly kissing her forehead. "You know I'm kidding. I can't wait to marry you."

A deafening crack interrupted the banter as a titanium driver connected with a golf ball at the 15th tee to their right. The white, dimpled sphere jettisoned off the tee at breakneck speed, and headed north up the fairway on the challenging par 4 hole. The couple appreciated the high-pitched whishing sound, indicating that they were already out of harm's way. Their home sat barely beyond the manicured grass of the tee box. It would take a laughingly poor shot to put them at risk of being hit. The couple was accustomed to the previously jarring sound, having spent many hours outside on the deck. Repetition had bred indifference. They were acclimated to the point where the piercing intrusion barely elevated their heart rate.

Gary slid around the glass table and sat across from his bride-to-be. Lauri grasped the hand painted martini glass and gently spun it around, admiring the vibrant tropical colors of the toucans adorning its surface. She successfully negotiated "a deal" with a vendor in Mexico for a set of two of these unique items. The other glass, currently nursing the doctor to her right, bore depictions of the sunrise and sunset. She was so excited after the friendly and engaging exchange with the pleasant middle-aged Mexican gentleman who repeatedly replied, "No, siñorita, not enough." Gary pretended to be looking at other items in the shop while Lauri and the proprietor debated the value of the wares. Judging by the broad smiles on both of their faces, Gary knew both the buyer and the seller were happy with their transaction.

8

Lauri lifted her glass and extended her arm toward her future husband. Like many couples preparing for their second marriage, compatibility was as essential as the emotional ties that bind. Their love had grown at a steady pace and they were confident of themselves and each other. Their wedding was six months off, they were in love, and they wanted to be together for the rest of their lives. Gary reached toward Lauri with his glass, and as optimism of the sunrise touched the beauty of the toucan, a melodious ring tone heralded their new beginning.

chapter 2

THE SWELTERING HEAT of mid-July even caused the plants to sweat. Like many couples, Lauri and Gary were incompatible when it came to defining a comfortable temperature. Venus loved it hot, and Mars loved it cool. They compromised inside with the air conditioning set with Gary on the verge of perspiring, and Lauri on the verge of shivering.

"If we don't get out of here, we're gonna hit traffic," Gary shouted, his voice fading as it climbed to the top floor.

"I'm coming. We'll be fine. I make this drive every day." Lauri's tone was confident, born of a month's experience commuting.

Gary heard the rhythmic thump of Lauri descending the stairs. He gathered the volume of pre-op forms off of the gray granite countertop in the kitchen, not a crumb to be found on the shining surface. The sink was spotless. Three red ceramic canisters were evenly spaced, almost touching the shining back splash. It had taken Lauri months to find them in just the right color to accent her choice of wall paint. Three metal bar stools were precisely positioned at the bend in the counter separating the kitchen from the dining room. The meticulously polished cherry formal dining table looked elegant with long, thin, white candles atop the two crystal candleholders, ready for the next sitting. The kids referred to their parents as "clean freaks."

Gary paused to marvel the expansive view of the sunrise. Two large banks of windows, one in the dining room and one in the living room, dominated the eastern wall of the main floor of the condo. The limited wall space was covered with two small pictures Lauri purchased at a local store for another "deal." They were hung, one above the other, at the corner intersection of the two rooms. The eight-inch square paintings depicted lush pastoral scenes from a European vineyard, location unknown.

The rolling hills of southern New Hampshire lay in the distance. The undulating contours were dense with trees, affording picturesque views on a daily basis.

Lauri correctly predicted the snarl-free drive into Boston. The couple was facing their first authentic health challenge, and like when he went to work, Gary wanted to get to the hospital early.

"Explain to me again what severe dysplasia of the cervix is," Lauri said as they crossed the state line. She received a call two weeks ago from her gynecologist indicating a significant change on her most recent pap smear. He was anxious to get her in for surgery.

Gary smiled at Lauri. "It's a condition where the cells of the cervix have mutated. They changed from normal to abnormal. The cells are not yet cancerous, but they are in a transitional phase between normal and cancer. No one can know how long it would take to go from this precancerous state to actual cancer, and for that reason—"

"I know. The cervix needs to be taken out."

"Would you like to finish this explanation, Dr. Lauri?"

"No thanks, Dr. Confer. You continue. You know a lot about women. Why is it you didn't become a gynecologist?"

"Feeling funny this morning are you, Dr. Lauri? You alone are more woman than I can handle."

"Now who's the funny one?" Lauri said, glancing to her left and grinning.

"I guess that would be me." Gary winked. "To complete the thought, along with the cervix, the uterus is also taken out. In your case, being only forty-six, your ovaries aren't coming out along with all the rest of your equipment."

"Thanks. I know you went over this before, but I'm a little nervous. I want to do the right thing." Lauri reached over, resting her left hand on Gary's shoulder. "Any chance it's already cancer?"

"You're going to be fine. Small chance. Not very likely as your earlier pap showed only mild dysplasia. Cancer of the cervix is typically a slower growing tumor. There are many worse cancers that you wouldn't want to have." Gary reached over and patted Lauri's knee. "Really Baby, it's all going to be fine. You'll see."

Lauri felt lucky to be riding to the hospital with her own live-in doctor. Taking her mind off the surgery, Lauri's thoughts focused on the real calamity currently facing the family. Jingles, Paige's seven-year-old tabby was missing, and Lauri was responsible. The cat made the interstate move along with the rest of the family. He had been an indoor/outdoor feline with a habit of abandoning half-mauled "treasures" on the doorstep of their Massachusetts home. Prior to leaving for camp, Paige corralled every member of the family. Lauri heard the warning playing over and over again in her head, "Don't let Jingles out. I mean it. He doesn't know his way around here yet."

Lauri, while carrying in some groceries, had given Jingles an opportunity he couldn't pass up. The quick and nimble feline skirted between her legs and out the door. Despite everyone roaming the neighborhood and relentlessly knocking on doors, Jingles was gone.

"Do you think we will every see the cat again?" Lauri said, her head bowed. "Paige will be home on break from camp in two weeks. I haven't had the heart to tell her."

"It's been three weeks since his escape. I think the four-legged furry fugitive is on the run and unlikely to return to his incarceration." Gary's attempt at levity failed to elevate Lauri's spirits or her face. He believed the cat was dead. "We can tell Paige about Jingles when she comes home on break. It won't be pretty, but she can handle it. With her going away to college, she wouldn't have even seen the cat that much." While trying to downplay the impact of the event for Lauri's sake, Gary knew the catastrophe would play itself out in Biblical proportions.

After the tension of the car ride, the remainder of the day went off without a hiccup. Lauri breezed through the vaginal hysterectomy and spent two uneventful days in the hospital. Before being discharged, they were relieved to find out the tissue was negative for cancer. After only five weeks of living together, Lauri felt bad that she had to burden Gary with a health problem. Now, it was behind them, and it seemed like the proverbial bump in the road.

chapter 3

In spite of Lauri's hopes and prayers, the fateful day arrived with Paige due home, and the cat still missing. Four weeks had passed since Jingles engineered his dastardly escape from his new home. To many, the place was, "the cat's meow." Jingles, however, had been completely unimpressed and was a feline with designs on a more open air, beyond the walls, come and go as you please, I've got the world by the paws lifestyle.

Lauri knew what the cat meant to her daughter. As far as Paige was concerned, Jingles was as much a part of the family as her brothers—maybe more. He was always there for her with a hug or a purr, a living, furry, security blanket. Seven years ago, he was her most cherished Christmas gift. She christened him with a seasonably appropriate moniker, and except for her summers at camp, they were inseparable.

As a young child, Paige sat on the floor eating her jelly sandwich while Jingles lapped up a saucer of milk. After their meal together, she would dab off his milky white whiskers and paws with her napkin. She cradled him in her arms for hours, transporting him from room to room. Lauri marveled at the cat's patience. Jingles was family, and now a family member was gone.

Lauri prepared an approach rooted in calmness and control. The plan dissipated into thin air once she told Paige that Jingles had been missing for almost a month. Tears flowed like April showers. Nothing short of a miracle could console her. She ran upstairs and collapsed onto her bed face first, her long silky blonde hair spreading out into a nearly perfect sunburst pattern.

"That went well." Lauri rolled her blue eyes skyward as she flopped back onto the couch.

"Neither of us expected her to handle it without a lot of emotion," Gary said, as he settled down next to Lauri. "And, if there is one thing Paige does well, it's emotion."

"I feel terrible," Lauri moaned. "She was as upset about me waiting to tell her as she was about the cat being gone. First, the fur ball escapes. Then, I don't immediately alert her, the media and the National Guard." Lauri turned toward Gary, her face drawn and wrinkled beyond her years. "Sometimes, I hate being a parent."

"Join the club." Gary extended his left arm around Lauri's shoulder and pulled her near. "You know what they say, if it's not one thing, it's your mother."

Paige spent every waking moment of her 48-hour break from camp searching for Jingles. She distributed flyers with his picture above his new address and his new home phone number. She even drove thirty miles south to Jingles' former digs, to look for him and inform their former neighbors to be on the lookout. She checked their old front stoop, his favorite place to display his night's catch. All for naught, Paige dejectedly returned to camp with the cat still missing, and feared dead.

Lauri received a call every day from Paige for the next week. "Hi Mom, any sign of Jingles?" Paige's tone strained to exude hope.

"No. Sorry," was Lauri's repetitive forlorn reply. Lauri dreaded each call, her heart breaking for her little girl. By the end of the week, with all prospects of finding Jingles exhausted, Lauri promised to take Paige to the shelter to pick out a new cat in four weeks, when she finished her counseling job at the summer camp.

Another week went by without any sign of the escapee. Lauri barely heard her cell phone ringing as she had left it on her nightstand plugged into the charger. She ran from the living room, climbing the stairs two at a time, grasping the oak stair rail, pulling herself forward. Reaching the top floor winded, Lauri looked at the caller ID that flashed MOM. She paused, took a breath, and flipped up the metal cover. "Hi, Mom."

"Lauri, they found Jingles!"

"Really. Where?" Lauri's heart was pounding.

"I just got a call from the animal shelter in Nashua. Someone turned him in. They identified—"

"You gotta be kidding me." Lauri collapsed into a chair, her rubbery legs incapable of support. "I can't believe it."

"Me either. Someone turned him in. They knew him from the ID chip I had put in him years ago. He looks really scrawny, like he's been living outside for a long time." Lauri's Mom, pleased to have saved the day and the cat, talked right through Lauri's attempted response. "I'm coming over. We can go get him together. Can I call Paige and tell her?"

"Thanks, Mom. Thank you, thank you, thank you. She will be so happy."

Lauri closed the phone cover and sunk back into the lavender colored fabric chair, the only seat in the bedroom, and her favorite place to read. She was happiest for Paige, happy for herself and the forgiveness of her sin, but not at all excited about the resumption of cat litter detail. *The sacrifices we make for our children.*

Lauri's Mom punched in the number to the counselor's cabin at the camp. A sultry voice answered the phone. "Hello. Greetings from Camp Pocahontas. If you are a strapping young brave who is interested in sharing a teepee with a lonely Indian maiden, come on up." Kathy's inviting monologue had been rehearsed and intended for her boyfriend, from whom she was expecting a call.

"Hello, young lady. Sorry to burst your bubble. This is Paige's grandmother. Is she there?"

"Oh! Sorry."

The jolting crack as the phone hit the table induced temporary deafness. A brief silence was followed by smack, smack, smack, as the phone landed on the floor. The line went silent as Kathy ran to the next cabin to get Paige.

Kathy ran up to Paige, nearly knocking her over. Placing her hands on Paige's shoulders, she recounted her mishap on the phone. "Do you think she'll tell anybody?"

Paige smiled and hugged her camp sister. The two had spent the last seven summers together and there wasn't anything they didn't know about each other. "Don't worry. You didn't give her your name, did you?"

"No."

"Then…no problem." Paige ran over to the counselor's cabin, picking up the phone from the floor. "Hi, Nana."

"Paige, I found Jingles."

"Where?" Paige's heart began to race. "Is he okay?"

"He's at the shelter. He's okay, a little thin, but he's alive. They identified him with the chip I put in him years ago. You must be so happy."

"Oh, Nana, thank you so much. I've missed him."

"Your mom and I are going to pick him up."

"Call me when you have him, please."

Paige's world order was restored as a potential tragedy was averted by a miracle. Twists of fate weave their way through the fabric of our lives, sometimes stitching us together, sometimes ripping us from seam to seam.

chapter 4

TWO MONTHS AFTER her partial hysterectomy, Lauri and Gary were told that her cousin, who was in her forties and who had a recent devastating recurrence of breast cancer, had been found to carry the BRCA mutation. The carriers of this genetic mutation possess a markedly increased risk of breast and ovarian cancer, significantly above the risk in the general population. With the overall risk being so substantial, and coupled with the likelihood of developing these cancers at an early age, many women with the mutation choose to have elective surgical removal of their ovaries and their breasts.

Lauri immediately pursued her own genetic workup at a major teaching hospital in Boston. By mid-September, the couple received the unwelcome results that she also possessed this mutation. After intensive research and counseling, as well as long heartfelt conversations between the couple, Lauri decided to have her ovaries removed in early November, after they returned from visiting Gary's son, Nick C, in London. He was studying abroad for the first semester of his junior year of college.

While stressful, the decision to remove her ovaries was not a difficult one. Aside from inducing early menopause, and giving only fleeting thoughts of laboring through another delivery, Lauri's ovaries were otherwise a threatening but obsolete intruder. Gary's medical background and tireless scouring of the latest medical literature gave Lauri supreme confidence in their grasp of the grave health risks of allowing her ovaries to continue residence in her body. Their combined efforts guided them forward, helping them to feel relaxed and emboldened with their chosen option. However, had they known of her genetic malady, she could have had her ovaries removed at the same time as her uterus, rather than requiring two separate surgeries only five months apart. Lauri wasn't happy with the way fate was twisting up her life.

The issue of considering an elective double mastectomy was burdened with significantly greater physical and emotional consequences. This decision was briefly postponed until after January, as Lauri was feeling the strain of wedding and honeymoon preparations. Lauri obtained an MRI of her breasts, which was negative. This reassuring result lessened the necessity to immediately consider the more extensive and disfiguring surgery. Gary was completely supportive of when and how Lauri wanted to proceed, but he felt removal of her breasts would ultimately be required.

Lauri, always upbeat, began to feel the weight of her recent health issues. She worried about the added stress on her relationship with Gary. "I can't believe this is happening," she said. "We have the week in London coming up, the wedding, and the honeymoon week with both our families in Cancun, all in the next few months. Now we have to deal with another surgery." Lauri sighed. "I feel like you got a real lemon."

There was a momentary silence. Gary tilted his head and grinned. "Yea, but I love lemonade. How about I give *you* a squeeze?"

"I'm serious." Lauri fought back the urge to laugh.

"So am I."

As he so often did, Gary broke the ice; transforming a cold obnoxious solid block of frozen water into jovial cubes.

A mountain of challenges and adjustments had piled up: the jobs, longer commutes, the kids, health concerns, the upcoming wedding, planning the honeymoon, and the escape of Jingles. It represented a rough few months by anyone's standards. However, Gary couldn't imagine a life without Lauri, or a life without the combined families.

The two families literally grew up together. Along with Nick C and Jack, Gary taught Ben and Paige to drive. Lauri taught Nick C and Jack how to play cribbage. Gary attended Ben's football games and took the pictures before Paige's junior and senior proms. Lauri made it to Nick C's basketball games and Jack's concerts. Both parents forged strong bonds with their soon-to-be stepchildren. The kids completely integrated and treated each other like siblings, which like in most families, wasn't always pretty. A few challenges weren't going to send Gary running for the hills.

The couple laughed, hugged, and Lauri had a good cry. They always had humor in their life despite the many obstacles in their shared past. Lauri partially drew back from the embrace. "I have been on the web looking at the breast surgery and reconstruction. It looks pretty intense."

"It is. But we'll get through it together."

Lauri nuzzled her face against Gary's neck. "I'm worried. Will you feel different about me?" Lauri said in a slow deliberate tone.

Gary turned in and smiled. "We're both going to be fine with this, you'll see." Gary playfully patted Lauri on her upper thigh. "You know, I'm a leg man…and man you have great legs."

Lauri gently kissed Gary's cheek. "I'm going to need a whole new wardrobe to go along with my new body."

"Is that right?"

"Yes. Most definitely."

Amidst all of the medical turmoil, Lauri and Gary thoroughly enjoyed living together. Despite feeling comfortable with their decision to move in together and their plans to marry on January 1st, 2007, they both entered this "next step" of their union with some anxiety. Remarriage was something neither thought they would ever consider, and statistics were not favorable. Typically, remarriages occur within a couple of years of divorce. Lauri was now eight years out; Gary was six. They had beaten the odds, and notwithstanding a combined span of protracted singleness, they would soon be husband and wife. An undying bond existed between them. It provided comfort and joy to know that this would be the last time they would exchange wedding bands.

chapter 5

THEIR MID-OCTOBER week "across the pond" visiting Nick C flew by faster than the traditional London Black Cabs negotiating the narrow back streets of the Royal City. The vehicles possessed an odd form with their elevated, bubble shaped roofline, originally a necessity to accommodate the bowler hats atop the heads of their bygone male patrons.

Nick C, thoroughly enjoying his semester abroad, met them at Heathrow's baggage claim and surprised them from behind. He slipped in between Lauri and Gary, wrapping his arms around their shoulders and pulling the trio into a tight circle. "Cheers," he uttered with all the flare and ease of a Chelsea native. "How was the flight?"

"Long," Gary said, as Lauri planted a kiss on Nick's cheek.

"You look great," Lauri said. "How are things going?"

"I love it here. The only drag is that everything is so expensive. I thought we'd take the tube back rather than a cab and save a few bucks."

Nick's hug slackened and Gary reached for one of the many suitcases. "What's the tube?"

"Oh. Sorry. That's what they call the subway. Don't forget to mind the gap." Nick chuckled. He explained that in all the tube stations, there is a recurring and annoying public address announcement about the danger of getting too close to the edge of the platform as the subway trains enter or leave the station. The space between the opposite platforms where the two train tracks run is called "the gap." Every few minutes, the PA system warns everyone to "mind the gap." In addition to the verbal barrage, there were signs everywhere. For all of the study abroad students, it became a humorous aspect of their experience which had weaved itself into conversation. Whenever they were parting ways, either to go to class or more likely when returning to their dorms after a rousing night at one of the local pubs, they would end the conversation with "mind the gap." It was their adopted way of telling each other to be careful out there.

Nick enthusiastically assumed the role as tour guide on weekends and evenings, filling their time with both enlightening and trivial anecdotes about his adopted home. He truly loved the hustle and bustle of the city and relished riding the crowded tube. He frequently uttered "cheers," and unwaveringly attended with friends Chelsea's raucous, pre-game, premier league soccer festivities. He was having the time of his life.

Gary and Lauri spent the weekdays investigating the abundance of historical sites while Nick was either in class or involved with his internship in the financial district. Lauri was particularly excited by the exhibits dedicated to Lady Diana at Kensington Palace. Gary loved the Tower of London and all its intrigue. They both enjoyed visiting the National Gallery in Trafalgar Square. The museum was packed, a consequence of the wealth of artwork and the lack of an admission charge. Many of the museums in London lacked an admission fee, allowing natives and foreigners unrestricted access to the national treasures.

They spent time milling around Trafalgar Square, named for the battle of Trafalgar, a pivotal naval victory for the English over the French and Spanish in 1805 during the Napoleonic Wars. Spiking skyward in the center of the square was Lord Nelson's Column. The 151-foot-high granite column had a 15-foot-high sandstone statue of the Admiral on top. The memorial commemorated the victory and the death of the Admiral.

Lauri and Gary were great companions on the road or at home, the antithesis of oil and water. To Gary, the enjoyment of travel was not only its entertainment value, but also learning about the people and places they visited. Consequently, Lauri traveled with her own personal tour guide.

Gary pointed to the top of the tall column. "That's Lord Nelson up there. He commanded the royal navy during the battle and was killed by a sniper's bullet at the very end of the fight. He was said to be a real blood and guts salty dog with an unquenchable thirst for glory." Gary paused and took a sip of cool diet soda. "He entered the navy at the age of twelve. By the time he died, he had already been wounded numerous times, losing his right eye and right arm in previous battles…what an animal!"

"He's really your kind of guy, isn't he?" Lauri smiled and reached for Gary's hand. "Where do you always come up with all this stuff?"

Gary released Lauri's hand and slipped behind her, wrapping both arms around her chest. "Listen up, lady. I have my sources, and if I tell you, I might have to kill you." Gary rested his face against Lauri's neck and deeply breathed in her fragrance. "On second thought, let's go back to my place."

Lauri spun around, leaned in and firmly kissed her guide. "I think we'll save the behind the scenes part of the tour for later." Lauri winked. She turned, grabbed Gary's hand, and they continued on through the square. "Speaking of battles, why haven't we ever had a big fight?"

A grin spread over Gary's face. "Because, neither of us likes conflict. We fought enough battles in our past." Gary turned toward Lauri. "Were both lovers, not fighters."

Lauri smiled knowing Gary was right. Prior to meeting each other, they had both been through some very rough times. Neither lost an eye or an arm, but they had sustained nearly fatal injuries to their hearts. Their primary methods of survival involved withdrawing and contemplating a strategy for compromise. Neither was prone to mounting a head on frontal attack and going for the jugular.

"I'm starved…I could use a pint or two," Gary said, as he and Lauri tried to make their way through the multinational and dense crowd in the square.

"Me too. Let's head in the direction of Harrods. I want to go there again after lunch." Lauri's voice was barely audible above the din of the multitudes. Harrods Department Store, in the Knightsbridge district of London, is one of the most famous stores in the world. There was no way Lauri could be in London without making several visits to its plush and unique departments. She loved to stroll through the massive, multilevel store, which was like a combination mall and food emporium under one very large roof. You could obtain anything there, from jellybeans to cars.

"Go ahead and buy it," Gary would say to her, as she examined a potential purchase.

"No. That's way too expensive, and I don't really need it." Lauri shared Ben Franklin's fondness for pennies and thus rarely made an extravagant purchase.

Reaching their destination, Gary held open the arched, weathered, heavy wooden door to the pub. The entrance was framed by large gray blocks of stone that gave the appearance of a castle. Capping the stone arch, and centered on the keystone, was a massive wooden sign emboldened with EAT DRINK AND BE MERRY. Large metal beer mugs provided the bookends to the motto of this authentic establishment.

Gary and Lauri wedged their way to a small open table for two in a dark back corner of the room. The aroma was unmistakable: centuries old musty wood and stout ale. After placing their own order at the bar, as is the custom in pubs, they settled in.

The couple noticed several professional men and women consuming a pint of ale along with their lunch before returning to their afternoon of toil. Nick C had told them this was acceptable behavior in Europe. Gary wondered if English physicians partook prior to engaging their afternoon of waiting patients. He felt the surgical patients might be particularly leery of this habit.

Gary read to Lauri the description on the back of the menu as she was too tired to read it herself. "For centuries, the 'public house' has been a place where people gather to celebrate life, share love, exchange ideas, and most importantly, drink ale. The term 'pub' was coined during the Victorian era as an abbreviation of 'public house'. Centuries ago, ales were sometimes brewed for church festivals or to raise funds for the church, and these were known as 'scot ales'. At the time of the festival, all those who brewed ales were required to give some of their stock to the church. Those who secretly brewed batches and failed to give a share to the church were said to be drinking 'scot free'."

"Do you get it?" Gary asked.

"Not really. I think I'm too tired to get it. Explain it to me."

"The expression 'scot free', used today to mean someone getting something without paying their fair share, originated with people brewing and drinking beer without paying the church what it was due, like a tax or debt that was avoided." Gary leaned his head toward Lauri with a hopeful look in his eyes.

"I get it," Lauri said. "Since you're paying for lunch, I am getting off scot free." Lauri felt some energy return, enough to support the wide grin now spreading across her face.

Gary smiled back. He adored Lauri's playful side and her ability zing one back at him when he least expected it. The couple quietly enjoyed their meal, consuming fish and chips chased down with molten thick ale.

As Gary gazed across the table at his fiancée, he reflected on how Lauri had changed his life. From an adult relationship perspective, their five years together were the happiest ever. This was not purely an internal assessment. It was an obvious external transformation reflected in his attitude which was noticed and commented on by those around him.

Lauri brought all the qualities of a master jeweler to bear on the jagged, tarnished qualities of Gary's life. She provided the steady and guiding hand to smooth the sharp edges of his behavior: the cut. She muted the glare associated with his own flaws as well those of others: the clarity. Lauri brought a new and iridescent brilliance to his life: the color. She imbued his life with love and hope and there was no adequate measure to weigh the positive and sustaining impact she had on him: the carat. Lauri was that rare gem that Gary had been searching for. She was truly a diamond in the rough.

chapter 6

LAURI AND GARY hurried south to Boston at 5:30 am for their appointment with the female oncologic surgeon who would be removing Lauri's ovaries. While Lauri didn't have a known cancer, her increased risk of ovarian cancer related to her BRCA mutation warranted the enhance skill and knowledge of a specialist.

"Hard to believe we're doing this again," Lauri said, frustrated over the latest medical intrusion into their life. "You know, I've always been a very healthy person. Before a few months ago, the only other time I was hospitalized was with complications while carrying Paige. I was in the hospital for a few weeks before the delivery."

"Don't worry. Today's procedure is easy compared to the partial hysterectomy or bringing Dolly into the world." Gary reached over, placing his right hand on Lauri's left knee, giving it a gentle reassuring squeeze. Lauri laid her left hand on top of his. Gary could feel the moisture from her sweaty palm. "Don't worry."

"That's the first time I've heard you call Paige, Dolly. You two have become really close. It's great how connected we've all become. It makes me so happy."

"How'd she get that nickname?"

"When she was a baby, I rocked her to sleep while singing 'Hello Dolly' to her. She would smile and coo up to me. Her beautiful eyes would open and close a few times, and then she would drift off to sleep. I miss those times." Lauri loved children. "I wish we could have a baby." Lauri slid her fingers in between Gary's and squeezed.

Gary felt the pressure and slight pain as Lauri's engagement ring dug into his hand. "Well that would be a miracle given your last surgery. Besides, four kids in college and five overall, is enough."

"You made your point." Lauri tightened her grip on Gary's hand for emphasis.

"Yeah, I got the point." Gary's voice was an octave above its normal range. "The point of your diamond is jabbing the side of my finger."

"Good. That's what I was going for." Lauri released her grip. "I'm sorry. I didn't mean to hurt you."

"No problem—only a flesh wound." Gary winked at Lauri. "You know, had things been different, it would have been great to have kids together."

Lauri returned her hand to Gary's, resting her soft palm on the back of his hand. "I know."

The couple arrived at the Boston hospital and made their way to the outpatient surgery building. After the volume of paperwork and pre-op assessment by the nurse, Lauri was taken away in a wheel chair.

The laparoscopic surgery proceeded flawlessly and Lauri was released later that afternoon in a groggy stupor from the residual anesthesia. Two surgical procedures and too many doctor's visits was more medical attention than Lauri wanted during their first five months of living together. For the foreseeable future, Lauri only wanted Gary to examine her.

The good news arrived three days later—no cancer in her ovaries.

chapter 7

THOUGHTS OF THE wedding crept into her mind on an hourly basis. Lauri and Gary were neither as young nor as naïve as they were at nineteen and twenty-two when they hitched their futures to their first spouses. A shared past failure made them both cautiously optimistic about the future.

The mid-November foliage lay strewn upon the fading green carpet of the fifteenth fairway. Lauri, perched on the second floor balcony, admired the pastoral scene. The rolling hills were covered with a patchwork of leafless crestfallen deciduous trees and stoic evergreens, both bracing for the impending wintry mix of plummeting temperatures and hellish varied states of water descending from the gray clouds above. Oh how she loathed the shortened periods of daylight and its attendant meteorological chaos. For now, Lauri was warmed to the core, wrapped in the muted browns and golds of an afghan retrieved from the closet. Her hands clutched a steaming mug of aromatic coffee. The location embodied supreme peace and comfort, and it was destined to become her personal sanctuary.

The couple decided on the simplest of ceremonies. They believed the second time around should focus on the immediate family with none of the pomp and circumstance of virginal vows. The sands of time had molded their maturity as well as their complexions. A justice of the peace would marry them in the suite of a downtown hotel bordering The Boston Common, a large tranquil park in the center of the historic city. Only their five children would witness the ceremony.

They spent a beautiful, clear, crisp, fall Saturday surveying hotels before settling on a location. A wristwatch with the inscribed date of January 1st, 2007 would be the keepsake for each child to mark the occasion, as well as symbolize the preciousness of time.

Lauri set down her red mug and picked up the freshly printed copy of the wedding ceremony reading that Gary composed. "Most writing is ten percent inspiration and ninety percent perspiration," he often said. Gary provided the sweat. He likened writing to bleeding. At times, thoughts trickled out at a painfully slow pace, one drop at and time. At other times, inspiration gushed forth with the urgency of a ruptured artery, the author having trouble momentarily containing and recording his thoughts. Gary penned many drafts along the path to the finished product. Lauri adjusted her afghan and began reading.

LAURI AND GARY
JANUARY 1, 2007
We come together today in celebration and recognition of the beginning of a new family. This ceremony is small and simple to focus attention on the most precious asset we have, each other. With this union, we both join two individuals and bond together two families. We move forward with acceptance and respect for the past, as it is our history that defines who we are today. We pledge to be a positive influence on each other's lives as we live and grow together. This pledge extends to each and every member of this family.

The cornerstones of any lasting and happy relationship are love, trust, respect and honesty. These attributes provide the foundation that fosters growth and prosperity of both the individual and the family. We are all now responsible for nurturing this union by investing ourselves completely towards its success.

A second marriage, with the union of two families, presents unique challenges and opportunities. The path to happiness is paved with the recognition that we are all bound together to support and encourage each other. The weight of the inevitable challenges we all must face will be lighter to carry, and the elation of the many triumphs ahead will be that much sweeter, by sharing the emotions with the ones you love and the ones who love you.

Lauri felt the transfer of emotion from the words to her heart. As a few tears moistened the corners of her eyes, the clank of the rotating door handle caused her head to snap to the left. Gary's form was slightly fuzzy through the full-length pane of glass. The door swung open, creating a breeze that wafted onto Lauri's face.

"Aren't you freezing out here?" Gary eased out onto the deck. He paused in front of Lauri and planted a kiss on her forehead.

"No. It's nice and crisp. This afghan and coffee are keeping me warm."

Gary moved around to the other side of the round glass table and plopped down. "You're home early. Fast commute?"

"I left a little early. Things were caught up, and I was feeling tired. The girls could handle the rest of the day." Lauri was the manager of a busy downtown office in the center of Boston.

Gary unbuttoned his collar and loosened his tie. He leaned toward Lauri, looking over the top of his glasses. "Are you all right? How about I—"

"Fine...I'm fine. A little tired with all that's going on. Do you think we can pull this all off? Thanksgiving, the wedding, the trip to Cancun. I don't think so." Lauri took a long sip of the hot java as a swirl of steam curled in front of her nose.

"Piece of cake...pun intended. The hard stuff is already done. Getting the trip organized was the worst. Everyone is really excited. The wedding plans are done. Thanksgiving is always a challenge, but a fun one."

Gary noticed the composition laying on the table and thought about going another round with the effort. The writer and the composition were in a boxing match. Sometimes the writer threw the knockout punch with all the thrill of victory. Sometimes, it was the writer that was knocked on his butt in defeat. "What did you think?" He motioned toward the paper.

"I just finished it. I was starting to cry when you came in." Lauri breathed deeply. "We are really becoming a family. I'm so happy."

"I will keep on it, never satisfied you know."

Lauri leaned towards Gary and smiled. "I think it's beautiful just as it is."

"Thanks." Gary reached across the table and pickup a manila envelope. "What's this?"

"Oh! You're gonna love that. It's the calendar I ordered with the blown up family pictures above each month. It's great."

Gary slid the treasure out and thumbed through it, one month at a time. With the advancing seasons, the corners of his mouth arched higher and higher. "That's spectacular. We've done a lot over the years."

The wind whipped up and Gary saw Lauri shiver. She pulled the afghan up to her neck. "How about we go in?" he said. "I'm getting cold."

Lauri looked at Gary and crumpled her face. "You're just saying that. You're never cold, even in the dead of winter."

Gary pushed himself to his feet, came around the table and reached out for Lauri. "Guilty as charged. Let's go in."

Lauri hated to surrender her freedom to the changing of the seasons. She fought tooth and nail to extend her time outside as far into the fall as possible, even if she had to be uncomfortable to do it. The air and sun were worth the cold. "All right. But you know, if we wintered in Florida, we could be outside in the sun everyday." Lauri shifted forward in her chair. "I would love that."

"Someday Baby…someday."

Lauri reached up for Gary's hands and he pulled her to her feet. Wrapping his arms around her, he pinned the afghan between them. He softly creased her lips with his own, savoring the softness of her skin. Lauri's heart gently fluttered.

Gary squeezed her tighter. "You know, it feels like there is less of you to hold on to. Lost any weight for the wedding?"

"I'm trying. My dress still seems too tight. I've got a ways to go." Lauri smiled. "Never satisfied, you know."

"Point taken." A large grin smoothed Gary's concerned expression. "Don't go too far. Let's get inside. Want some wine?" Gary released the hug, grabbing the afghan before it hit the deck. He picked up the calendar and the sheet of paper.

"Great." Lauri shivered again as a breeze enveloped her exposed body.

The couple retreated into the living room, and Gary ignited the gas fireplace. The erratic flame darted between the stone logs. Lauri settled down on the dark red fabric couch that resembled crushed velvet. The color nearly matched the paint on the kitchen and dining room walls. She swung her feet up on the cushions. Her head drifted down onto the pattern fabric of the pillows that matched the two classic, high-back accent chairs.

Gary covered her with the afghan. "Why don't you rest for a minute while I get showered. You know how much I love a good shower." Gary started toward the stairs. "I'll get the wine after."

"Great. Thanks."

The couple felt fortunate to be together. The odds of any two individuals in the global mass of humanity finding each other are infinitesimally small. Lauri saw it as fate while Gary thought it was just dumb luck. No matter the director of their destiny, their futures were now locked together. The wedding plans were complete, as were the honeymoon festivities. They were bringing their five children, nine members of Lauri's family, and eight members of Gary's family to Cancun for a week following the wedding. It would be a great opportunity for everyone to meet as they lived on opposite coasts of the country. Gary had spent eight months organizing the trip to accommodate the needs of everyone's demanding schedule.

Life was good, really good. They easily and joyously acclimated to cohabitation. Six months and two surgeries were behind them. They had the rest of their lives to look forward to. For the first time in their adult lives, Lauri and Gary were truly in love… and loving every minute of it.

chapter 8

THE AROMA OF turkey and sausage stuffing filled the home. While they had more than a literal full plate to digest over the past few months, Lauri was committed to providing sustenance to the expected twenty-one family members joining her and Gary for the holiday. Twelve precisely placed chairs encircled the fully expanded dark cherry dining table with only its legs visible beneath the smartly pressed holiday pattern tablecloth. The blue bordered family china, given to Lauri by her grandmother years before, was stacked in organized pyramids with a gold charger for their foundation. Water goblet, wine glass, and nearly butler-perfect ruler measured silverware placement completed the military precision ensemble.

Traditional wooden pilgrim statues were the table's centerpiece, their detailed hand painted surfaces slightly marred from years of dedicated service. Within twenty-four hours, they would be cocooned in the guarded embrace of bubble wrap, sequestered in lonely attic storage for the next eleven months. All items, functional and decorative, rested upon the white cotton tablecloth, its fabric accented with colorful turkeys that looked surprisingly calm despite their fated association with the gathering. A smaller, equally manicured, table bridging the opening between the dining room and living room accommodated eight. Throw in three spots at the counter and everyone had a place to enjoy the holiday spirit of love and family.

"Gary," Lauri screamed. "I've got a problem."

"Coming." Gary logged off the computer. Lauri recently convinced him to switch to electronic banking. She had set up all the account information, including entering all of their recurring payments. She was right about how much easier it was compared to the manual method. Lauri's command of the computer always impressed Gary.

"What's going on?" he asked, passing through the arched opening on the way from the living room to the kitchen. The painters produced a precise line, dividing the deep red kitchen from the muted gold paint covering the living room wall. Lauri had spent months thinking and rethinking the colors in the home. The kitchen and dining room had taken six coats of the red paint to cover properly.

Lauri stood at the sink, hands dripping wet. She wore only a short nightgown. Her enticing long thin legs were nearly completely exposed. Since her surgery and the premature advent of menopause, her internal thermostat was all out of whack, and despite the traditional low temperatures of Thanksgiving Day, she was hot. Mars was even more confused than normal about the needs of Venus.

"The sink is clogged." Lauri reached for the autumn colored dishtowel. "I still have a lot to do before everybody gets here."

As Gary approached from behind, his thoughts were drawn to her form rather than the predicament. Exercising better judgment, he re-focused on the problem. "What happened?"

"I've been peeling potatoes and now they're stuck in the disposal."

"How much?" Gary asked, having already concluded it was more like a bushel than a peck.

"Ten pounds." Lauri dropped her head and closed her eyes. "I'm really, really sorry. I was rushed." Lauri's face, now crimson in color, was nearly indistinguishable from the paint on the walls.

The guests were due to arrive in two hours, and the couple had a drainage disaster on their hands.

"Don't worry. I'll get it. But you're gonna owe me." Gary smiled, easing Lauri's tension.

"Thanks."

Despite his adeptness around the house, many passes with a plumber's snake, and volumes of drain cleaner, Gary was unable to relieve the blockage. He retreated to the shower, attempting to make himself presentable to the arriving entourage.

It is at times like these when possessing a family with both ingenuity and a sense of humor is like manna from heaven, sustaining on both a physical and an emotional level. Everyone pitched in to complete the meal preparation with water from alternate sinks in the home. The meal and fellowship were a colossal success.

After an unimaginable variety of cholesterol laden, artery clogging desserts, Lauri's two brothers and Gary retired to the basement. They were determined to relieve the tuber-induced constriction. Gary, being merely an apprentice and better equipped to diagnose and cure human aliments, filled the journeyman role. He assisted the two seasoned veterans as pipes were dismantled between conflicting sibling banter on the "right" course of action. The mixture of profanity and insults were good-natured with "moron" and "idiot" uttered with the frequency of rain showers in the Amazon jungle.

Between "serious" considerations of some truly harebrained ideas, the trio laughed their butts off. The keen solution involved a garden hose shoved down deep into the drainage pipe and turned on full force, with towels and hands plugging the gap between the open pipe and the hose. In theory, this should force the offending potato peels down into the city drain.

Gary chuckled as he envisioned debris spraying back throughout the basement and drenching the holiday attired trio in potato peels and globular starch droplets. It would give the family a renewed appreciation of an old classic—Mr. Potato Head. After two failed attempts and only a minor mess, relief was achieved just in time for the pots and pans to be washed in the kitchen sink by the traditional combined efforts of more hands than you could shake a stick at. It turned out to be one of the most heartwarming and hilarious holidays anyone could remember; a story children and grandchildren will want to hear over and over again.

chapter 9

WHILE THE PILGRIM portion of the holiday season was literally draining on many levels, Lauri was at least in spirit joyously invigorated, directing her attention to her favorite celebration of the year, Christmas. All members of the family knew Lauri's voluminous collection of holiday music would now solely occupy the compact disc players both at home and in the car. It would be a month-long marathon of countless renditions of holiday classics, as well as new-age festive compositions, an eclectic collection from rock to Bach.

Lauri's body was not in sync with the approaching season of good cheer. She felt constantly queasy, as if she were traveling by ship in rough waters. If she weren't missing all the necessary equipment, she would have bet the farm, including the rabbit, that she was pregnant. The fantasy crossed her mind many times over the past few weeks.

A week after Thanksgiving, Lauri contacted her surgeon and drove to Boston for a visit. Her complaints were non-specific, and it was assumed that the combination of multiple surgeries and the demands of the holidays, as well as justifiable nervousness about her impending wedding and honeymoon, had worn her down. She was also likely reacting to the lack of estrogen, as surgically induced menopause had started. After another week and another visit, a bladder infection seemed the likely culprit. Ten days of antibiotics and follow-up negative urine cultures confirmed definitive eradication of the bacterial invader. However, Lauri's fatigue progressed. Plausible explanations were followed with ineffectual remedies. An outside observer would never suspect her level of sheer exhaustion. For Lauri, public displays of physical or emotional illness graced her personal world only once in a blue moon.

She returned to work only three weeks after her last surgery and nearly completed all of her normal pre-Christmas Day tasks. Mountains of presents circled the eight-foot Douglas fir, adorned with ornaments spanning the history of the combined family. Grade school craft time, hand-painted dough creations of candy canes, stockings, and stars were the most cherished possessions. An inviting pine aroma filled the home.

The tree sat in front of the ten-foot by eight-foot floor to ceiling window, which typically allowed for majestic views of the sunrise. For now, the view from inside and out was of an intensely illuminated, multi-colored, conical beacon of hope and happiness. Christmas cards were neatly displayed on windows, doors and shelves. Handmade oversized empty stockings were hung on the mantle, yearning to be filled by Santa. Lauri, many years before, made Gary's, Nick C's and Jack's to match the rest of the family. The children, while grown, were well aware and sensitive to Lauri's warning of the perils of being naughty. This home, their home, like her home every year before, was a "ten" on the holiday scale, and the envy of many visitors.

Gary returned home from work Monday to find Lauri sleeping on the couch. She awoke as he attempted to quietly cross the room to the den. "How are you feeling?" He went to the couch and sat down next to Lauri's partially bent legs.

"Not good," she said, in a weary voice. Her face, drawn and pale, peeked out from beneath her favorite afghan. "I can't seem to shake this nausea. I'm so tired I can't get up. What's wrong with me?"

Over the weekend, Gary begged her to make an appointment with Dr. Thompson, her family physician. She refused as Christmas and their wedding were both fast approaching. She believed the weight and worry of everything was responsible for her current state of exhaustion. Now, physically and mentally beaten down, she was more receptive. The mild nausea of a few weeks ago now came in waves, at times reaching a high note crescendo that literally dragged her down to her knees.

Gary shook his head and furrowed his brow. "I don't know, but we'll find out." He reached down, patting Lauri's legs. "I know you've been trying to lose weight for the wedding, but you may be overdoing it. Have you been eating at all? You really look thin. How much have you lost?" Gary paused, feeling bad because of the rapid fire verbal attack on an obviously defenseless victim. "Sorry. I didn't mean to hit you with so much at once."

"About fifteen pounds over the last few weeks. I can't eat with all this nausea. The thought of food makes me want to throw up." Lauri's voice trailed off as she even lacked the energy to hold a conversation. The final straw had fallen. Gary had Lauri in Dr. Thompson's office the following morning.

✻ ✻ ✻

Gary and Lauri silently listened to her holiday music during the forty-five minute drive. A dreary, gray, December sky blocked the sun, an omen of snow flurries to come. A white Christmas was sure to heighten Lauri's spirits. Lauri intermittently dozed off during the ride, something she often wished she could do during her long daily commute into Boston. An early morning phone consultation between Dr. Thompson and Gary, doctor-to-doctor, precipitated the appropriate response, "Bring her right in."

Dr. Thompson's waiting room overflowed with patients despite the typically slower time of the year in most physician offices. Lauri's family received their care at this same location from before the time she was born. Dr. Thompson came from a long line of physicians, having joined his father after completing his medical training fifteen years ago. For a ten-year stint, father and son shared the office, blending old school know-how and new age technology. The elder Mrs. Thompson ran the office with the tenacity of a drill sergeant, keeping her husband and son in line and on time. Her softer side was reserved for the sick children who received a fresh homemade chocolate chip cookie when they left, rather than the traditional lollipop. The younger Mrs. Thompson gave the elder a wide berth, a necessity on both a physical and emotional basis.

The office occupied a majestic Victorian home in the suburbs of Boston. A diversity of patients sat in ornate chairs, reminiscent of the parlor that the room more accurately represented. Lauri felt both relieved and frightened to be once again in the embrace of the medical profession. Christmas was only a few days away, and while she knew she was ill, she desperately wanted to joyously celebrate her first Noel sharing the same home with Gary. All the kids were home, four on winter break from college. The last thing she needed or wanted was more health problems.

The modern medical furniture in the exam room sharply contrasted the waiting room décor. The stiff, white, uncomfortable sanitary paper of the exam table crumpled as Lauri strained to shift her leaner body.

"Lauri, how long have you been nauseated?" Dr. Thompson's eyes scanned her face while his hands felt her neck. He adeptly examined Lauri while listening to her history.

"Almost daily since Thanksgiving—really bad the last couple of weeks."

"Any vomiting?"

"No, but I almost do several times a day. There is nothing to bring up because I'm not eating."

Lauri felt Dr. Thompson using both hands to thump on her back, up the right side and down the left. Gary would later explain to her that he was listening for a change in the character of the sound. The lungs, being filled with air, resonate with a high-pitched sound if you firmly rap on the patient's back. If there is fluid or infection in the lungs, or in the space around the lungs, the sound has a lower pitch, dull character. A high-pitched tone followed every rap on her back.

"Any pain with or after meals?" Dr. Thompson pulled his stethoscope from his white coat pocket and slipped it around his neck.

"No pain at all. Hardly any meals either."

"Let me listen to your heart and lungs." Dr. Thompson adjusted the earpieces and methodically moved the stethoscope around, instructing Lauri on her breathing. "You sound clear." He replaced the instrument in his pocket. "I'm sending you to the lab for stat blood work and an ultrasound to get a look at your gall bladder. After the tests, come back to the office and I will go over the results with both of you." Dr. Thompson extended his hand toward Gary. "It was nice to meet you, Dr. Confer."

"Call me Gary."

"Well Gary, you're a lucky man. Lauri has always been one of my favorite patients."

"I know. She's something special."

Dr. Thompson put his hand on Lauri's shoulder. "Don't worry. We'll figure this out."

The lab work and ultrasound were performed at the outpatient facility associated with the hospital just down the street. The couple returned to Dr. Thompson's office to discuss the findings. The results showed complete obstruction of the biliary system, which drains bile from the liver. Bile is produced in the liver and stored in the gall bladder. The bile is excreted into the intestine through a system of ducts to aid in the digestion of fatty foods. It seemed to Lauri that the family already encountered more than their share of blockage issues at Thanksgiving. Now she had a very personal plumbing problem. It couldn't have happened at a worse time. What she needed was the medical equivalent of her two brothers to adjust her own pipes and unblock her biliary drain.

The couple left the medical office carrying fear and concern on their shoulders, but no cookie in their hands. Gary knew the most likely explanation was disease of the gallbladder, probably small gallstones blocking the biliary ductal drainage system. However, he was concerned as no stones were seen on the ultrasound. The other possible causes for obstruction in this region were much more ominous, not amenable to creative plumbing solutions her brothers might be able to execute.

"How worried should I be?" Lauri asked, as she waited for Gary to unlock the car.

"Not very. It's probably small gravel type stones causing the blockage."

"Can this wait until after the wedding and the honeymoon? You know, I'm really tough. I can do whatever it takes."

"I wish it could." Gary pulled on the door handle. "If we get you in for treatment right away, this could all be taken care of quickly. Hopefully, everything will work out." Lauri slid past the open car door and settled down onto the tan fabric bucket seat. "Watch your legs," Gary said, as he carefully shut the door. By the time he rounded the SUV and got in, Lauri was sobbing. Gary reached over and eased her head onto his shoulder. "It'll be okay."

"I guess I'm not as tough as I thought." Lauri attempted to gain control while choking out the words. The combination of fear and disappointment made her cry, an emotional outburst as rare as an oasis in the Sahara Desert.

Lauri's blockage was severe. Intervention needed to be pursued immediately. As fate would have it, her sister-in-law was a gastroenterology nurse, and the necessary procedure, an ERCP, was expeditiously scheduled for the next day.

Lauri's revelation of her condition to Gary allowed her to shed her previously tough exterior. She now appeared much more fragile. She had wanted to lose weight for the wedding, and now, they both knew the "success" was primarily due to ill health rather than willpower. Her health was off, as was her color, a complexion of plaster white. She was not yet jaundiced, a yellowing of the skin caused by increased bilirubin in the blood, a consequence of a backed up biliary system.

Gary spent the evening preparing Lauri for the next day's procedure. The ordeal involved sedation, which allowed the gastroenterologist to negotiate a garden-sized hose down your throat, through the cavity of your stomach, and into your small intestine, where the bile duct connects and drains bile. The end of the tube has a camera to allow the doctor to see inside the patient. There is also an opening to allow the physician to pass tubes and instruments into the patient for diagnostic and therapeutic pursuits. It took quite a bit of dexterity to perform this maneuver. Lauri tensed at Gary's explanation. In less than twenty-four hours, an additional installment of the marvels of modern medicine would be unleashed upon her.

Lauri was scared to death.

Neither of them found relief that night in their four-corner post, old English style bed. Each spiral was an ornate pattern of carvings that spiked toward the vaulted ceiling on the third floor of their spacious but physically demanding condo. The three levels and three and one half sets of stairs had not initially germinated a second thought for the physically fit man and woman in their late 40's. The location was perfect, the view was breathtaking, and the companionship was more than either could hope for. However, the new reality of their first six months of living together made them both wish they had opted for a less mountainous personal escape.

They tossed and turned until dawn. Gary and Lauri pondered their future as they gazed at the clouds and faded stars through the two skylights in the vaulted ceiling.

chapter 10

"WE HAVE TIME," Lauri said, as she dumped large bags of treats and essentials onto the glass coffee table. Several of the plastic deodorant canisters dropped onto the hardwood floor with a resounding thump.

"You sure?" Gary thought they should head to the hospital.

"Christmas is only four days away. I want the stockings filled… just in case."

"That's a mountain of stuff."

"I know, but I couldn't resist. I've been picking things up for weeks."

Gary laughed. "Looks more like months." He started segregating the items on the table into piles: jelly beans, candy canes, chocolates, bathroom essentials, socks, gift cards and scratch-off lottery tickets. If anyone uncovered a big prize, over one hundred dollars, by house rule, it was spit between the five kids. For five years running, the rule never had to be enforced as the tickets were duds—long on hope, short on payoff.

The joyous task traditionally occurred late on Christmas Eve with holiday music in the air and eggnog with a touch of brandy not far out of reach. Not this year. In the light of day, Lauri tried to sip coffee, although, her nausea dulled the pleasure. Gary drank a diet cola, his preferred method of caffeine intake.

Gary followed Lauri's explicit instructions, distributing a precise equal share of rewards to the four boys of the brood. Paige had a few unique, gender-specific treats. Lauri's female intuition incited this deviation from her standard holiday protocol.

The stockings were quickly filled. Gary hung them beneath the lip of the painted white mantel surrounding the gas fireplace. "Ready to go."

Lauri pushed off the arm of the couch to stand. "Ready."

"I'll grab the coats and help you down the stairs."

"I can do it. I'll meet you in the garage."

The glaring sunlight penetrated the windshield of the SUV, necessitating sunglasses. The attire was more characteristic of Gary's upbringing in Southern California where Christmas was celebrated with snow-free, high-temperature days and nights that made children wonder about Santa's choice of a sleigh for transportation. A spacious large-engine, high-performance convertible, like Lauri had always wanted, might be a more appropriate delivery vehicle for the jolly gift distributor who was facing his own impending sleepless night on the 24th.

Gary fought to focus on the road as his mind rehashed the information gleaned from a middle of the night web search of the other potential causes of Lauri's blockage, and their possible consequences. He kept this frightening data to himself.

"Lean back and try to take a nap." Gary knew Lauri's tendency to fight to stay awake in the car to keep him company.

"No thanks. How much is this going to hurt? You know I'm a big baby."

"You're one of the toughest people I know. It shouldn't hurt at all. They'll knock you out with higher doses of the same meds I use when I do biopsies on patients. You probably won't remember anything, either."

"You're sure?"

"Trust me."

Lauri reached over and gently poked Gary in the side. "You almost had me convinced. Right up to the 'trust me' part."

Gary chuckled. "Really, it'll be fine."

"Okay, I'm trusting you on this one."

The ride continued in silence for the next fifteen minutes. Out of the corner of his eye, Gary saw Lauri sleeping peacefully with her head perched on her right hand, and her elbow resting on the doorframe. The positioning looked shaky, but at least she was resting. He pondered their fate for the remainder of the drive.

Lauri shifted beneath the white sheet on the stiff hospital bed awaiting her ride to the procedure room. Gary and other family members had been ushered to the waiting room and she had a brief moment of solitude. She earlier met and immediately liked Dr. Allen. He was a tall, friendly, good-looking man with a comforting, confident bedside manner. Lauri felt reassured by her doctor.

The remainder of her life was in turmoil. The holidays, the wedding, and the honeymoon were approaching fast and there were places to go and many things to do. At this moment, Lauri was confined to the hospital with no hope of completing any of the tasks on her long list. She wondered what she had done to deserve this fate.

"Lauri, they are ready for you now," the nurse said. "I'll wheel you into the procedure room." The stretcher lurched forward. "The sooner we get you in, the sooner you will be out. You'll do great."

Gary's previous reassurance faded as the nurse's voice trailed off. Lauri reached up and grabbed the metal railing, her thoughts directed at propelling herself off the stretcher and out of the hospital. Her nurse, sensing the upwelling of paranoia, placed her hand on Lauri's cheek. "I will be with you the whole time. Nothing bad is going to happen. If you need me, I'll be right there."

Lauri relaxed her death grip, keeping her hand and thoughts at the ready if she decided to make an escape. She almost smiled as she thought of Jingles and his unplanned exit from the condo. She extended her neck, tilting her face toward the nurse. "Thank you."

The procedure took longer than anticipated and didn't go smoothly. Despite heavy sedation, Lauri woke in the middle, frightened and choking on the scope going down her throat. She required more and more sedation to keep her settled down so the procedure could continue. She and Gary later joked that this was characteristic of her high tolerance, requiring several shaken, not stirred, martinis to feel relaxed. She wasn't a cheap date when it came to non-medical sedation, and today, in the sterile environment of the hospital, she wished they were serving double rather then single shots of prescription, mind-altering drugs.

A nurse entered the waiting room and approached Gary and the gathered family members. "Dr. Confer, Dr. Allen would like you to join him in the procedure room. We are done. He would like to discuss his findings."

Gary rose from his chair, replaced the outdated magazine on the already cluttered table, and followed the messenger into a portion of the hospital normally off limits to patients' family members. Being a doctor had its privileges. Gary showed the same professional courtesy to colleagues whose family members required his services interpreting their imaging studies.

Dr. Allen extended his right hand, revealing a perspiration soaked armpit. His long and grueling day had ended with a challenging case on a colleague's fiancée. The betrothed would celebrate Christmas in four days, and begin the New Year with their wedding. Dr. Allen wondered how the plans would play out. The alignment of the stars was definitely not working in anyone's favor on this day.

"It was a difficult case," Dr. Allen said, while firmly grasping Gary's hand. The two avoided introductory pleasantries as they both knew there were more pressing issues to discuss. "Lauri has a tight stricture at the ampulla which was difficult to cross. I ended up doing a papillotomy. I debated on stenting her but decided not to. Time will tell if I made the right choice." Dr. Allen showed Gary an image he took through the scope, which demonstrated the ampullary region. "I only saw one tiny stone as you can see on this image. I am hoping Lauri has small, gravel-type stones that are causing the obstruction. The papillotomy should allow the stones to pass into the duodenum. I also took several biopsies."

"Any chance the obstruction is secondary to an alternative etiology?" Gary asked, not having to articulate the word cancer, as the implication was obvious to both physicians.

"Given her age, I don't think so." Dr. Allen put his hand on Gary's shoulder and ushered him down the hall. "Lauri is doing well in recovery. Let me walk you over. And by the way, congratulations on your upcoming wedding."

"Thanks. We're both hoping it all works out." Gary's tone was a murky blend of optimism and doubt.

Lauri lay silent as Gary stood alongside the gurney. He clutched the metal side railing with both hands, transferring his mental anguish to the physical structure. The fully elevated railing prevented the heavily sedated patient from rolling out of bed. While recumbent and immobile, Lauri's facial expression was tense. Gary reached down and tucked her cold hands under the three blankets the nurses had used to cover their patient, a genuine attempt to provide comfort in a time of need. Lauri would have lots of questions, so in his mind, Gary composed the translation of doctor-to-doctor medial jargon into a more colloquial doctor-to-patient discussion.

He would explain to her that Dr. Allen had found the site of blockage at the point where the bile duct connects to the intestine (the ampulla). The narrowing (the stricture) was very tight, and he tried to open the blockage by cutting through the tissue (a papillotomy). He did see one tiny stone and took several samples of the tissue at the point of the blockage (a series of biopsies). The opening created by cutting through the tissue should allow any small stones to pass from the bile duct into the intestine (the duodenum). Dr. Allen considered placing a plastic drainage tube (a stent) across the blockage after cutting through the tissue, but he felt it wasn't necessary at this time. *That should suffice*, Gary thought.

The long day neared its end. Lauri's procedure, being an emergency add-on, was performed at the end of the regular day's schedule. She was transferred from the recover area to her room at eight pm—it was now ten.

Gary sat at the bedside and gently grasped her hand. Lauri's eyelids barely opened, revealing blue eyes without their usual sparkle.

"Hey Baby," Gary said. The combination of exhaustion and medication prevented Lauri from responding. Her eyes shut without a hint of recognition. At eleven, Gary left the hospital. It was a lonely drive home, one of many he was destined to make.

chapter 11

LAURI'S PAIN RIPPED at her abdomen as if an angry internal invader was trying to claw its way out of prison. The gnawing discomfort she tolerated previous to the procedure was replaced by intense spasms of sheer hell; making three natural childbirths seem like a walk in the park.

Over the evening, Lauri required higher and higher doses of morphine that made her babble incoherently. Her brief episodes of clarity were punctuated with desperate cries for additional pain meds. Tears streamed down her face, which was now a brownish yellow hue, as jaundice had arrived as a coconspirator. Lauri's new skin tone and worsening pain indicated that the attempted treatment for her obstruction had failed, with the boomerang effect of worsening the biliary blockage, and causing pancreatitis. Despite all she had to live for, this was the first time Lauri contemplated death as a favored alternative to life. And, it wouldn't be the last.

Gary's early morning consultation with Lauri's nurse and Dr. Allen incited another early departure from his own hospital responsibilities. He raced down Interstate 93 to his second hospital stop of the day. The previous day's sunshine was gone, replaced by ominous dark gray clouds that spat out large thick unflattering snowflakes that haphazardly pounded the windshield. The first day of winter, Friday December 22nd, arrived with the ferocity of a starving African lion on the hunt. Lauri favored a grazing lamb to the king of beasts any day of the week—preferably every day of the week.

Gary focused on the highway as the environmental conditions had soured along with Lauri's situation; the roads were now slippery with slush and ice. Exhausted from the combined emotional and physical stress of his home life and his job, Gary felt like he was on a perpetual 24-hour call rotation. His workday involved the interpretation of images of the inside of the human body. He saw disease everyday in the faceless, emotionally neutral, internal organs of his patients depicted on their CAT scans, Ultrasounds, and MRI scans. Gary's occupational exposure to the devastating consequences of illness heightened his concern for Lauri's fate.

He thought about the necessity for doctors to maintain some separation between their emotion and their intellect when caring for patients. This enables the doctor to focus on how to cure the disease without letting an emotional attachment cloud their judgment. This is why many physicians don't treat family members or friends.

In the subspecialty of radiology, patient contact is rare except under the circumstances of interventional procedures such as biopsies. Gary performed hundreds of biopsies on patients, always attempting to comfort them as much as possible while removing potentially cancerous tissue from various parts of their bodies. The patients' fear of the pending result was always palpable during the procedure, an emotion rooted in the symbolic relationship between cancer and death.

A wise physician Gary trained under clarified the distinction between a physician treating a patient with an illness, and being the patient with the disease. The discussion focused on the difference between being "INVOLVED VS COMMITTED." The physician is "involved" with the illness while the patient or their loved ones' are "committed" to the illness.

Over breakfast, Gary's mentor fiddled with his ham and eggs as he made his point. "It is like this meal," he said. "The chicken was involved, supplying the egg." He pierced a thick piece of ham and held his fork in the air with a sly grin on his face. "Now the pig, he was committed—sacrificing his life." He drew the fork toward his mouth. "Get it." Gary got it.

The early morning session of "spinning yarn" and filling stomachs combined education and necessity. Gary, at this much earlier stage of his career, understood that the patient has their entire existence invested in and dependant on the outcome of a life-threatening illness. Close family members are also very concerned, given the threat to their loved one. Both the patient and their family are fully "committed" to the illness.

On the other hand—the one not holding the fork and the ham—the physician is "involved" with the patient and treating their illness. In reality, and by necessity, the doctor is not at mortal risk of either losing their own life, or the life of a loved one. This level of detachment allows the physician to focus on the solution, rather than the suffering.

With Lauri's illness, the situation was both personal and professional for Gary. As a doctor, he was involved; as a loved one, he was committed. He simultaneously played the role of the fowl and the swine.

Gary hurried down the hall past the nurse's station toward Lauri's room. He stopped short at the door, encountering Lauri's nurse who was exiting the room. "How's she doing?"

The nurse shook her head. "She's having a really tough time. She's in and out from the morphine. Dr. Allen is on his way. He's been back and forth all morning."

Gary momentarily felt immobile, cemented in place by fear and concern. Instincts kicked in, and he instantly regained momentum and composure, rushing into the room. Lauri thrashed around in the bed. Her faced, soaked with perspiration, looked unfamiliar, contorted. The light from the window illuminated her frankly yellow skin, giving her a cold-blooded almost inhumane aura. Gary grasped her hand. Her eyes snapped opened.

"Please help me!" Lauri said. "The pain is killing me."

Before Gary could respond, Lauri's eyes shut and she faded back into oblivion. Dr. Allen hurried into the room and moved to the side of the bed across from Gary.

Dr. Allen gazed down at his suffering patient who was temporarily unresponsive, a result of pain, fatigue, and narcotic-induced stupor. "We need to do another ERCP immediately. Lauri's block-age is worse. She now has severe pancreatitis. We need to relieve that blockage right away." Dr. Allen raised his head and looked directly at Gary. "I should have put that stent in yesterday. I was up half the night second guessing myself…I'm sorry."

Gary and Dr. Allen were colleagues, both members of the fraternity of physicians. Gary knew all too well the professional pain of making a difficult judgment call, and then having it come back to bite you in the ass. Unlike in sports where instant replay gives you the opportunity to calmly consider all alternatives and make the correct call, often in medicine, time is of the essence, and there are no tapes to review and no others to consult. You are on your own and must make the crucial decision at that instant in time, and deal with the consequences if you are wrong.

Gary looked at Dr. Allen. "Don't be. Under the circumstances yesterday you did what you thought was best for Lauri. How could I fault that?"

"Thanks. We'll get it right this time." Dr. Allen extended his right hand. The two men who shared a profession and a genuine concern for the patient between them, clasped hands above Lauri's ravaged body.

Lauri, confused from the combination of pain and medica-tion, mercifully would have only vague scattered recollection of these events. Gary waited at her bedside until she was taken back to the procedure room for her second ERCP in less than 24 hours. She faded in and out of consciousness, frequently babbling inco-herently and spewing disjointed thoughts about unrelated events and people. Gary had seen this chaotic display many times before by patients whose minds and bodies were beyond their own con-trol. Both prescription medication and illicit drugs had the power to severely distort reality.

The morphine, in conjunction with the heavy additional meds given by the ever compassionate and vigilant nursing staff, allowed Lauri to survive her second procedure without waking up. Dr. Allen again visualized her blockage where the bile duct emptied into the intestine. It had dramatically worsened since the prior procedure. He struggled and ultimately succeeded in placing a plastic stent, much like a firm straw, across the blockage in hopes of providing a route for the bile to drain into the intestine. He aggressively took another series of biopsies. Because he shared Gary's concern that cancer might be the cause of Lauri's blockage, he ordered blood to be drawn for a C19-9 test, a biochemical marker sometimes found in the blood of patients with pancreatic cancer.

Gary once again joined Dr. Allen inside the procedure room. Lauri had been taken to recovery and the staff was performing the post procedure cleanup.

"I think she's out of the woods for now." Dr. Allen rose from the stool and dropped his pen atop the patient order sheet; his scrub top soaked with sweat. "I was able to stent the stricture. I'm happy about that."

"Looks like it was tough."

"It wasn't easy. I didn't see any more stones so I took additional biopsies. I also ordered a C19-9." Dr. Allen knew he didn't need to elaborate about the specifics of the uncommon lab test as he was sure Gary already knew the details.

"That's good," Gary said in a weary voice. "I went over Lauri's CAT scan with one of the radiologists downstairs. He was nice enough to give me access to their system so I could look over all her studies. Neither of us sees a cancer, but we also don't see much evidence of stone disease. I'm worried."

"Me too." Dr. Allen reached down and retrieved his pen. "I still think it's unlikely she has cancer, but you never say never in medicine."

"That's for sure. Thanks for all your help." They shook hands for the second time that day and Gary headed to the recovery room.

While both of Lauri's doctors were fearful of the possibility of cancer in the pancreas as the cause of the biliary obstruction, an inflammatory condition associated with small stones was still a possibility. Lauri's CAT scan showed signs of obstruction, but no defined mass within the pancreas. The draining bile duct passes through the pancreas on its way to connecting with the intestine, and while uncommon, cancer in this region was devastating and responded poorly to treatment. Thankfully, Lauri was young, and the likelihood of her having pancreatic cancer was remote.

Dr. Allen's efforts were rewarded. Lauri slowly improved. Her bile was draining into her intestine through the stent. This reduced her pain and nausea. Her skin color improved, returning to its non-jaundiced tone. Her morphine-induced stupor was lifting and she could now converse intelligently between her frequent periods of sleep. She started on clear liquids with the prospect of advancing her diet to gelatin for her Christmas dinner in three days. While these were only baby steps, they resurrected both hope of recovery and a desire to survive.

With the physical challenges temporarily on the mend, the emotional strain took its toll. Lauri would be residing in the hospital during her most cherished of family gatherings. Her fate was in jeopardy, along with her wedding and honeymoon plans. She wondered what she had done to deserve such a calamity. Why was everything in her life suddenly ending up "jelly side down"? If she could get to her stocking hanging on the fireplace mantle, Lauri was sure Santa had filled it with coal.

chapter 12

WELCOME VISITS FROM the immediate family filled the daylight hours of the weekend as Lauri begrudgingly adjusted to the concept of melding hospital sterility with holiday cheer. Gary and Lauri spent the evenings discussed how they might adjust their plans. They contemplated postponing the wedding and the honeymoon, as she would not be able to travel within the next couple of weeks. Gary began the laborious task of calling everyone to cancel the flight and hotel reservations that had taken months to coordinate. The honeymoon with twenty-one guests in Cancun was off, and this reality caused Lauri's heart to ache more than her abdomen.

The kids decorated Lauri's room with a small, lighted table-sized Christmas tree and a few decorations, attempting to elevate her spirits. A portable CD player cycled through a diverse collection of Lauri's favorite holiday tunes. Being enthusiastic members of the technology generation, they hatched a plan to take advantage of the instantaneous information era with the theme that if Mom couldn't come to Christmas morning, Christmas morning would come to Mom. This would be the first Christmas in the lives of her three children that Lauri wasn't at their side sharing the emotion of the intensely joyous occasion. She would desperately miss the spontaneous hugs and smiles.

Christmas morning was devoid of sunlight as smoky dense gray clouds cast a dreary shadow on the beginning of the holiday celebration. The family did its best to elevate their spirits above the bland environmental conditions.

At 10 a.m. the gathering was set. Gary, Nick R, Nick C, Ben, Jack and Paige were determined to put on the best show possible for Lauri. The DVD recorder was on when Lauri called home. Paige's pink cell phone, set on speaker, was strategically positioned on the coffee table in the middle of the living room only a few feet from the twinkling lights of the family tree they had all decorated two weeks ago. Outside, a gentle snowfall descended, granting Lauri's annual wish for a white Christmas.

"Hello." Lauri's voice was crystal clear as the speaker volume on the phone was at its maximum.

Gary's hand went up: 1 finger, 2, 3, and everyone yelled, "Merry Christmas, Mom."

Alone in her hospital room, a silent stream of tears etched Lauri's face. Refusing to spoil the occasion, she responded in her most joyous tone, "Merry Christmas." Lauri patted her face with the bed sheet. "From the looks under the tree, Santa thought all of you were very good."

"Oh, we were," Paige and Jack responded, causing them to turn toward each other and cast a knowing smile. The gifts were opened and the traditional family banter gradually gained momentum with Lauri's voice directing the event with little awareness of her physical absence. As was her habit, almost all of the gifts were signed from Santa. She frequently commented on how clever he was to know just what they all wanted.

"Thanks, Mom, for all the Patriot barbeque gear. This will be great for tailgating," Nick R said. He was a rabid professional football fan. He attended all the home games and caroused with the other fans all decked out in authentic jerseys. The local carnivores packing the stadium parking lot relished the smell of fresh cooking meat in the air, and salivated at the prospect of bone crushing tackles on the field.

"You're welcome, but it was Santa, not me," Lauri said with a frivolous yet slyly serious tone to her voice. She loved making every attempt to perpetuate the fantasy of the gathering, which becomes increasingly difficult as children mature. She couldn't wait to have grandchildren to invigorate the magic of the holiday season.

"Thanks Santa for the Red Sox hat," Ben said, putting it on his head.

Lauri heard the crunching of Christmas paper. "Nick C, what are you opening?"

"I'm working my way through all the stuff in my stocking. Thanks for the coffee and donut gift card."

Despite the mountain of gifts, it took only fifteen minutes to expose all the treasures. Gary and Lauri felt fortunate to have the ability to bestow such a bounty on their children. They also felt blessed to have a group of kids who genuinely appreciated all they received.

The at home festivities were transported to Lauri's hospital room. The clan of children all wore oversized red velvet Christmas stocking caps with a snow white ball on top. The brood, who would normally utter a few complaints about donning the traditional and slightly humiliating attire, were following their hearts and willing to extend themselves to any length to make their mother smile.

The hospital staff pointed, laughed, and shed a few tears as they witnessed the four strapping, good looking, sharply dressed young men, Nick R 6'3", Nick C 6'1", Ben 6'1" and Jack 6'4", lumbering down the hospital corridor, four abreast, arms filled with Lauri's gifts. Their comical, and somewhat menacing appearance, looked like the holiday incarnation of burley football players marching down the gridiron. The less conspicuous duo of Paige and Gary followed close behind, assured of a clear path to Lauri's room. Gary anticipated that the spectacle of the four GQ attired brutes, with the appearance of a dysfunctional group of elves on steroids, would incite Lauri to broadly expose her pearly whites. He was not disappointed.

The sterile hospital room environment was temporarily transformed into a joyous holiday family gathering complete with a twinkling tree, seasonal music and good cheer. While it warmed her soul and lifted her spirits, after an hour, Lauri's strength was evaporating. Her eyelids descended to shade her crystal blue eyes, closing the curtain on this unique Christmas morning family celebration. It wasn't the holiday they had hoped for, but the family was together. While the honeymoon was off, the wedding would go on as planned in seven days on January 1, 2007, location to be determined. Like in many families, it was adversity that formed and accentuated the bonds of commitment and love. Lauri's and Gary's fate was bound by forces that mortal events could never put asunder.

chapter 13

THE GENTLE SNOWFALL of Christmas Day strengthened into a near blizzard, sure to challenge and frustrate ever the most ardent Boxing Day bargain hunter. Lauri awoke braced to battle her illness and the inclement months ahead. She felt a modest sense of hope and happiness this morning as she felt better than in days. Her stomach churned with a gentle and more familiar gnawing—hunger pains—a pleasant alternative to her prior gut wrenching spasms. Despite the bland meal on its way, she looked forward to the impending consumption, which realistically could be adequately devoured by even a toothless individual. The previously simple and pleasurable act of eating now assumed a dominant and formidable role in her life. This challenge was destined to grow in the months ahead.

Gary slipped out of the hospital office, where he and his fellow radiologists interpreted patients' films, to take Dr. Allen's call. The chaos of the past week made him deviate from his more familiar routine of separating his work life from his home life. His attitude and work ethic were engrained from an upbringing where his single parent mother juggled a career while raising four children. He could still hear his mother's constant refrain, "Don't call me at work unless you are bleeding." All the kids knew she was talking hemorrhage, not oozing. She died a couple of years ago, at a less challenging time in her life when a phone call from one of her children was a highlight of her day, rather than an intrusion.

Dr. Allen called Gary to relay the good news that all the biopsies from the two ERCP's were negative. While they both felt relieved and optimistic as Lauri's condition improved, there remained no defined explanation for her blockage. They decided to transfer her to one of the major teaching hospitals in Boston to continue her evaluation. Dr. Allen believed cancer was unlikely, but he felt the complexity of Lauri's case warranted the best care medicine had to offer. "The top medical minds hang their shingle in Beantown," Dr. Allen said.

Gary took another moment away from his work schedule to call Lauri and relay Dr. Allen's thoughts and recommendations. She reached for the cell phone vibrating on the laminate covered nightstand and unplugged the charger. She looked at the caller ID, flipped up the cover and said, "Hi, I was hoping it was you." Lauri's voice was sweet and strong. By opening her blockage, the drainage stent was relieving her symptoms and restoring her spirit.

"Hey, you sound better," Gary said, keeping the volume of his voice down as he stood in the hospital corridor with staff moving around him. "I just got off the phone with Dr. Allen. We both feel it would be a good idea to transfer you to a teaching hospital in Boston. There are a couple of choices he is looking at. Remember, we thought this might be necessary."

"I know." Lauri's voice trailed off. "Looks like I'm not getting out any time soon."

"I'm sorry, Baby," Gary whispered, trying to achieve a modicum of privacy while in a very public setting. "But we really need to figure out what's going on. They will transfer you later today by ambulance."

"All right." Lauri heard the beep, beep, beep, of Gary's pager going off. "You've got to go. I'll see you later. Bye."

The appropriate contacts were made, and while she lay recumbent in the unfamiliar confines of the back of an ambulance, Lauri was once again in the familiar bumper to bumper traffic of Boston. Looking out the back window, she saw they were crossing the expansive, modern, Leonard P Zakim-Bunker Hill Bridge; the widest cable-stayed bridge in the world. Passing over the Charles River, Lauri entered the city she loved, and the site of the most famous tea party in history.

Gary knew the necessity of the transfer, but equally appreciated the downside of being a patient at a quintessential center for medical care delivery and training. He not so fondly recalled the four years of his radiology residency at an equally gargantuan hospital in Detroit with over 1200 inpatient hospital beds, and as many, if not more, staff.

Facilities of such size are like mini cities with people running around in all directions. He, like all doctors in training, spent the years in an exhausted stupor. His cloudy state of judgment was more conducive to being an ideal candidate for participation in a study on the ill effects of sleep deprivation, rather than to be responsible for the well being of sick patients depending on his medical acumen to help them. Perhaps it was appropriate to refer to it as the "practice" of medicine, particularly when referring to the formative years of a physicians' career.

Gary remembered the commonly uttered adage at teaching hospitals, "SEE ONE, DO ONE, TEACH ONE." This referred to the method of learning a new task in the medical field. As a physician in training, the first time you watched someone perform the task, the second time you did the task yourself, and the third time you taught another physician in training how to do it. In three short steps you graduated from inept student, to competent performer, to expert teacher. See one, do one, teach one, repeated over and over in his mind, raising his concerns along with his blood pressure. While see one, do one, teach one was often said tongue in cheek as a funny oversimplification of medial training, there was an element of truth to it that was not at all humorous or comforting. It reflected the challenge involved with learning how to quite literally be responsible for the life of another human being. At some point, even in pivotal matters of life and death, a doctor in training has to perform a task for the first time. Otherwise, there is no practical way for them to progress to the point of becoming competent. Gary would do his best to smooth out Lauri's potentially bumpy journey through this teaching hospital. He wanted to ensure more expertise, and less practice, when it came to her medical care.

The late afternoon sun strained to pierce the dense clouds as Lauri's gurney was wheeled out of the elevator onto the eighth floor medical ward by the brawn duo entrusted with her transport. She felt entombed on the stretcher, unable to move under the crushing weight of several thick nap blankets and three tightly pulled reflective yellow retention straps. The enthusiasm with which Sam and Martha had restrained her made Lauri wonder what shackles they might experiment with during their leisure time pursuits.

Gary left work early and simultaneously arrived on an adjacent elevator with his mummified fiancée. He moved to the side of the transport stretcher and placed his hand on Lauri's covered shoulder. "How was the ride?" he asked.

"Smooth as silk," Martha said, not giving her patient a chance to respond.

Gary smiled at Martha. "Thanks for bringing her down."

"No problem," Sam chimed in.

"I'm tired and I'm in pain," Lauri said.

"We'll get you to your room pronto," Martha said. "Sam, let's move it."

The talkative duo negotiated the crowded hall with the precision and pace of a NASCAR driver. While appreciative of their enthusiasm, the twists and turns accentuated Lauri's nausea. Even when feeling well, she was not one to jump on carnival rides.

The series of subsequent events over the next few hours confirmed Gary's worst fears. The confusion could have been adeptly ushered in by a master of ceremonies in hospital scrubs, one arm raised, hand clutching a caduceus proclaiming, "LET THE MEDICAL CHAOS BEGIN."

Lauri still required pain medication. Upon entering her room and meeting her nurse, she requested some. The polite and genuine response was, "As soon as I have a set of orders from your doctor." After an hour of inaction, Gary gave Lauri some of her prescription narcotics he had smuggled in. He had anticipated the potential delays related to her transfer. Lauri's hospital sanctioned medication would be administered four hours later.

The series of discussions that followed was mindboggling. They were told that no one on the nursing or medical staff knew they were coming, and that they were lucky to get one of the last remaining beds in the oldest wing of the hospital. Lauri and Gary were asked by at least half a dozen different individuals what hospital they were transferred from, what doctor had transfer them, and to which doctor they had been transferred. This went on for hours. It was the medical admission equivalent off déjà vu. The couple felt destined to relive this experience until the next morning's sunrise. There might be another night of insomnia in their immediate future.

Finally, a person wearing a white coat walked into the room. Thankfully, the red coats had been chased out of Boston over two hundred years ago. "Hi, I'm Dr. Simms. I'm the intern on the medical team. Sorry about the delay in getting up to see you. I'm swamped with admissions tonight." She looked down at the 3X5 white index card in her hand and drew a line across it. *Only three new patients to go,* she thought.

Gary had earlier explained to Lauri that an intern is a doctor in their first year of medical training after completing four years of medical school. A first year intern is the quintessential example of "practicing" medicine. The joke at teaching hospitals is that the most dangerous day of the year is July 1st, the beginning of the medical training new year. This is the first day in the life of a physician when they are ultimately held accountable for the life of another human being. It is a day of sheer terror, both for the doctor and the patient. As an intern progresses thru their first year, the learning process continues with a step by step march to mastering their chosen profession. Gary was relieved that it was six months into the training year. He would have been petrified if today was July 1st.

"What brings you in today?" Dr. Simms asked.

Lauri, frustrated by the pain, the nausea, and the delays, thought about flinging back a sarcastic response like, *an ambulance driven by a racecar duo that fancies shackles.* However, exercising personal rather than recreational restraint, she held her tongue. Gary had prepared her for some of the challenges she would face at such a massive institution. Gone was the personalized care of the small community hospital where, as the formally popular TV show set in Boston used to claim, "Everybody knows your name." Lauri took a deep breath. "I was transferred to be seen by Dr. Carpenter," she respectfully replied.

"I will contact the gastroenterology (GI) team. Dr. Carpenter is the attending on that service. However, the GI team will consult on your case, and the medical team will oversee your daily care." Dr. Simms lifted the stethoscope from the deep and overloaded pocket of her white coat and flung it around her neck. She began to take Lauri's medical history.

Dr. Simms looked bedraggled. Gary guessed she was several hours shy of the halfway point in her thirty-six hour shift. Gary remembered being told during his training that you can survive on call without sleep, or without food, but not without both. Dr. Simms looked like a ravenous insomniac in search of a bed next to an all-you-can-eat buffet. Lauri, one of the many patients blocking Dr. Simms' rendezvous with chow and rest, represented one more name to check off her admission list. In order to expedite the process for the benefit of Lauri and Dr. Simms, Gary stood up from the uncomfortable vinyl chair. He extended his right hand and said, "Hi, I'm Dr. Gary Confer. I'm a radiologist in New Hampshire. Lauri and I are engaged. Maybe I can help out with her history."

"Thanks. That would be great." Dr. Simms shook his hand.

Dr. Simms greatly appreciated Gary making her job easier by succinctly recounting all the relevant events of the past few weeks. He explained to the intern the details of Lauri's procedures and imaging studies as only a trained physician could. Dr. Simms said she would be sure to let the medical staff know that Lauri's husband was a doctor. Neither Lauri nor Gary bothered to correct the social history error, as it would cease to be an issue in a few days, as long as they could work out the nuptial details.

Dr. Simms replaced the tools of her trade into the bulging pockets of her white coat. "I'll see you again first thing in the morning, before rounds. Only six months to go and my intern year will be over. Thank God. Then I will start my Dermatology residency." Dr. Simms headed for the door and the next name on her 3 X 5 index card.

Just what Gary didn't want to hear. Lauri had a first year doctor in training who was just killing time. He hoped she would not inflict the same apathy and result on her current patient.

Lauri finally settled in for the night around 10 p.m. with orders written, medication administered, and a sparse scraped together clear liquid dinner. She received a weary kiss on the lips from Gary, her far beyond the intern level personal physician.

Gary left the bedlam of the city and drove one-hour north to the relative tranquility of their home. The atmosphere of the home had changed with Lauri's latest medical challenge and prolonged hospitalization. There would be many more nights of sharing his bed with desolation and loneliness as his only companion.

chapter 14

LAURI AWOKE BEFORE dawn in preparation for what Gary had dubbed the "Parade of White Lab Coats." She was five days away from her wedding, and instead of fussing over the final nuptial details, she was wedged into an undersized hospital bathroom washing her face. As she patted her skin with a poor facsimile of a soft cotton towel, she starred at the foreigner reflected in the mirror. Her face was drawn and bland as she had gone several days without makeup. The hospital issue drab blue johnny hung to just above her knees while the matching bathrobe prevented unwanted and unintentional wardrobe mishaps. Lauri grabbed her brush and began taming the wayward strands of hair that seemed to be reacting to her scalp the way she felt about her medical confinement; escape in any possible direction.

Gary had prepared Lauri for the endless flow of physicians in training that would be asking her questions and examining her, all wearing white lab coats. As Lauri settled back into bed, first through the door was the intern, itching to become a dermatologist, Dr. Simms at 6:30 a.m. As she already knew Lauri's story, her visit was brief. Large coffee cup in hand, she raced to her next patient, hoping with all her heart that they had a skin condition.

The resident, in his second year of post medical school training, exuded confidence. He asked a few questions not articulated by the intern, did an exam with dexterity and ease, and departed, never even telling Lauri his name. In and out between 7:05 and 7:15.

Next up at 7:30, the fourth year medical student, Dr. Lee. She would graduate from medical school in six months and then move on to the next level of training, her intern year. Her clothes were neatly pressed and her eyes sparkled, indicating that she had not rotated with Dr. Simms on call last night. "Good morning. I'm Dr. Lee," she said, simultaneously extending her hand when she approached Lauri's bed. She was meticulous and measured in her history assessment and physical exam, thinking her way through a rehearsed pattern of information retrieval, compartmentalization, and processing. She spoke clearly and listened intently, recording notes for later reference. Dr. Lee explained her status as a medical student, indicating that while medical students are referred to as "Doctor", they have not yet completed their educational require-ments to warrant the M.D. designation. That title is given after successful completion of medical school and a battery of exams.

Dr. Lee worked under the supervision of Dr. Simms. Dr. Simms, the intern, was supervised by the resident, Dr. Battle, who had just previously examined Lauri. Dr. Battle was supervised by the attending physician at the top of the medical team of Ward 8, Dr. Drew. Dr. Drew was a "real doctor", no longer in training.

Gary previously explained to Lauri that the attending physi-cian represented the "alpha dog" of the medical team concept. Stray beyond the parameters of your leash, and you were likely to incur the bite of the leader of the pack. Dr. Lee said that Dr. Drew would lead the entire team on group rounds at 10 a.m. Rounds was the term used to indicate a group of doctors going from patient to patient and discussing their medical care. Dr. Lee thanked Lauri for her time. As she turned to leave the room, Lauri returned the complement. Lauri, impressed with this medical student, felt sure she would become a competent and respected physician.

The final face occupying the bottom rung on the medial team ladder was Dr. Tatum, a third year medical student. He rep-resented the polar opposite of Dr. Lee. His entrance into the room was unflattering as he caught his right shoulder on the door jam, spinning him half way around, giving Lauri a perfect profile view of the back of his white lab coat tucked into his pants. As he righted himself, Lauri viewed his wrinkled collared shirt with a tie knotted so ineptly that he would have been better served with a clip-on. His tennis shoes had long ago worn out their welcome, and the right one wasn't tied. Midway through their encounter, he rushed out of the room retrieving a stethoscope from Lauri's nurse. The history and physical he performed was so disjointed that it caused Lauri's nausea to return. She welcomed his departure. Lauri assumed that Dr. Tatum had been a frequent recipient of the alpha dogs' wrath.

After a short rest, Lauri awoke to the arrival of the entire medical team for rounds. Dr. Drew led the sterile procession of white coats into her room, and in a confident, firm, and slightly condescending voice stated, "Good morning. I'm Dr. Drew and I will be supervising your treatment." He extended his hand.

Lauri reached out and shook it. "Hi, I'm Lauri. Nice to meet you."

"Nice to meet you as well. I understand your husband is a doctor."

Lauri smiled. "Actually, we're engaged."

Dr. Drew shot an irritated glance at Dr. Simms for misinforming him. Dr. Drew tolerated mistakes as well as most of us enjoy the shrill sound of fingernails on a chalkboard. He returned his gaze to Lauri, forcing a tight smile. "Sorry. Congratulations. When is the big day?"

Lauri's smile quickly faded. "In five days. Do you think I will be out by then?"

Dr. Drew paused. "We'll have to see how things go. Let's remain hopeful."

Dr. Drew turned toward the third year medical student, Dr. Tatum. He tipped his head slightly down while raising his somewhat manicured eyebrows, allowing his charcoal eyes to peer over the top of his metal rim glasses in his infamous "double supralenticular" body-piercing stare. Long ago, one of the less intimidated medical students had coined the term to refer to Dr. Drew looking at you above his glasses in a manner that begged the question, "Do you have what it takes to be a good doctor? Show me."

The third year medical student knew the routine. Dr. Drew slid his right hand down deep into the empty pocket of his white coat. "Let us begin by Dr. Tatum educating our team on your condition."

Lauri sensed the terror the third year medical student felt. It was an odd consciousness, like feeling the heat of the mid-day sun while not being able to comprehend how that transfer can occur over such a distance. Try as he might, Dr. Tatum floundered with the chronology of events leading up to Lauri's transfer from the community hospital. His performance was the stellar equivalent of a black hole—no illumination.

After several perspiration-provoking minutes, and with Dr. Tatum now sporting a moistened face and collar, Dr. Drew broke in. "Dr. Tatum, you are obviously ill prepared for this task. And frankly, you look worse than your presentation. Let us have Dr. Lee show you how a competent medical student presents a patient."

Dr. Lee cast a compassionate glance at her junior classmate tying to preemptively, and non-verbally, apologize for the ensuing intellectual blood bath. With the precision of a seasoned butcher dexterously dismembering an entire steer, Dr. Lee succinctly articulated Lauri's current and past medical history with flawless cataloging of symptoms, physical findings, lab results and imaging findings.

At completion of the task, Dr. Drew nodded at Dr. Lee and said, "Excellent. Exemplary display." Dr. Drew then turned toward Dr. Tatum and scowled. Mercifully, the look was the only lashing the student had to endure.

Dr. Tatum had only minutes to compose himself, as he knew he would get first crack at presenting the next patient on their rounds. He would need to keep presenting patients until he got one right. The struggling third year medial student was well aware of Dr. Drew's belief that adversity was the mother of invention. Dr. Tatum was preparing himself for the regurgitation of the next patient's medical data, hoping to avoid another embarrassing and grade lowering display.

Dr. Tatum needed an immediate reincarnation of himself as the male equivalent of his more senior and supremely capable classmate, Dr. Lee. Scott Tatum, fictitiously referred to as "Doctor" by his patients, had spent too much time living the theme, "If you can't dazzle them with brilliance, baffle them with bullshit." It was a tenuous anthem that had thus far enabled him to squeak by. Dr. Drew, aka Alpha Dog, was neither impressed nor confused by the lack of focus and commitment displayed by the student under his charge. Now, the more appropriate cliché was, "Money talks and bullshit walks." Dr. Tatum knew there was precocious little time remaining for him to clean up his act, as well as his appearance, or he was in danger of walking himself right out of medical school.

Dr. Drew turned toward Lauri. "Thank you for being a patient patient," he said, smiling as he always did when he uttered that line. The "patient patient" phrase was Dr. Drew's trademark. Even Dr. Lee rolled her ebony eyes when she heard it, although not so obviously that Dr. Drew would notice. She didn't want to get bit.

Dr. Drew explained that the medial team would provide her general medical care while the gastroenterology service, the GI team, would primarily direct her further workup. "Dr. Carpenter is the attending physician on the GI service. He is a close colleague with exceptional skill. When I need a gastroenterologist, he's the one I see."

This statement elevated Lauri's confidence and confirmed the appropriateness of her transfer to this mecca of medical knowledge. Dr. Tatum, still wounded by the attack of the alpha dog, wished he could be the one to aggressively insert the endoscope when Dr. Drew needed his next colonoscopy.

Early that afternoon, the intern and the resident on the gastroenterology service visited Lauri, her sixth and seventh white coats of the day. They each performed another history and physical exam. The resident stated that she would be going down to the endoscopy lab that evening for another ERCP, which would be performed by Dr. Carpenter. Dr. Carpenter would discuss this with her and her fiancé later that evening.

Lauri placed her third call of the day to Gary, updating him on the latest news of another procedure. Gary had discussed this possibility with her during their first call of the morning. He knew her current physicians would want to get a good look for themselves. She was also scheduled for another CAT scan prior to the evening's unpleasant and unwelcome invasive festivities.

"I know it's necessary," Lauri said. "But, it's no fun. I want to be home with you, getting ready for the wedding."

"I know," Gary said. "Soon Baby...soon."

chapter 15

WHILE ANTICIPATED, THE news of another procedure zapped what little strength and hope Lauri built up since her last ERCP five days ago. Emily, Lauri's nurse, was friendly and energetic. She had been attentively in and out of the room all day between the endless doctor visits. A young and petite woman, Emily's signature feature was her long flowing mane of black as night follicular overachievement. She kept her stunning hair tightly constricted at the back of her scalp, and it swished from side to side with equine fervor as she galloped around the hospital.

She was the highlight of the day providing compassionate care and welcome companionship. Lauri and Emily clicked immediately, sharing local roots and pleasant unassuming personalities. Between the parades of white coats, her flower-print nursing smock provided a colorful and soothing interlude, reminding Lauri of the warmer and happier times of the previous summer. Lauri gradually recounted her medical and social history to her newfound friend. Emily wanted to help with both the physical and emotional needs of her suffering patient.

In the late afternoon, Lauri thought about her wedding, only five days away. She had spent countless hours planning and organizing what evolved into an intimate romantic weekend in Boston for her and Gary, complete with an evening of touching and rousing holiday music with the Boston Pops on Saturday night. On Sunday night, they would have been attending a formal New Years Eve party with dinner and dancing. Lauri had investigated local hair boutiques and paid handsomely to have her hair done early New Years Day, in preparation for the 11 a.m. ceremony in their hotel suite. Flowers would be arriving that morning to adorn the tables and the mantle in the spacious sitting room and adjacent beautifully decorated bedroom. There was ample space for the justice of the peace, the couple sharing their vows, and their five children. The kids all had New Years Eve plans and would be driving into the city the following morning, arriving at 9 a.m. They were all sternly warned about not overdoing it the night before the wedding, despite what was more typically an evening of excess. Lauri wanted them all to look "sharp." The boys would handle the audio and video setup, and Paige would assist her mom getting ready for the big day.

As Lauri recounted the details of the holiday weekend wedding to Emily, tears streamed down both of their faces. The pair simultaneously recognized that this was a fantasy that would fail to make the leap to reality. The seriousness of Lauri's current illness and her level of utter exhaustion were enough to cut back on the festivities. The continuing uncertainty about the cause of her illness necessitated additional tests, which also would take time and consume her energy. All these issues were conspiring to bring down the curtain on what would have been a blessed event. Lights were always out in the theater district on Monday—dark Monday. This included January 1, 2007. Likewise, there would be no spotlight shining on Lauri's wedding.

Lauri and Gary were formulating contingency plans for the wedding. As a last resort, they would have a brief ceremony in the hospital room. This would be followed, at a later date, by a more appropriate exchanging of their commitment.

"I have a better idea," Emily said. "There's a beautiful chapel on the first floor where I often go during lunch to grab a minute of peace and comfort. If you want, I will show it to you on my break."

"I would love that." Lauri reached out and grasped Emily's hand.

Emily bent down and hugged her new patient and friend. "Try to get some rest. I'll be back in about an hour." She quickly turned to leave with her hair casting a wide dark arc, leaving the right side of her back and coming to rest on the left.

"You know," Lauri said, "women would kill to have your hair."

Still moving forward, Emily turned her head revealing a sly smile as if to say, "Eat your heart out."

During the elevator ride down, Emily told Lauri she would contact the Chaplin the following morning to discuss the details. The chapel was appropriately quiet with a solitary man kneeling in prayer in the front left corner. *Emily was right,* Lauri thought. *If I have to be married in the hospital, this would certainly be the best place.*

The chapel had monastic nondenominational spiritual décor with several chairs and kneeling stands. Emily gently rolled Lauri to the right side of the sanctuary. She stopped half way up to the diminutive altar, next to a red velvet kneeling stand. "Let's pray," she whispered to Lauri.

Lauri, too weak to support herself on her knees, remained in the wheelchair clasping her hands together on her lap. She bowed her head and closed her eyes. Emily reached into the left pocket of her nursing smock retrieving an engraved wooden box. She slowly opened it and carefully removed three sets of beads. The faint scent of cedar filled the air. Emily intertwined the beads between the fingers of her left hand and then joined her hands together. She assumed the position of submission on the kneeling stand next to Lauri, her arms resting on the plush fabric. As Emily settled in, the beads initially rocked back in forth. They gently came to rest, emblematic of the calming and focusing of the thoughts of the two worshipers.

While their petitions were silent and personal, Lauri was certain there were shared thoughts expressed by the new friends. After fifteen minutes of reflection, Emily rose and wheeled Lauri out of the chapel.

"Thank you so much," Lauri said. "The chapel is really beautiful. I hope we can use it."

"I know the Chaplin. I'm sure he can work something out." Emily pushed the wheelchair toward her second favorite spot at the hospital. The new friends were in a quite secluded area on the north side of the first floor. The outside wall consisted of large glass panels that afforded unobstructed views of the Charles River and allowed bright sunshine to illuminate the room. "Boy I love the sun," Emily said, directing her face toward the windows while closing her eyes for a moment. She elevated her chin to allow its rays to caress her face.

Lauri assumed a similar posture. "Me too. I can't get enough." After a few moments of silence and solar absorption, Lauri asked, "What are those beads you're carrying?" Lauri had recognized one of the strings as rosary beads.

Emily pushed Lauri toward a solitary chair closest to the glass. She sat across from Lauri and pulled the wheelchair close, so their knees were touching. She laid the beads across her patients' lap and proceeded to enlighten Lauri about their origin and significance. Emily explained that they were three sets of prayer beads, which had been given to her. The first set, an iridescent string of amethyst rosary beads, had been given to her by her best friend's mother. The thirty-three beads signified the thirty-three years Jesus Christ spent on Earth. The ivory *misbaha* beads, Muslim prayer beads, were a graduation gift from her college roommate. The ninety-nine beads represented the ninety-nine names of Allah. The coral japa mala beads, Hindu or Buddhist prayer beads, one hundred eight in total, were a gift from her high school guidance counselor, Satya. "Her name means truth," Emily said. "Satya immigrated to the US from India. She became my surrogate mother after my Mom passed away during my sophomore year of high school. I was so lucky to have her in my life."

"I'm so sorry about your mom." Lauri reached over and gently stroked the side of Emily's face.

"Thanks." Emily looked skyward. "It's a wound that slowly heals, but never scars. She's always in my thoughts."

"I'm sure you're always in hers." Lauri was touched by Emily's honesty and compassion. She wished she could someday bring comfort to her new friend.

Emily explained that the significance of the 108 *japa mala* beads was too involved to get into. The number reflected a mixture of religious and mathematical associations.

"Prayer beads help the worshiper keep track of the number of times a prayer is repeated," Emily said. "With each time, the hand is advanced along the continuous circle of beads. When the circle is complete, the prayer is over." Emily adjusted her hands in Lauri's lap, which allowed the beads to drape over Lauri's thighs. Lauri brought her hands down on top of Emily's. "The prayer beads are a simple way of counting. They enable us to focus on the words, allowing our mind and soul to be receptive to the spiritual gifts."

"You are an amazing person." Lauri's fingers became gently intertwined with Emily's fingers and the beads.

"Thanks. So are you."

Emily, through the people she encountered, and instigated by her own quest of spiritual discovery, had been exposed to all the major modern religious practices. She also researched many of the past ways that humans expressed spirituality. The diversity of Boston and its surrounding suburbs housed every imaginable structure of worship. Emily attended both organized and impromptu faithful gatherings at many of them. No matter the content of belief or the method of expression, she always gleaned some enlightenment and comfort from the experience. As Satya, her surrogate mother had told her, "There are many paths which can lead to the unity of mind, body and spirit. The more tolerant and inclusive one can be, the more likely the enlightenment of the individual can be expanded to unite humanity."

Satya used the example of tributaries of a river to describe the different forms of worship practiced around the world. In the end, when all human imperfection and skepticism is cleansed, we will realize that we are all flowing in the same direction. The joining of these smaller bodies of belief will form a mighty river of harmonious communal enlightenment and contentment. Satya would frequently say, "The path to individual grace is achieved by cradling the hearts and souls of all humanity."

Emily gathered her precious prayer beads and safely returned them to the engraved wooden box that had belonged to her mother. Every time she grasped the box, her body was filled with the love, warmth, and comfort of her own mother's touch. Sometimes, she just sat quietly, both hands grasping the box, allowing her mother's sprit to embrace her entire being. Like the box protecting the prayer beads, her mother's spirit provided eternal shelter for Emily, her mother's precious little lamb.

Emily wheeled Lauri back to her room and gave her a long and rejuvenating hug before helping her back into bed. "Try to get some rest before your procedure. Is Dr. Confer going to make it?"

"He hopes to; if he can get away from the hospital on time. Long drive and all."

"I'm sure he will do his best."

"Emily."

"Yes, Lauri?"

"Thanks for being here." Lauri's eyes welled up and she partially choked on the words.

Emily bent down and kissed Lauri on the forehead. "We are going to watch over you." Emily wiped a tear from Lauri's face.

"We?" Lauri asked.

"Yes, we," Emily said. "Me, my mom, and my prayer beads."

chapter 16

DR. PETER CARPENTER, the alpha dog of the GI service, clad in a slightly wrinkled long white coat, walked swiftly toward the couple. The unbuttoned front flaps fluttered back and forth, revealing royal blue scrubs with the hospital's name in large black letters across his chest. The young recently trained gastroenterologist came highly recommended. He received particularly stellar accolades for his skill with a scope during difficult procedures. He was short in stature, the only trait that would position him on the below average side of the bell curve. His impeccable credentials included the authorship of many articles and book chapters in his field, acknowledgments Gary retrieved from the Internet in the wee hours of the previous morning.

"Hi, I'm Pete Carpenter," he said, at the abrupt termination of the rapid pace he set approaching Lauri's gurney. His hands remained in the deep pockets of his coat.

Despite her exhaustion, Lauri forced a smile. "Hi, I'm Lauri."

"I know all about you, Lauri. I talked to Dr. Allen earlier today. He filled me in on the details from your hospital stay prior to your transfer. Nice guy and great physician. We trained together." Dr. Carpenter removed his right hand from his pocket and extended it across the gurney toward Gary. "Nice to meet you, Dr. Confer. I understand you're a radiologist."

Gary reached out and gave Dr. Carpenter's hand a firm squeeze. "Yes. Call me Gary."

Dr. Carpenter was focused and unhurried during his discussion with Lauri. His earlier phone call with Dr. Allen brought him up to speed on Lauri's previous care, including the results of her two prior ERCP's and biopsies. Dr. Carpenter spoke with a clear, confident, reassuring tone, and, despite the late hour of 9 p.m., he looked fresh and raring to go. "I'm sorry to put you through another ERCP, but I'd feel more comfortable if I can look for myself. Sometimes, I am able to get a little better look at the obstruction." Dr. Carpenter carefully balanced the tone and inflection of his statements so as not to disparage a prior colleague's efforts. Pete Carpenter had many unique qualities, but arrogance wasn't one of them.

"Thanks for expediting Lauri's care," Gary said. "It's late. We appreciate you adding her to the schedule."

"Glad to help. We'll talk after the procedure." Dr. Carpenter's pager went off; beep, beep, beep. He casually reached down and pulled it off the edge of his white coat pocket. "It's always something," he said with a shrug and a laugh. He looked down at Lauri. "We doctors are always on the run. I'm sure you know all about that, Lauri. I'll bet Gary gets paged all the time, too."

Lauri smiled up at the latest addition to her parade of white coats. *This white coat is a keeper,* she thought.

Dr. Carpenter was the reason Lauri needed to be at a teaching hospital. Centers of excellence in medicine attract and are sustained by the medical equivalent of the cream of the crop. Dr. Carpenter represented a physician at the top of his game. Both Gary and Lauri were reassured after their discussion. Dr. Carpenter reached down and grasped Lauri's hand. "I'll see you in the room. Don't worry, we'll take good care of you."

"Thanks," Lauri said.

Dr. Carpenter looked up at Gary. "We can go over the results later."

"Great. I appreciate it."

Dr. Carpenter turned and headed down the hall. He looked at his pager, recognized his home phone number, and smiled. It was time to call home and say goodnight to Melissa, his three-year old daughter.

What a nice alpha dog, Lauri thought. *I'm sure he doesn't bite.*

While the hour was late, the staff in the GI lab was pleasant, even jovial. When Gary apologized for keeping them there so late, they all chuckled indicating that tonight was a "slow one."

"We're usually here past eleven doing exams," a nurse said.

Lauri worriedly explained to the staff her need for extra sedation and her prior experience of waking up during the previous procedure.

"We'll really knock you out," they said. Lauri hoped for a crushing and mind-numbing uppercut to the jaw.

An hour after Lauri entered the ERCP suite, the third time in seven days, Dr. Carpenter emerged and led Gary to his office to review the study while Lauri recovered from the sedation. Gary would later learn that she again awoke during the exam gagging and heaving on the scope. The staff was apologetic and amazed at the volume of sedation she required.

The two doctors stood in the exam room. Dr. Carpenter pointed to the image on the monitor. "See the long irregular narrowing to the distal common duct?" Dr. Carpenter used a pen to trace the area of concern. "As you know, this is the segment of the bile duct which passes through the pancreas before it empties into the intestine."

Gary looked on in silence.

"I first removed the stent and then did the procedure. The tight opening made it difficult to get the stent back in place, but we succeeded." Dr. Carpenter replaced the pen in his pocket. "I took biopsies before replacing the stent."

The slightly ashen and featureless expression on Dr. Carpenter's face was all Gary needed to see. Words would bring the hammer down, but Gary could tell it was poised to deliver a devastating blow.

Pete Carpenter hated this part of his job. "I'm sorry, but I believe it is very likely that pancreatic cancer is the cause of Lauri's blockage. The combination of the length and irregularity of the narrowing is highly suspicious. I wish there was some other likely cause."

Gary was stunned, momentarily mute, but not totally surprised at the news. Dr. Carpenter's declaration was matter of fact, but Gary knew he was genuinely sorry for the bad news.

"I was very aggressive in there. I was able to get some very deep biopsies, which I hope are good enough for a diagnosis. Diagnosing cancer in this region can be very difficult."

Despite a family member being involved, physician to physician interactions were always more direct than the typical discussion between doctors and patients or their families. Gary, while fearing this diagnosis, was still temporarily shocked to have his fears realized and the word CANCER articulated.

Dr. Carpenter's facial muscles were taut. His head slightly shook from side to side. He knew the challenging circumstances Gary and Lauri were about to venture into. He had far too many times seen the devastation that cancer wrought. *A very deep abyss*, Pete Carpenter thought. "Lauri is in recovery. I will come over and talk to her in a few minutes."

"Thanks for all of your help," Gary said. "There's no need for you to break the news. I will do it."

"Are you sure?"

"I'm sure. She would rather hear it from me." While Gary loathed being the messenger, he knew Lauri needed him to be.

Gary appreciated the oppressive weight that the diagnosis of pancreatic cancer levied on its victim. In the arena of cancers, there are varying degrees of lethality. Pancreatic cancer, if viewed from a sports perspective, is the undefeated heavyweight champion of cancers; the cancer that wins every fight.

Part of pancreatic cancer's lethality relates to its stealth quality. It typically grows undetected during the early stages, not causing any symptoms. Commonly, when diagnosed, pancreatic cancer has already aggressively spread beyond it initial site of origin. This represents metastasis of the tumor. Cancer in the pancreas represents a hard working, hard charging tumor, whose goal was to kill the supremely unfortunate individual inflicted with it.

In addition to its malicious star quality for growth and destruction, it is highly resistant to any forms of treatment. Every year about 34,000 people in the United States are diagnosed with pancreatic cancer with upwards of 30,000 of them dying before the anniversary of their diagnosis. The average life span after diagnosis is eight months. While cancer in general incites fear because of the risk of death, the diagnosis of pancreatic cancer assures mortality, most commonly within one cycle of the seasons.

Lauri, 47 years old, coming out of sedation, five days away from being married, the only biologic parent involved in the lives of her three children, likely had an illness that would take her life before she could experience Christmas as the wife of the man she truly loved. It was Gary's responsibility to deliver this devastating news.

Lauri returned to her bed on the 8th floor medial ward just before midnight. She remained dazed and confused from all of the drugs administered over the last procedure, to say nothing of the volume of sedatives and narcotics she had been given over the last week. She was a child of the 60's and 70's, and if you hadn't known better, you might assume her high medication requirement stemmed for recreational drug use while growing up. Nothing could be further from the truth. While she was no Pollyanna, Lauri was also as far from an abuser as anyone could get. She drank a few beers and smoked some cigarettes during adolescence. She smoked pot a few times, always making sure to fully inhale as instructed by her friends, because what was the point if you didn't? As an adult following the national elections, she guessed that a former commander in chief failed to inhale because he and his friends were less well informed.

Lauri's young adult moderation was on practical, not moral, grounds. Her friends' battle cry of "Better living thru chemistry" never offended her, but it also never intrigued her. Her problem with these substances was physical. They induced a cloudy, amnesic, blunted approach to life that she didn't enjoy. Thus, she rarely partook of self-inflicted mental status changes.

As the grip of medical alchemy lessened, she gradually gained awareness of her return to the medical ward. Lauri again appreciated the repetitive disturbing cough of the male patient across the hall. His thunderous reverberating hacks bellowed forth with the resonating strength of the tenor parts in the opera Othello. Gary thought his bravo worthy performance might cause him to bring up his entire lung, rather than just copious amounts of phlegm.

"Oh, I see 'Mr. Hacker' is still here," Lauri said, in a slow deliberate voice. As the couple didn't know his name, Lauri had labeled him "Mr. Hacker." Her speech was scarcely audible over several more of his loud rumbling offerings.

"Yes. If he's contagious, we're all going to be infected." Gary rapidly walked toward the door, which he shut. The clap of the door against the jam registered a decibel level between moderate irritated and really pissed off. The coughs continued but were now muffled. By the time he returned to the bedside, Lauri had fallen back to sleep.

Prior to her procedure, Lauri commented on how much noisier this hospital was compared to the prior one. If she wasn't disturbed by the constant chatter of personnel and guests, it was the intermittent IV alarms chiming on and off. If it wasn't the alarms, it was Mr. Hacker across the hall. Lauri was tempted to ask Gary to resurrect his Lamaze skills and go coach Mr. Hacker. Perhaps, with Gary's comforting but persuasive bedside manner, he could help this laboring gentleman deliver forth the spoils of his pulmonary confinement. Hospitals are 24/7 service centers producing a veritable cacophony of irritating auditory intrusions, stealing slumber from those who need it most.

Neither Lauri's mind nor her eyes could focus long enough to comprehend Gary's explanation of the ominous results of her last procedure. Gary gently kissed his bride-to-be goodnight and told her he would be back in a few hours. He proceeded down the corridor, stepping in time to the medically inspired musical accompaniment of hack, hack, hack and ding, ding, ding.

The sultry blue lights that draped the suspension poles of the Zakim Bridge were becoming an all too familiar and frequent beacon at the beginning of Gary's long drive home. He struggled not to succumb to the hypnotic enticement of the illumination set against the background of the intensely glowing full moon. Only a couple of months ago, he felt perched atop the pinnacle of joy and contentment. He and Lauri had connected on so many levels. While it seemed cliché to say it, they were as close to soul mates as either had ever been, all previously encountered souls considered.

The beginning of Gary's ride home was complete and utter decompensation. Alone in the car, and beyond the need or desire to fake control and unwavering composure, he was free to crumble under the increasing weight of exhaustion and terminal despair. Maintaining barley enough coordination to avoid a collision, he wept like he had only done once before, after his mothers' death two years ago. The tears streamed down his face and he wiped them on the sleeve of his brown winter coat. The unabsorbed heat and humidity fogged the windows. His heart ached for Lauri, and for himself. However, he felt the greatest searing pain for her children who were destined to lose their mother to the relentless and lethal attack of pancreatic cancer.

chapter 17

THE RENDITION OF Frosty the Snowman blaring from his cell phone startled Gary into consciousness. His hand first banged into the clock radio on its way to retrieve the phone attached to the charger cord atop the mahogany nightstand. Lauri insisted on his unwavering participation in the holiday festivities that included the ritual of ring-tone conversion. Every morning he converted back to the more mundane and professionally appropriate standard ring on his way into the hospital. When he failed to make the adjustment, the radiology staff smiled at the jovial jingle emanating from his pocket.

His rapid transition from sound asleep to wide-awake was honed to perfection from the twenty-six years of night call, dating back to medical school. His blurry vision took only a second to sharply focus on the illuminated digital numerals of the bedside clock, annoyingly proclaiming 3:15 a.m.

He grasped the cell phone, flipping open the smooth aluminum cover. Before he could utter a sound, Lauri's frightened voice screeched, "There's a mouse in my room! Come down here right now!"

"What happened?" Gary propped himself up on his left elbow.

"The IV alarm woke me up. When I sat up, I saw the little creature coming around the trash barrel." Lauri took several breaths. "He stopped in front, stood up on his hind legs, and looked right at me. He wiggled those whiskers and I felt my skin crawling." Lauri's voice increased in volume and irritation with each passing sentence.

"Did he at least smile?"

"That's not funny. I hate those things." Lauri tried to catch her breath. "You could see that brown narrow face twitching at me, and, he had one of those long thin tails that drives me crazy. I need you to come take me home…now…please."

"Slow down." Gary reached for the light switch. "Did you call a nurse?"

"Yes. She told me there are mice all over this old part of the hospital from all the construction going on. She gave me a flashlight and told me to rattle the trash barrel to scare him away. I can't stay here."

"Lauri…just try to calm down." Gary attempted to sound comforting, but insistent, as he had to be at work in only a couple of hours. He had already missed more time in the last few weeks than in the preceding twenty years. While he understood Lauri's panic, the excuse of a mouse wouldn't incite compassion and tolerance with his partners at his own hospital. There was no way he could make the one hour commute each way and be back at work on time. "I'm sure there aren't that many mice running around. Maybe we can get you transferred to a newer part of the hospital. Is he still in the room?"

"He disappeared into the bathroom, but not before the little bugger stopped at the doorway and looked back at me again." Lauri's voice was laced with more irritation and less panic. Gary thought the transition toward anger was a good sign, making it less likely he would have to rush south to save the day.

"I'm sorry to wake you. I'll be fine." Her voice and breathing returned to normal. For the moment, her unsanitary roommate was gone, hopefully never to return. As Lauri regained her composure, her thoughts shifted to the procedure performed only a few hours ago. "What did Dr. Carpenter think?"

Gary paused. "Well—"

"He thinks I have cancer, doesn't he?" The rattling hesitancy of Lauri's voice matched the shuddering of her body. Her heart pounded rapidly in her chest.

It was the second time in only a few hours that the articulation of the word CANCER had temporarily rendered Gary speechless. He quickly garnered his faculties. "He is very concerned…nothing is for sure…we need to wait for the results of the biopsies."

Gary recounted Dr. Carpenter's thoughts presenting them with a less emphatic and a more sensitive delivery, reflective of a doctor to patient rather than a doctor to doctor interaction. Gary was both involved and committed to this patient and her illness. The conversation was fragmented with a staccato on again off again presentation as Gary gingerly selected his words, attempting to convey honesty and some hope.

Gary lay in the bed they lovingly shared, while Lauri reclined in the not so sterile environment of the hospital room she shared with her furry roommate. Their greatest fears were apparently confirmed. A physician at the top of his profession felt Lauri had one of the most lethal forms of cancer known to man. A fearful aura descended upon them. With the back of his head sunk deep into the pillow, tears gently eased out of the corners of Gary's eyes, pooling there, and causing a stinging sensation as he suffered in silence.

Lauri had a more audible expression of her distress, whimpering into the phone. Tears flowed down her face in many streams of fear and despair, moistening the front of her hospital gown. She was days away from being married; she had expected to be joyously crying into a bouquet of flowers in celebration of a new beginning. Now, it was an ending she was thinking about.

"What should we do?" Lauri asked.

"I'll be right down."

"What about work?"

"Don't worry. I'll contact one of the guys. We need to be together."

"Thanks. I love you," Lauri's said.

"I love you, too."

chapter 18

LAURI FELT CONSUMED with loneliness and grief. The sun attempted to break through the gray skies of another wintry morning, inching its way above the horizon as a faintly glowing crimson ball set against the backdrop of Boston harbor. The contrast of the red sphere against the dark blue water was intense and beautiful. Gary had already come and gone, with the couple sharing a short period of much needed comfort. He departed without disturbing Lauri's slumber and headed back to his own hospital. He would return later that afternoon.

The New Year was only a few days away. All her dreams and plans, along with her life, were at risk of being lost. Lauri desperately wished this were all a dream. Just as she was poised to surrender to desperation and sorrow, her mortal ray of sunshine, Emily, bounded into the room. Her white teeth twinkled in the dawn's subtle light, and her flowing ebony hair blew in the breeze she generated by her quicken pace. Emily moved around the hospital at one speed, lightning fast.

"The Chaplin gave his okay for you to marry in the chapel," Emily said. When the news failed to arouse a smile from Lauri, Emily grasped her patient's hand. "What's wrong?"

"They think I have cancer." Lauri choked on the words as tears filled her eyes. "The procedure yesterday was not good. Dr. Carpenter told Gary it's very likely I have pancreatic cancer. There's no reason for me to get married." Lauri's last remnants of optimism vanished. Throughout her life she had been a treasure chest of hope and good cheer. Now, that bounty was gone—stolen by the words that her fate had been sealed. "I can't expect Gary to go through with the wedding. It would be best for everyone if I called it off."

When Lauri's verbal surrender was complete, Emily bent down and kissed her forehead. "Lauri, I believe in combining the power of medicine and the power of prayer to battle illness. As long as you have life, you have hope. And, as long as you have hope, you have a future."

Emily retrieved a tissue from the nightstand and wiped Lauri's tears. "Your future is spiritually and physically bound to Gary's. No challenge can alter that connection. You should get married on Monday. It will be a blessed gift you give each other."

"Thank you so much for being here." Lauri reached out and grasped Emily's hand. "I just don't know what to do."

"Let's just take one thing at a time. I'll help you."

Lauri felt blessed to have Emily for her nurse and newfound friend. Emily possessed maturity and wisdom well beyond her twenty-two years. Lauri reflected on how all the nurses she encountered had helped her. They were the true worker bees of the medical profession, and doctors were completely dependant on them. Nurses were the eyes and ears of the doctor, gauging a patient's progress and determining when to alert the doctor for assistance. This sentry function was invaluable, as the doctor couldn't remain at the patient's bedside indefinitely. In addition to this surrogate sensory role, the nurse was also the hands and legs of the physician, performing all the duties required to promote the physical well being of the patient. Most importantly, the nurse was the heart and soul of the medical team, providing comfort and emotional support. While many patients respect their doctor, more often, they love their nurse.

With her dampened spirits starting to dry, Lauri's maternal instincts kicked in. She thought her oldest son, Nick R, might benefit from being introduced to Emily, a modern day Florence Nightingale.

"Emily."

"Yes, Lauri?"

"Are you seeing anyone?"

Emily laughed. "You're already feeling better. Well, yes, I am. A medical student. Why, did you have someone in mind?"

"Caught me. I thought you'd be a good match for my oldest son. He's nice."

"I'm sure he is, just like his mother. Sorry, my heart belongs to another." Emily reached for Lauri's chart on the wall.

"Too bad. You'd be a great addition to my family."

"Thanks," Emily said. "I feel the same."

The remainder of Thursday was filled with a repeat performance of the parade of white coats. Lauri regurgitated the same answers to the same questions. She was poked and prodded by a literal battalion of medical soldiers, all on the look out for the next diagnostic mountain to climb and conquer. Instead of nylon braided ropes, carabiners and crampons, they wielded stethoscopes, pocket sized medical reference books, and a small army of tools of the trade, stuffed into the deep and sagging pockets of their sterile suits of honor. Lauri smiled broadly as she envisioned what Gary would have looked like as a medical student, making his rounds and skillfully avoiding the bite of the omnipotent and menacing Alpha Dog.

Dr. Carpenter arranged to meet with Lauri and Gary early Thursday evening to accommodate the demanding schedule of both doctors in Lauri's life. The meeting was professional and cordial with Gary alternating between medical colleague, during the professional dialogue, and compassionate and concerned fiancé, during the doctor/patient interchange. It was a split personality Gary was very familiar with from the years of being the intermediary between family members and the health care system.

"I asked for a stat reading on yesterday's biopsy," Dr. Carpenter said, with a tone that suggested it was rare for his requests not to be met. "They came back negative."

"That's good news," Lauri said.

Dr. Carpenter forced a tight smile as he carefully chose his next words. "I am very concerned…But in my experience, it is rare to get three back to back negative biopsies from a patient with pancreatic cancer. I was very aggressive in there yesterday. After talking to Dr. Allen, I know he also made every effort to get a good sample of the tissue with the two sets of biopsies her performed." Dr. Carpenter raised his right hand and removed his glasses. He looked directly at Lauri. "While I am still concerned about cancer, there is a rare entity called autoimmune pancreatitis which is a possibility. It is a serious condition which has fooled us in the past, but it is not cancer, and it is not lethal."

Gary reached down and grabbed Lauri's hand. "That possibility is good news. How is the diagnosis made?"

"There are some lab tests as well as other things to consider. I would like to make one more attempt at a biopsy using endoscopic ultrasound before we proceed with the workup of autoimmune pancreatitis. I would like to do it tomorrow."

"Okay," Lauri said, her voice drawing the word out as if it had many syllables. "What's involved?"

"It's like an ERCP, but we use ultrasound to guide us. We put the scope down your throat and into the stomach. We biopsy the pancreas by putting needles through the stomach wall and into the pancreas which sits next to the stomach."

Lauri tilted her head to one side. "And…you've done this to other people?"

Dr. Carpenter chuckled. "Hundreds of them. Don't worry."

"That's easy for you to say. You get to hold the needle."

"It's easy. I promise. You'll see."

"Okay," Lauri said. "I trust you."

"Good. We'll do it tomorrow. Get some rest." Dr. Carpenter replaced his glasses and stuck his hands into the deep pockets of his white coat. "Any questions, Gary?"

"No, Pete. Thanks again for all your help."

"You're welcome. Let's keep our finger crossed."

Dr. Carpenter left the couple much more optimistic than he found them. This ray of hope, autoimmune pancreatitis, did not come without many associated challenges. Dr. Carpenter was also going to draw a sophisticated lab test for autoimmune pancreatitis, an IgG4, which took three weeks to process.

Lauri's upcoming biopsy procedure, the fourth in seven days, would be performed late Friday. The results wouldn't be available until early next week, after January 1st. Dr. Carpenter also arranged for a consultation with the best pancreas surgeon at the hospital for early next week. If autoimmune pancreatitis wasn't the cause of Lauri's condition, and if this final biopsy was also negative, the next step would be surgical removal of the part of the pancreas thru which the blocked bile duct passed. Surgical removal of the duct, along with the surrounding part of the pancreas, would both relieve Lauri's blockage, and allow for a definitive diagnosis of her condition.

As Dr. Carpenter walked down the hall, the announcement from the overhead speaker informed all listeners that it was now 8 p.m. Visiting hours were over. No need to say goodnight to his little girl on the phone tonight. His next stop was home.

Gary looked down at Lauri, expecting a smile of relief to be adorning her face. Her eyes were closed. The physically exhausting and emotionally draining day had taken its toll on her weakened body and spirit. He gently released her hand without disturbing her peace and quiet.

As she drifted off to sleep, Lauri reflected on her nurse's earlier comment. Emily was right. Lauri was still alive, and now she had hope.

Gary's mood on the hour ride home was a far cry from that of the previous night. What a difference a day made. At least there was a possible non-lethal explanation for Lauri's blockage. He crossed the bridge spanning the Charles River and headed north back to New Hampshire. He made his usual litany of calls, starting with the kids, followed by several members of Lauri's family, and then onto the west coast relatives, his two brothers and his sister. Still on the phone as he drove into the garage, he completed the last call before depressing the button on the automatic door control attached to the visor. It was a rare occurrence to have hopeful news to convey, and everyone was able to go to bed for the first time, in a long time, with optimistic thoughts and a hopeful heart.

chapter 19

GARY PULLED THE ringing cell phone from his right pants pocket, keeping his left hand on the steering wheel. He didn't need to look at the caller ID. The sun had not risen, but his fiancée had. Prior to Lauri getting sick, the couple was always up before dawn, efficiently scurrying about as they prepared for their respective workdays. They had long commutes in opposite directions. It was a good thing they were both morning people.

"Hey, you're up early," Gary said.

"I know. It was the first good night's sleep I've had in awhile." Lauri's voice had hints of her more familiar pleasant and energetic tone. Gary loved her ability to bounce back from adversity. She always attempted to view the world through rose-colored glasses. That tendency became harder and harder to adhere to these days, but Gary knew she wasn't giving up or giving in any time soon.

Lauri's tremendous inner strength might go unnoticed by the casual observer. When upset, which was a rarity, she never exploded in rage. She internalized her anger or frustration and rechannel that energy in a positive direction. Her personal history had more than its share of unsavory events that would have soured the average individual's taste for life. Lauri always chose the comfort of the rose over the pain of the thorn. Gary was lucky such a beautiful flower had blossomed into his life.

"I looked over the literature on autoimmune pancreatitis last night," Gary said. "As Dr. Carpenter said, it can mimic cancer. It's not an easy diagnosis to make."

"Is that why he's doing another biopsy?" Last nights' discussion was still cloudy in Lauri's mind.

"In part. He can't make the diagnosis of autoimmune pancreatitis from the biopsy. That's dependant on the lab test. He wants to make another attempt at getting tissue to see if he can find a tumor. The more negative biopsies you have, the less likely it is to be cancer. Also, the ultrasound will give him another look at the pancreas to see if it looks like there's a mass."

"I'm amazed we can't figure out what's going on." Lauri's voice was more vigorous, and it had an edge to it.

She really is feeling better, Gary thought.

"I'm not looking forward to another biopsy. I hope they give me enough meds this time."

"I know. They will." Gary lowered the window to enter his code on the keypad to open the gate to the hospital parking lot. A subzero wind shot into the car, refreshing the stale air from the long ride. "I will try to make it down before you go in for the biopsy. I'll definitely be there by the time you come out." While at first he hesitated to ask, she was feeling better. "Any more visits from your furry roommate?"

"I can handle the mouse. If I have too, I'll ask Paige to visit and bring Jingles."

Gary laughed. "That will go over big with the nursing staff."

"I'm sure they would love having a cat around. Maybe that's what's needed to clean up the vermin."

"Good luck with selling that idea. I'm at the hospital and have to get going. I love you."

"I love you too. Bye."

Lauri forgot to pass on the news from Emily that the couple could use the chapel on Monday for their wedding. The up and down struggle between cancer and any alternative pulled at every thread of her being. Lauri remembered reading once that the two greatest motivators of man were hope and fear. She had her fill of motivation for the time being. Right now, she felt better than she had in several weeks. Had she not been prevented from eating solid foods because of her impending procedure, she would have loved the chance to fill her stomach with more sustenance than the clear liquid plus gelatin diet she was allowed.

Lauri spent much of the day on the phone attempting to return the mountain of voice mails logged onto her cell phone. It was uplifting to personally reconnect with family and friends as well as a joy to offer a non-lethal option for the cause of her current health crisis. In addition to the army of physicians on her case, she was scheduled for an appointment with Dr. Marks, the surgeon, on Wednesday January 3rd. Lauri felt a momentary emotional stab of regret. *I should have been honeymooning on a tropical beach sipping margaritas rather than meeting another doctor.*

The day flew by, pushed forward by more happiness and less awareness of her health than Lauri had experienced in a long time. Lauri slid onto the gurney, her chariot to the procedure room for her fourth encounter with scopes and needles in the past eight days. Gary and several members of the family arrived as she was being wheeled down the sterile white hallway toward the elevator. Stilted conversation punctuated the crowded ride down as everyone attempted to distract Lauri's thoughts from the impending, and all too familiar, challenge ahead. Lauri's frail frame looked even more fragile as she lay motionless, fearing this repeat encounter with doctors and their instruments of investigation.

In addition to her fears of physical discomfort, her emotional state felt as frayed as the cuff on the pants of the male patient services representative in charge of her transport. He, like many young men at the time, was in the habit of low riding his pants that caused them to be trampled under foot. The fractured stands of material dragging along the floor apparently represented an in-fashion look of the day. Lauri suppressed the desire to offer to trim the young man's trousers.

Gary held Lauri's hand as the elevator descended. He reflected on his unique profession and the seeming contradictions it involved. Patients often go to see their doctor because they are in pain. In the process of attempting to diagnose their patient's problem, doctors inflict more pain with medical procedures. It is often the case that patients must first suffer at the hands of the healer, as a prerequisite to be healed.

Lauri couldn't understand why it was taking so long to figure out what was wrong with her. She was preparing for her fourth biopsy in eight days and she desperately hopped this would determine whether or not she had cancer. She felt she had suffered enough; it was time to get on with some healing.

Lauri previously articulated her frustration to Gary. Having spent decades in the field, Gary knew medicine was as much an art as a science. There were often times when it wasn't easy to arrive at a yes or no response to patient's justifiable, but at times, unanswerable questions. His field of radiology illustrated the uncertainties often encountered in the "practice" of medicine.

Patients are sent to radiology to literally have pictures taken of the inside of their body. A variety of modalities are utilized such as sound waves, x-rays and magnetic waves to reproduce images of the internal confines of the patient to determine if there is an abnormality present. Sounds simple! Take a picture and either the patient is normal or abnormal. With over twenty years of on the job experience under his white coat, Gary knew it was not that cut-and-dried. Medicine in general, and radiology in particular, is ripe with uncertainty. The human body is unimaginably complex, and at times seems to resist all attempts at unveiling its mysteries. Professionally, Gary had plenty of frustrating experiences trying to determine a patient's diagnosis. Now, personally, he was on the receiving end of that frustration in his role as the loved one of a patient with an undiagnosed illness.

Mammography, one form of imaging the breasts to look for breast cancer, illustrates the challenges of making a diagnosis. The breasts are composed of a combination of glandular and fatty tissue. Often the combination of elements presents a chaotic mixture of densities that confound the radiologist's ability to quite literally separate the cancer from the normal tissue. Gary always felt that reading mammograms reminded him of the exercise of locating "Waldo" in the Where's Waldo Books he had often looked at with his children. Waldo, like a breast cancer, can be the proverbial needle in a haystack, only obvious after you sit on it.

Breast cancer, like many ailments searched for in medicine, can often have a "waldoesque" character. Despite the best of intentions, the diagnosis cannot be readily discovered. Once you know the patient has breast cancer, you can sometimes go back and "see it" as a subtle, but initially imperceptible finding, on a prior mammogram. Just as once you know where Waldo is in the picture, it is child's play to find him.

Lauri's frustration, while overtly expressed to Gary, was limited to her interactions with him. She was respectful of all the physicians that were striving to diagnose her illness. Her case was unique and challenging, two ominous characteristics for any disease. While weary, the couple was confident answers to their questions were on the horizon. Waldo's days in hiding were numbered.

chapter 20

DR. CARPENTER GREETED the entourage as they entered the procedure staging area. His scrubs were crumpled from another long day of using scopes to look inside patients. After shaking several hands, he walked over to the side of Lauri's gurney. "Ready for another go round?"

Both Lauri and Gary sensed the enthusiasm in his tone.

"Please make sure I don't wake up this time. I'd rather sleep through this one," Lauri said, loud enough so the nurse coming up from behind Dr. Carpenter could hear.

A burly nurse with the name Paul monogrammed on the pocket of his scrubs slid in next to Dr. Carpenter. "Don't worry, little lady. I looked at you last procedure sheet. I'm gonna up your meds, no extra charge. But, no driving for you tonight."

Lauri grinned, and a few chuckles rumbled through the crowd. Lauri thought, *if the meds don't work, this hulk could knock me out with just his pinky.*

"This procedure will take longer than just the ERCP," Dr. Carpenter warned. "We should get a good look at the site of the obstruction. I will do my best to get a deep set of biopsies. This should answer some of our questions."

"That would be good," Lauri said. "I like you a lot, Dr. Carpenter, but we really have to stop meeting like this. I don't want your wife to get suspicious."

Dr. Carpenter smiled. "Lauri, my wife is a saint. I am lucky to have her." Dr. Carpenter slightly turned toward the nurse on his right and reached up, stretching to place his hand on Paul's massive shoulder. "We call this guy Tiny. He is my brother-in-law. Would you do anything to hurt his sister?"

The crowd burst out laughing.

"I wouldn't dare," Gary said.

"Me neither," Lauri said. "Nice to meet you, Paul."

"My pleasure. We'll bring you right in." Paul pointed at Dr. Carpenter while looking at Lauri. "Don't worry; you're in the best hands in the hospital." Paul turned and headed back to the nurse's station.

"Seriously, Lauri," Dr. Carpenter said. "You'll have to meet my wife someday. I'm sure you'd hit it off like two peas in a pod."

Lauri smiled back. "I'd like that."

Dr. Carpenter eased away from the gurney. "I'll see you inside. And Gary, I'll talk to you after."

As he passed the nurse's station, Tiny handed Dr. Carpenter a mug of steaming coffee. "Thanks."

Lauri looked over at Gary. "He sounds excited."

"I'm sure he is. Docs like him like a challenge." As soon as the words left his mouth, Gary wished he had chosen a better way to express himself.

"Do you think this is going to be difficult?" Lauri asked, her voice slightly trembling.

"No, sorry. That's not what I meant." Gary searched for words to ease Lauri's concern. Unfortunately, none popped into his head. "From my reading, this procedure is only done at the top medical institutions by doctors at the top of their field. Working at the cutting edge of his field is what motivates guys like Dr. Carpenter." Gary paused again. "You know what I mean. Maybe I should just shut up for now."

"It's okay. I know what you're trying to say. It'll be all right. Like Tiny said, I'm in the best hands in the hospital. Who'd be dumb enough to argue with that giant?" Lauri reached up and pulled Gary down, kissing his lips. She turned to the crowd and gave a subtle wave. "I'll see you all soon."

What Lauri understood, but Gary had a hard time conveying, was that challenging diagnostic dilemmas were what drew top physicians to upper level teaching hospitals. Dr. Carpenter was excited by obscure medical cases that required the skill of a detective to discover their cause. There was an adrenalin rush associated with the most difficult cases. Dr. Carpenter was an adrenaline junky, a Sherlock Holmes in a long white coat.

Dr. Carpenter completed the latest installment of medically sanctioned torture and met with Gary and the family to discuss his findings. He was perplexed. "I don't see an obvious mass in the pancreas." He paused, choosing his words carefully. "In my experience, that is unusual. Given all we know thus far, I would expect to see a mass if there is cancer present."

"Does the lack of a defined mass make autoimmune pancreatitis more likely?" Gary asked.

"It does, but that diagnosis is one of exclusion." While Dr. Carpenter knew his statement had registered with Gary, for the benefit of the non-medical relatives in attendance, he continued, "We first must prove cancer is not present. If the next set of biopsies I just took is negative, cancer is less likely. We also need to wait for the results of the IgG4 blood test, which will be positive if autoimmune pancreatitis is present."

"How did the sedation go?" Gary asked.

"Fortunately, thanks to Tiny, she slept like a baby. It'll be sometime before she is awake." Dr. Carpenter started to turn and walk away. "I'll check on her later and I'll call you with the biopsy results a few days after the wedding. Good luck. I hope it's a happy new year."

"Thanks. Same to you."

The start of the eighth year of the new millennium signaled the beginning of a new life, a life that Lauri and Gary would share as husband and wife. It was also a signpost that would mark the specific challenges the new legally sanctioned couple would jointly contend with. The revelry in Times Square was only a couple of days off, and Dr. Carpenter was hopeful that the new year would usher forth answers to the couple's, as well as his own, questions.

Doctors feel added pressure when treating someone with a connection to the field of health care. The motivation and effort to cure the patient is no different. The additional burden stems from the feeling of having someone watching over your shoulder, much like a car mechanic might feel if he were attempting to repair the vehicle of another mechanic. There was little wiggle room when it was obvious that efforts to diagnose the patient's condition had failed. Both Gary and Dr. Carpenter were feeling the strain of an undiagnosed problem. Everyone involved were desperate for answers.

As much of her recent past, the weekend was shrouded with considerable uncertainty. Lauri at times felt like a ping-pong ball in a match between the cancer team and the non-cancer team; batted back and forth without mercy. Her body and her mind had suffered many a menacing paddle marks over the last several days. Lauri was searching for an answer, and the journey was taking its toll. She was yearning to call out, "GAME OVER—EVERYONE GO HOME."

Lauri made slow but steady progress on Saturday and Sunday. Visits from family and friends brought about a rapid botanical transformation with numerous vibrant bouquets of flowers adorning the windowsill and nightstand. Her large window provided expansive views of the Boston skyline causing friends to joke that with some remodeling, the place would make a great condo. The joyous reconnection with family and friends nourished and revitalized Lauri's depleted spirit and soul.

The gastroenterology weekend staff physician covering for Dr. Carpenter, substitute alpha dog, had met Gary and Lauri on Saturday morning and returned again on Sunday, New Year's Eve. He was optimistic, elevating Lauri's spirits, as it was his opinion that it was unlikely for Lauri to have pancreatic cancer. He felt autoimmune pancreatitis was the most likely cause of her symptoms.

Lauri's diet was advanced to solids, and while she still had little appetite, she forced small quantities of food down in hopes of improving her strength and stamina. Much to their surprise and delight, Dr. Carpenter had been in contact with the weekend hospital staff, and they agreed to release Lauri from the hospital that afternoon. While still quite ill, she was now only on oral medications. Her improvement, coupled with Gary's ability to take care of her at home, enabled Lauri to escape the confines of her medical prison eight hours before the stroke of midnight.

Before being discharged, Lauri tightly hugged Emily. "Thanks for everything. I couldn't have made it without you." Their patient/caregiver relationship had rapidly evolved into a close and supportive friendship. They were both happy for Lauri's release, but saddened to be parting ways. Their embrace lasted minutes with tears gently descending the smooth sloping curves of their slightly reddened cheeks.

"Lauri," Emily said, "never ever forget, where there is life there is hope, and where there is hope, there is a future. There are many pairs of hands supporting you. You will continue to be in my prayers as I clasp them together with the combined strength of my prayer beads and my mother's spirit." Emily kissed Lauri's forehead. "You are a part of my life, and I will always be there for you. If not in body, then in spirit."

Lauri's mouth quivered as their embrace ended.

"Have a beautiful wedding." Emily smiled. "I know you will." She turned around and walked away at her normal accelerated pace. This drew her ebony equine-like mane away from her back. As the distance between their linked souls increased, Emily's signature hair began its rhythmic back and forth sway.

While one individual in her thoughts and in her deeds, Emily embodied all the goodness of the nurses and health professionals who had cared for Lauri. While excited to be going home, Lauri was eternally grateful to everyone who had participated in her care. The gift of healing and support passed from their hands to Lauri's heart. What Lauri received, she hoped to someday pass on to others in need, completing another small circle of the gift of giving and receiving, the gift of grace and gratitude.

chapter 21

THE METAL FLOWER baskets along the deck railing were barren. The Christmas decorations had been returned to their storage boxes and the house lacked the visual stimulation of the festive season Lauri so cherished and enjoyed. The scene mirrored the emptiness she felt as the holiday season had come and gone amidst a life, her life, dominated by illness and uncertainty.

The inaugural sunrise of 2007 crested above the patchy white and green rolling hills with warmth and brilliance as the rays of sunshine bathed the easterly facing rooms of their condo. The evening's wintry precipitation created an ivory and emerald patchwork as the snow intermittently obscured the stoic pine needles. They appeared frozen in silence and solitude, bound to their supportive wooden perch. The evergreen branches sagged under the added weight of snow and ice. The deciduous trees were bare no more as a white ribbon crested each brown branch, looking like a meticulously adorned topping of icing had been hand painted on them.

Gary stared out the window, his breath condensing on the surface. On the trees just beyond the panes of glass, ice crystals frosted the un-orphaned pinecones still clutching to their maternal branches. The less fortunate of the brood lay strewn about the base of the tree, most covered in a blanket of crystalline opaque water. When winter succumbed to spring, new life would germinate from the seeds cast out from their fall.

While there were plenty of reasons to be somber, Lauri cleared her mind of the recent calamities, joyously focusing on her wedding day. Her brother and sister-in-law had insisted the wedding take place in their home. Lauri and Gary felt blessed to have such an understanding and accommodating family. In truth, her siblings and their families were thrilled to attend what had previously been slated to be an intimate ceremony with only the couple, their five children, and the Justice of the Peace.

"Paige, don't forget your dress," Lauri said, as she slowly descended the steep stairs down from the top floor of the condo; her fatigue magnified by their multilevel home.

"Mom, I've got it. Don't worry." The sliding closet door made a loud crashing sound. "I'm just grabbing it."

"I want to make sure everyone is set. We don't have time to come back for anything." Lauri struggled to catch her breath as she stepped down onto the main floor.

"Why didn't you tell me you were coming down?" Gary asked, slightly irritated as he had told Lauri he would help her down the incline.

"I need to build up my strength," Lauri said, barely able to get the words out as she drew in another deep breath. "You shouldn't have to help me. I don't want you marrying an invalid."

"You're doing great. Just give it some time." Gary slid his arm around her shoulder and helped Lauri over to the couch. "Take a rest for a minute while I load the car." Gary turned toward the flight of stairs down to the finished walkout basement. "Are you guys ready?" he shouted. "Come give me a hand."

The four boys were watching the first of several televised college football bowl games. "We're coming," several voices echoed up the stairs. "Right after this play."

"Get up here, now. We need to get going."

The four avid fans knew there was no room for negotiation. The remote button was pushed and the clan jockeyed for position. They wedged into single file to get up the stairs to the living room. The four brutes loaded the two cars and the family headed south for the ceremony that would legally join them together.

Lauri's brother's home, which on its own stood as a beautiful two story colonial, had been internally transformed in less than twenty-four hours into a wedding chapel. The vows would be exchanged in the formal living room with the couple clutching hands as they stood next to the mantle. A gentle fire blazed in the hearth. Three large white flickering candles were evenly spaced along the mantle with their bases obscured by the intertwined stems of white roses. The reflections in the mirror of the three defined flickering torches appeared as a multitude of conical embers, illuminating the hopes and dreams of a new beginning.

Lauri's extreme weakness made her initially consider forgoing formal attire. However, she was bound and determined not to let her illness confiscate all of her plans. She battled through the weariness and nausea, and with the support of all the women gathered, she looked radiant as the blushing bride-to-be. She wore a stunning ivory gown with sewn in beads. Her hair was perfectly arranged by her second sister-in-law. She opted to forego shoes, as her weak muscles couldn't steady her frame perched on heels. Gary wore a tuxedo and chuckled when the boys all greeted him as The Emperor Penguin. The four boys looked sharp in their neatly pressed shirts, sans ties, as per their request. Paige looked breathtakingly beautiful in her full-length lavender satin dress.

Lauri and Paige shared a lifetime together. Now, mother and daughter were both adults, and as such, possessed a common fear of what the future held. The maternal/child bond reflects emotions and commitments, both spoken and silent, which reverberate with a harmony born of similar blood and history. As the rose petal doesn't fall far from the blossom, the two eternally linked souls were the picture of excited anticipation. For the moment, they tucked away their communal concerns beneath the surface of their skin. Neither was naïve of the concerns at their doorstep, but neither would surrender to their fears. They stoically employed makeup and fortitude to cover up their mutual worries.

The justice of the peace, in her full-length black robe, orchestrated the abbreviated ceremony. She stood to the right of the decorated mantle while Gary and Lauri were positioned to the left.

The opening comments, while composed by the soon to be betrothed, were read aloud by the licensed officer of the state.

> *LAURI AND GARY*
> *JANUARY 1, 2007*
>
> *We come together today in celebration and recognition of the beginning of a new family. This ceremony is small and simple to focus attention on the most precious asset we have, each other. With this union, we both join two individuals and bond together two families. We move forward with acceptance and respect for the past, as it is our history that defines who we are today. We pledge to be a positive influence on each other's lives as we live and grow together. This pledge extends to each and every member of this family.*
>
> *The cornerstones of any lasting and happy relationship are love, trust, respect and honesty. These attributes provide the foundation that fosters growth and prosperity of both the individual and the family. We are all now responsible for nurturing this union by investing ourselves completely towards its success.*
>
> *A second marriage, with the union of two families, presents unique challenges and opportunities. The path to happiness is paved with the recognition that we are all bound together to support and encourage each other. The weight of the inevitable challenges we all must face will be lighter to carry, and the elation of the many triumphs ahead will be that much sweeter, by sharing the emotions with the ones you love and the ones who love you.*

The words were composed at a previous juncture when the emotions of love and commitment were not so intimately tied to life and death. The thoughts assumed greater meaning to all gathered for the hallowed occasion. The uncertainty of recent events caused tears to be shed that were laced with equal parts celebration and worry. Every single heart beating in the room raced on the combined stimulation of joy and fear. This was a wedding where bliss and despair were strange bedfellows.

chapter 22

GARY EASED THE SUV into the fast lane, accelerating past drivers with less pressing engagements. The southbound traffic flowed smoothly as the morning commute ended hours ago. This trip to the hospital was unique for the pair, their first drive to the Boston medical center as a married couple. Lauri found the title of husband and wife comforting. There were common concerns, some spoken and some silent, which loomed over their heads. They had both considered postponing the wedding until the current crisis matured into a defined illness with proposed treatments. The uncertainty of Lauri's illness scared them both to death.

Lauri, on a number of occasions, told Gary she would completely understand if he wanted to postpone the wedding. While this was her verbal declaration, her underlying emotions were more tenuous—if they waited, she feared it might never happen. *Would Gary want me if he knew I was really sick?*

Gary's view was skewed in a different direction. While he hoped her illness would not be related to cancer, his medical knowledge dictated a level of grave concern for Lauri. He knew what he was getting into if pancreatic cancer was the final diagnosis. He chose to proceed with the wedding because, quite simply, it was the right thing to do. Moving forward with the wedding gave Lauri hope of a future. This was a gift he would never deny her.

The couple drove for ten minutes with only the sound of the radio tuned to Lauri's favorite country station. "I looked up Dr.

Marks' bio on the hospital web site last night," Gary said. "He's one of the top pancreatic surgeons in the area."

Lauri reached down to lower the radio volume. "I wish I didn't need to see him. We should be in Cancun, not going back to the hospital. This whole thing's a disaster."

"I know, but we need to figure out what's going on. The stent is only a temporary fix."

"Is it is more or less likely I have cancer? Is Dr. Marks going to answer that?"

Gary maneuvered the vehicle out of the fast lane and turned toward Lauri. "He's a very smart guy with a lot more experience in this area than I have. Boston is a mecca for medicine. You couldn't be in better hands. Let's see what he says."

Lauri didn't press, allowing Gary to forgo giving his own opinion. She sensed that while he was hopeful cancer was not the cause, he had his concerns.

Nature was particularly cross. The combination of bone chilling cold and biting wind could peal the paint off of an automobile, to say nothing of the damage it inflicted on the surface of the human body. Lauri's fingers were chapped and cracked, skin ailments her previous medical intern, the budding dermatologist, would have been happy to treat.

The red brick medical office building was located adjacent to the hospital Lauri had left only four days ago. The walk from the parking garage to the surgeon's office was a brutal test of will and fortitude. Gary wrapped his right arm around Lauri's shoulder, pulling her tight in a futile effort to shield her from the mind numbing frigid conditions. At the end of the grueling trail, there was a line of patients and companions stalled outside the building. The revolving door was motionless; a consequence of a mishap with an elderly woman's purse strap wedged between the previously spinning door and its stationary metal frame. A motionless glass barrier now separated the visibly shaken owner from her belongings. Despite multiple layers of clothing, it was obvious that this woman was a skin and bones replica of her former self. Cancer had ravaged her body, and now, she was faced with an additional, more mundane challenge.

It wasn't enough that she had to shoulder the burden of her cancer; she also had to endure the traumas of everyday life while depleted of the personal resources to deal with them. The jammed revolving door was emblematic of how life can be going along seemingly without a care, and then, there is a glitch, an interruption in the flow of relative normalcy, and you are faced with an encounter that changes your life. Illness is often abrupt and unexpected, altering your life immediately, and sometimes permanently.

A receptionist escorted the couple into the corner office of the surgeon, Dr. William Marks. He rose from behind his desk revealing his lanky frame. His deep-set dark brown eyes were accentuated by precisely chiseled facial contours. He wore surgical scrubs as this was his normal day in the operating room. He had graciously agreed to see the couple between cases.

Windows with majestic views of the Boston skyline and harbor formed the northeast corner of the office. The remaining walls were obscured by floor to ceiling bookcases packed with meticulously arranged volumes of surgical texts and medical periodicals. The corners of his desk were occupied by the non-medical passions of his life, photos of his wife and three children.

"Dr. and Mrs. Confer, it's nice to meet you. Please take a seat." The couple settled into the adjoining tan fabric chairs facing the surgeons' desk while Dr. Marks waited for them to get comfortable before he eased back down into his oversized leather chair. "I have reviewed all of the workups and talked to Dr. Carpenter."

Beep, beep, beep, beep. Dr. Marks reached down retrieving his pager and reviewed the display. "That can wait." He set the pager on the desk. "It has been quite an ordeal for the two of you. Let me just say, Mrs. Confer, I think it is unlikely that you have pancreatic cancer."

Lauri's shoulders relaxed down and Gary heard her exhale. A broad smile illuminated her face. "Oh thank you," she said. Gary reached over and grasped her hand.

"However, as your husband will tell you, we never say never in medicine. I think the likelihood of cancer is small, but additional workup is required to prove that."

Gary turned toward his lean colleague, whom he sensed was pressed for time. "What do you think is the most likely diagnosis?"

Dr. Marks shifted in his chair, bringing his left hand up to his chin. "I believe chronic inflammation, either from small stones or possibly autoimmune pancreatitis. Autoimmune pancreatitis is a rare entity that can mimic cancer. We have done surgery on patients thinking they had pancreatic cancer and later found out they didn't."

Beep, beep, beep, beep. Dr. Marks snatched the pager from the desk with his right hand as his facial muscles tensed. He drew in a deep breath. Obviously, this surgeon was in high demand. "My plan is to administer high dose steroids for two weeks and then recheck your CAT scan and ERCP." He leaned forward looking intently at Lauri. "If there is no improvement on the follow-up studies, and if your IgG4 blood test is negative, I will be much more concerned and we will need to do surgery to remove the diseased area."

Gary leaned toward Lauri while looking at Dr. Marks. "How extensive of a surgery would you perform?"

"I would do the Whipple Procedure. I am sure you are familiar with it, Dr. Confer. Mrs. Confer, I don't want to discuss the particulars right now. We can cross that bridge if we come to it. I apologize for all of the interruptions, but I am needed in the OR."

Dr. Marks had been direct without being abrupt as he had a series of patients waiting for him to work his magic. He possessed the quintessential surgeons' mentality. For him, there was no greater challenge and thrill than taking the life of another human being quite literally into his own hands. His daily routine was filled with decisions that were absolute when it came to earthly decisions.

A surgeons' confidence can be misconstrued by others as cockiness. They can be viewed as self-absorbed champions of self-promotion and self-gratification. The truth is, there is no other profession in the world with this level of responsibility and stress. Their actions can either give life, or take it away—an ability sometimes claimed by mothers when their children misbehave: "I brought you into this would, and I can take you out of it."

Surgeons are often the last barrier between a dying patient and their maker. It is a pivotal battle with the talents of the surgeon matched against the adversary of the patients' illness. To the victor go the spoils—life lost versus a life resurrected. This is a specialty in medicine where supreme self-confidence is a necessity, as an element of doubt could spell disaster with the patient exiting the operating room feet first for the morgue. There was no greater failure than losing the life entrusted to your care, and there was no doctor who hated failure more than Dr. Marks.

Dr. Marks rose from his chair. "I must go. Pick up your prescription for the steroids at the front desk. See you in a couple of weeks." While a man of science with supreme confidence in his abilities, Dr. Marks appreciated the limits of human medical intervention. He walked around the desk and paused next to Lauri, placing his hand on her shoulder and leaning down. "If surgery is necessary, I will do the best I can to help you. There are three factors that will control the outcome. There is me, there is you, and there is faith."

Dr. Marks' spiritual reference surprised Gary; Lauri felt comfort. He was a man of science who wielded razor-sharp metal instruments. His amazing manual dexterity enabled him to open the human body, remove the offending agent of ill will, and reconstruct the supremely grateful patient to a physical condition vastly improved prior to his handiwork. Despite all his earthly accomplishments, Dr. Marks was, above all, a humble man when it came to comparing his powers to the spiritual influences in his life and in the lives of his patients. While he rarely asked for or needed the assistance of other surgeons to perform his intricate mortal miracles in the operating room, he frequently solicited spiritual support and guidance in both his professional and personal life. He was a renaissance man with both feet firmly on the ground, but his heart and soul remained open and receptive to the spiritual miracles and influences that lacked a scientific explanation. Lauri's spirit and her spirituality were enhanced by her appointment with Dr. Marks.

The morning's blustery conditions had calmed. The couple's exit from the building, through a fully functioning revolving door, revealed a cold, tranquil, winter afternoon in New England. Lauri tilted her chin up, directing her face skyward into the bright sunshine, letting it bathe her entire being. "I love the sun." She nudged Gary. "When are we going to winter in Florida?"

Gary chuckled. "That's what I love about you, always looking on the bright side." He very gently hip-checked Lauri as he wrapped his arm around her shoulder and pulled her close. He planted a kiss on her cheek. "Soon Baby."

Lauri kissed him on the lips. "Not soon enough. Baby."

The clear blue skies were an infrequent but greatly appreciated alternative to the depressing dreary gray atmosphere that routinely dominated the first three months of the year. The winter blues were easier for everyone to shake when the light and warmth of the sun had an unobstructed path to the surface of the Earth. The couple hurried out of the city, avoiding the evening rush of workers that routinely converted a flow of traffic into a crawl.

Recently, Lauri's hopes and dreams shifted between peaks of joy and cavernous valleys of despair, a rollercoaster of emotion that accentuated her baseline nausea. Lauri desperately wanted relief. With her latest doctor believing cancer was unlikely, hopefully, the ride was about to end.

chapter 23

GARY AND LAURI WALKED arm in arm along the uneven brick sidewalk from the hospital parking garage to Dr. Marks's office. The prior two and a half weeks were a blur as Lauri had been too fatigued and medicated to appreciate the many sunrises and sunsets. Two days ago she had her follow-up CAT scan and meeting with Dr. Carpenter who repeated the ERCP and biopsies.

Lauri arranged to have a large gift basket of cookies delivered to the endoscopy suite on the day of her procedure. Dr. Carpenter marveled at her thoughtfulness given her weary condition. The staff referred to her as the "cookie lady" for the entire next week.

Seated in Dr. Mark's office, Lauri dozed off while Gary's mind raced with thoughts of their next challenge. She awoke to the reassuring touch of her surgeon who momentarily rested his hand on her shoulder as he moved past the couple. He eased around the side of his massive light maple desk and took his seat. Lauri sensed a change in Dr. Marks. Gary thought he knew what had happened, and he braced himself.

The spring mechanism of the chair squeaked as Dr. Marks rocked back and forth. As he shifted his body, the leather creaked despite his lean form. His arms were folded across his chest. He slowly leaned forward, resting them upon the desk. "Things did not work out as we would have hoped. Your CAT scan and ERCP are unchanged, indicating no response of your disease to the steroids. Also, the IgG4 marker just came back this morning. It's negative, ruling out autoimmune pancreatitis."

Dr. Marks maintained a fixed gaze directly on Lauri, their eye contact never wandering. Lauri leaned in slightly, heaving a sigh. She then unconsciously recoiled, attempting to deflect the anticipated verbal assault.

"Mrs. Confer," Dr. Marks said, "I am now forced to believe that you have pancreatic cancer."

Neither Gary nor Lauri could respond. Gary had feared this diagnosis for quite some time, but he was still momentarily muted. Lauri was stunned and speechless. She was blindsided by Dr. Marks' emotionless declaration of her supreme misfortune. He offered no apology for previously raising her spirits.

Gary recalled his previous warning: "We never say never in medicine." Gary sensed that Dr. Marks felt as if he had failed, as his first impression did not withstand the test of time or further investigation. Often, the greater one's talents, the harder it is to accept our own shortcomings. Dr. Marks didn't acknowledge the distraction of his previous miscalculation. He had a job to do, and that job was dealing with his patient's current surgical needs.

"You will need to have the Whipple Surgery to remove the diseased tissue. This is a very complex surgery, but in the right hands—my hands—the mortality risk is less than five percent."

Dr. Marks retrieved his day planner from the top right drawer of his desk and thumbed through the pages. "I would like to schedule it for January 31st. You need to be off the steroids for at least a week."

Gary reached over and tightly grasped Lauri's hand. He could see she was fighting to gain some composure, fearing that if she tried to speak, she might completely lose control. Lauri had an endearing habit of sometimes speaking for Gary, most often finishing his sentences if he paused and she was certain what came next. While she wasn't always correct, it was always funny. The current circumstances were in no way humorous, but this was a time when Gary would speak for Lauri. "Have you had any similar cases in patients Lauri's age that didn't end up having cancer?"

Dr. Marks leaned back, separating his arms as he withdrew them from the maple surface and resting them on the chair. "Yes… Rarely."

"Would you do an intra-operative biopsy before going forward on the chance that it isn't cancer and you may not need to do such an extensive resection?" Gary pressed ever so slightly to be certain that only what truly needed too be done, would be done. He knew the risks of the Whipple Surgery, and he didn't want Lauri exposed to more risk than necessary.

"Each case is unique." Dr. Marks' eyebrows now were raised. "You can be sure I will only do what is in the best interest of my patient."

Despite his ginger approach, Gary had hit a nerve, and it was a sensitive one. He had pressed to heavily on this surgeon's medical judgment. "I'm sure Lauri is in the best of hands," Gary said.

"Mrs. Confer, let me explain what needs to be done. We still don't know with certainty what is causing your blockage. The surgery will both give us an answer and relieve the obstruction."

Lauri remained speechless. Dr. Marks retrieved a pad of paper and pen from the center drawer of his desk and proceeded to draw an anatomically accurate picture of Lauri's problem area. His long arms easily reached across the desk. He adeptly drew upside down as he spoke, so Lauri and Gary had an accurate, right side up, depiction of the area of anatomic concern. He labeled each structure in precise block print, also penned upside down from his side of the desk. Gary knew that all talented surgeons had a detailed, committed to memory, three-dimensional knowledge of the complicated anatomy of the human body. The medically unsophisticated might view this artistic display as nothing more than a parlor trick, a talent born of repetition rather than photographic recognition. Gary's field of radiology hinged on knowing the anatomy of the human body, and he viewed this display as confirmation that Dr. Marks vision was multidimensional, frontward or backward, right side up, or up side down. While operating inside a living, completely exposed, and venerable human being, this surgeon knew in intricate detail the internal confines of the human body. He knew how to avoid mishaps that stemmed from being unprepared. Unprepared was not a recognized word in Dr. Marks' vocabulary.

Lauri's obstruction of her biliary tract had been temporarily bypassed by the stent. Now, she needed a permanent repair of this blockage. The area of concern was literally in the center of her abdomen where many major structures intersected. The stomach, small intestine, biliary tract, pancreas, gallbladder, as well as too numerous to count arteries, veins and nerves, were all involved with this surgical endeavor. The surgery involved cutting out and removing parts of all of these structures, and then rerouting the connections in order for Lauri to have a reasonable ability to digest the food she consumed. In addition, the surgery would allow Dr. Marks to look for any spread of the suspected cancer. The procedure involved between five and six hours of operating time, a supreme test of skill, patience, and stamina. A pathologist would examine the removed structures under a microscope to definitively determine the cause of Lauri's illness.

The extreme gravity of her situation pressed down upon Lauri with the combined weight of several elephants. She was compressed into physical immobility and emotional stagnation. Dr. Marks' belief that she now likely had cancer so surprised her that his detailed description fell on despair induced deaf ears and his artwork failed to etch an impression on her frenzied mind. She knew Gary could explain it all later. Right now, she had questions, and she was dammed if she wasn't going to ask them. Lauri focused on her breathing. She gently raised both arms slightly away from her sides and drew in a long intentional inspiration while riveting her eyes on Dr. Marks. "If this is cancer…how bad is it?"

"Mrs. Confer. Until we are sure I—"

"Dr. Marks," Lauri raised her voice while trying to maintain a respectful tone. She grabbed the framed photo at the edge of the desk. "Be honest with me. I see these pictures of your children. I have children, too. I need to know."

Dr. Marks turned toward Gary. Gary nodded. Dr. Marks spoke in a calm unwavering voice. "Cancer in this region, cancer of the pancreas, is very, very serious. I would by lying to you if I didn't tell you that. The goal now is to remove it, all of it, and give you the best chance at survival."

"I need to know how serious," Lauri said. "How much time do I have?"

"Until we operate, there is no way to tell. We will know more on January thirty-first."

"It isn't much time, is it?"

Dr. Marks slightly bowed his head.

Gary leaned over, wrapping both arms around Lauri while fighting back his own tears. "No one, not even Dr. Marks, can give you an answer at this point. Let's go home. We need to talk to the kids."

chapter 24

"As WE TALKED ABOUT last night on the phone," Gary said, "your mom and I—Lauri and I—met with Dr. Marks, the surgeon, yesterday." Lauri and the kids sat quietly. "So you hear it from us and not from someone else in the family, we brought you all together. Sorry to bring four of you home from college mid-week."

Gary looked around the living room. Paige was leaning shoulder to shoulder with her mother, both of Lauri's arms wrapped around her. Nick R was next to Paige, leaning toward his sister, with his left hand on her knee. Ben and Jack sat on the adjacent couch, both leaning forward with their arms resting on their knees. Nick C was in a high back chair, hands clasped on his lap, his body pressing against the fabric.

All eyes fixed upon him, Gary stood before his silent family. "Your mom is going to need major surgery to open the blockage. While we can't know for certain, her doctors are very concerned… concerned that cancer is the cause."

Gary scanned the room. Paige turned away, burying her head in her mother's chest. Lauri tilted her head down attempting to comfort and shield her baby. Nick C cleared his throat, never raising either hand. Jack and Ben each leaned further forward, anticipating more information. Nick R stood up, took two steps away from the couch and leaned against the wall. He starred directly at Gary. "Why do they think that, after all the negative biopsies?"

"Cancer in this region can be very hard to diagnose. They are all a little baffled, but right now there is no other explanation.

Surgery needs to be done. It will open the blockage and remove the diseased tissue which will be evaluated to find out the cause."

While never releasing her grip on Paige, Lauri raised her head, revealing a few tears trickling down her face. "We don't want you to worry. Whatever we face, we will be there for each other."

"When is the surgery?" Jack asked.

Gary moved over next to Nick C and put his arm around his shoulder. "January thirty-first. Your mom and I want to be sure you all stay focused on school. When we need you, we will call."

"I think I should cancel my spring break plans for Mexico," Nick C said.

"Me too," Ben said. The stepbrothers had plans to spend a wild week in the sun and surf of Cancun with a bunch of college friends.

Lauri shook her head. "Don't. You need a break. All the plans are made, and you both worked hard to earn that money this summer. We'll fly you home if we have to."

"Your mom and I discussed this," Gary said. "We both don't want this to disrupt your lives any more than it has to." Gary moved away from Nick C and took his seat. He leaned forward. "For now, we need to get through the surgery. After that, we will know what else we need to deal with."

Lauri gently released her grip on Paige and their bodies slowly separated. Lauri reached up, wiping the tears from her only daughter's face. "You okay, Dolly?"

Paige's voice cracked as she wasn't able to utter a response. She collapsed back onto her mother, now sobbing uncontrollably. The eyes of all the males were moist; their facial muscles taut as they struggled not to reveal their own vulnerability.

Lauri held tight to Paige, wishing her arms could encircle the entire family. She thought back to when her children were small and their fears could be dispelled with a simple hug. Now it was different. Now their concerns were real, not the imaginary traumas that disrupted their dreams. Lauri remembered what a friend had once told her, "Being a mother is the perfect antidote for self-ishness." While she was afraid for herself, she was deathly afraid for everyone else in the room. She would fight to survive, but most importantly, she would fight to make sure that her children could survive, with or without her.

chapter 25

FROM THE FAR corner of the large surgical waiting room, Gary barely saw Dr. Marks as he entered and looked around. Eight hours had elapsed since Lauri and Gary passed through pre-operative registration, seven hours since he had to leave her frightened side. "I love you" were the last words they exchanged.

Gary spent the time viewing movies on a portable DVD player while Lauri's mother knitted. As the hours passed, several other family members arrived. Gary stood up and caught Dr. Marks' eye with a wave of his hand. The surgeon motioned Gary to the opposite side of the room where there were private consultation rooms. As the others rose to their feet, Dr. Marks glanced at the group, raised his right hand with only his index finger pointing toward Gary, and then curled it toward himself. "Looks like he only wants to talk to me," Gary said, his tone mirroring the concern on his face. "I'll be right back."

The consultation room was sparsely furnished with a small round table surrounded by five metal and plastic chairs. There were additional chairs stacked in the corner. Dr. Marks motioned for Gary to take a seat and then followed suit. "Lauri's in recovery, doing well. The surgery took a little longer than expected. I first encountered two areas of discoloration on the surface of the liver. I always look around for metastasis before doing the resection. As you know, Dr. Confer, if the cancer has spread beyond the pancreas, surgery most often isn't indicated for pancreatic cancer, as chemotherapy and radiation are the favored treatments. Having the surgery after metastasis has occurred, doesn't improve the length of survival."

"Yes, I know."

Dr. Marks ran his hand over his face, bring his hand to rest under his chin. "The pathology on the liver lesions was benign so I proceeded with the surgery. Oddly, I couldn't feel a tumor in the pancreas. This is very unusual. Makes me wonder." Dr. Marks picked up a Styrofoam cup filled with steaming black coffee and swallowed hard, his mouth oblivious to its temperature.

"What do you mean? Can you usually feel the mass?"

Dr. Marks took a second slug of the java, consciously raising his caffeine level as he had another surgery to follow. "Usually. It is rare when I can't. I took out ten lymph nodes, none of which looked abnormal." Dr. Marks twirled the cup in his hand. "Very little of Lauri's case has followed the textbooks. I'm hesitant to make any predictions. It is a bad sign when I can feel the tumor. For now, we need to wait and see what the tissue shows. The pathology report will take a few days."

"Is Lauri conscious yet?"

"Barely, intermittently. It was a very long surgery with, as you can imagine, a lot of anesthesia. Blood loss was minimal. We avoided a transfusion. All in all, it went well." Dr. Marks rose from his chair.

Gary pushed back from the table extending his right hand as he stood up. "Thanks for everything."

Dr. Marks reached out with both hands, clasping Gary's between his own. "You're welcome. Lauri will be in recovery for about two hours. The staff will come get you when she heads up to her room." Dr. Marks released his grip. "She was very tough in there. She's quite a lady."

Gary's throat constricted causing him to choke on his reply. "I know." Gary swallowed hard. "Thanks again."

Gary followed Dr. Marks out of the consultation room. He motioned to the family members to come join him. After all were seated, he closed the door. "Lauri did great. We can't see her in recovery. She will be in there for a couple more hours. They will come get us when she goes up to her room."

"What did he find?" Lauri's mom asked.

"He's a little puzzled. He didn't see or feel a cancer, which he said is odd."

"That's great," Lauri's mom said. "Does that mean she doesn't have cancer?"

"Not exactly."

"What does it mean?" Lauri's mom fidgeted in her chair. "I'm confused."

Gary, who had been standing, pulled out the last remaining chair and sat down. "In his experience, as an expert in pancreatic surgery, Lauri case is unusual. This doesn't mean she has or doesn't have cancer. It means we don't know yet. To him, to his feel, the tissue wasn't typical for cancer. The pathologist needs to look at the tissue. It will take a few days."

Worn out but relieved the surgery was over, Gary pushed back in his chair. One more battle victory in what had grown into a health war of attrition had been weathered. Lauri and Gary were fighters, surviving her third surgery in six months. The latest challenge was one of the most complex abdominal surgeries performed. She met the challenge head on. She rested in recovery, already starting to heal. "Why don't we get something to eat," Gary suggested. "I'll leave my cell number with the staff. It'll be a couple of hours before we can see her."

The nurse and orderly transferred Lauri from the gurney to her hospital bed. She was vaguely aware of her surroundings. On the heels of the orderly removing the gurney, the nursed waved the family in.

Lauri sat up in bed looking dazed but momentarily alert. "Can I get some ribs? I'm starving."

Gary laughed. "I doubt they'll let you eat this soon after surgery."

Lauri smiled. "Worth a try." Lauri feel back on her pillow and didn't speak another word until the next day.

"That's the anesthesia talking," Gary said, to the gathered family members. "Coming out of it makes people say strange things...although, she does love ribs."

Over the next hour the family gradually left, leaving Gary alone with his thoughts and his wife. He slid his chair up to the metal side railing and reached between the bars to grasp Lauri's hand. *Not the honeymoon I would have chosen, but definitely the right woman.* Only one month into their marriage and they'd already conquered a life or death situation. There were many more challenges ahead. They would fight all the battles the way they always did—together.

As the long day came to an end, Gary thought, *Don't you die on me.*

The following morning, Lauri awoke stiff and hurting. "Nurse, could I get some pain meds, please." Lauri spoke into the microphone on the call button twisted around the bed railing.

"Be right there."

Gary walked into the room. "You look great."

Lauri forced a smile. "I'm in a lot of pain."

"You should be, considering what they did to you. Did they ever get you those ribs you wanted last night?"

Lauri raised her eyebrows and tilted her head to one side. "What are you talking about?"

"I thought that might be your answer." Gary bent down and kissed her forehead. "When they brought you up from recovery, your requested ribs, and then you conked out."

"Are you kidding? That's what I said?"

"You did. It was all the meds talking. Don't worry about it."

Lauri reached out and wrapped her arms around Gary's neck, pulling him toward her. "Thanks for always being there for me. You mean so much to me."

"We're in this together."

Lauri released her grip and settled back into the bed. "Tell me how the surgery went. None of the docs have been in yet."

Gary explained how Dr. Marks was somewhat puzzled by her case and the fact that he couldn't feel a mass in the pancreas. "There you go again, being unique," Gary joked. "You're in one the top hospitals in the world and you're messing with the heads of your doctors. And, the way you pretend to be a doctor at home, you should know how to behave, medically speaking."

Lauri's facial muscles relaxed and an unforced smile creased her lips. "Not feeling a mass, that's good news, right?"

"Much better than the alternative. Dr. Marks said we have to wait a few days for the pathology reports."

Gary looked toward the door and Dr. Marks walked in. "How are you doing, Mrs. Confer?"

"Okay. I'm in a lot of pain."

Dr. Marks turned back to the door. "I'll fix that."

He left the room for less than a minute and returned with Lauri's nurse and pain meds. As the nurse injected the meds and apologized for the delay, Dr. Marks checked Lauri's chart. He handed the chart to the nurse as she exited the room. "Mrs. Confer, you have been quite a challenge, and I mean that in a good way. Each time I think I have you figured out, you surprise me. I met with Dr. Carpenter and the pathologist. We reviewed your tissue from the surgery. I can't explain it, but we don't see a cancer. There is more tissue to review, but at this point, I would say there is a chance you don't have cancer."

Lauri shook her head, and despite her considerable discomfort, she forced herself to sit up again. "Really! Now there's a chance I don't have cancer?"

"Yes…a chance," Dr. Marks said. "There is nothing routine about your case. Before we can be certain, the pathologists have a lot more work to do. I'll be back to check on you at the end of the day."

"Thank you Dr. Marks. Thank you," Lauri said, as her surgeon left the room and hurried down the hall to his next patient.

Lauri settled back into the bed. The combination of exhaustion, medication, and reprieve, drew her toward a deep and needed slumber. The perpetual rollercoaster ride of emotion continued, with hopefully only one more twist or turn to go. With the terminal prognosis associated with pancreatic cancer, Gary felt that they may have literally dodged a fatal bullet.

It had been a physical, emotional, and spiritual challenge. They frequently prayed for relief. Perhaps, their prayers had been answered.

Gary now was the one shaking his head. "Can you believe it? We have gone back and forth with this. Let's hope this is a thought we can hold on too."

Lauri reached out and grasped Gary's hand. "I know...let's hope."

chapter 26

SIX DAYS AFTER her extensive surgery, Lauri left the hospital, her right hand clutching a bad full of medications. The sensation of being so tethered to the health care system was foreign and disturbing, an unfamiliar and uncomfortable piece of clothing she wished she could return. Six months ago, questions of her health were the furthest thing from her mind. Now, health issues dominated her daily existence. She was determined to break free of her shackles, get healthy, get back to work, and get back to life.

While still in the hospital, Lauri had not so subtlety broached the topic of getting a dog. Prior to moving in together, she joked about them having a baby. When that issue lost steam, she'd started on the baby canine substitute. "I have the perfect name," she said. "We'll call him Whipple."

Gary thought, *Yeah, that's all we need. Your challenging health, four kids in college, my job, and you think we can swing house training and caring for a puppy.* However, he took a diversionary approach. "How about we compromise? We'll get you two hundred and forty horses—horsepower that is—the convertible you always wanted. We'll consider the dog sometime down the road. You can name the car Whipple."

"That sounds like a good compromise to me." Lauri smiled. "I get something I want, and you don't get something you don't want." Lauri winked at Gary.

"Seems fair to me…and somewhat familiar." Gary grinned.

Lauri adjusted to being home, spending most of her time in bed. Her pain gradually subsided, and while she truly wasn't hungry, she forced herself to consume small quantities of solid food. Her nausea acted like a frightened child; always her constant companion.

As usual, Gary left for work early on Friday February 9th. After a few hours of reading films, he slipped out of the radiology reading room in response to the ringing of his cell phone. The display window flashed a number with a 617 prefix; a call from Boston. Ten days of waiting for the pathology results from Lauri's surgery had taken its toll. Several conversations with Dr. Carpenter and Dr. Marks indicated that the results were still pending. Gary's emotions swung like a pendulum from cautiously optimistic to suspiciously pessimistic. For Lauri, there was no pendulum; she focused on a stationary, positive outcome.

Gary felt like the codefendant in a murder case with the jury deliberating their fate—freedom versus death row. Was it a good sign or bad sign that it was taking this long to decide? Lauri, not fazed by the wait, felt that the declaration of acquittal was just a delayed formality; her hope sprung eternal.

From personal as well as professional experience, Gary knew there was little difference between the health care system and the judicial system. The good die young, and the bad seemingly live forever. Often, the innocent suffer more than the guilty. Justice, medical or legal, had little to do with sainthood. It was rare in life to get what you deserved, either reward or condemnation. Sometimes, the only time you get patted on the back is when you were choking. And, that is if you are lucky.

Gary flipped open the cover on the cell phone as he hurried along the corridor to its dead end. The spot provided a little privacy and he sought refuge there while at work and dealing with personal issues. He had made many daily calls home, or to the Boston hospital, depending on where Lauri's head had hit the pillow the night before. The pace of Gary's respirations quickened and he felt flushed with warmth. "Hello."

"Dr. Confer."

"Yes."

"This is Dr. Carpenter. Did Dr. Marks get hold of you yet?" The somber tone of Lauri's doctors' voice immediately registered that the scales of justice had not tipped in their favor.

"No."

"I'm sorry to tell you. I can't believe we have gone back and forth so many times. We've shown Lauri's tissue to several expert pathologists in the area. They all agree that it is pancreatic cancer...I'm so sorry."

Gary opened his mouth but no words came out. His chest strained to draw in enough air to respond. He turned away from the open hall, facing the dead end corner. "You know, I was worried. Can't believe it..."

"There's more, Dr. Confer." Now, Dr. Carpenter's respiratory rate speeded up. Gary could hear each individual sigh. "The final results on the liver tissue were positive for metastatic disease. Also, four of ten lymph nodes showed cancer. I'm sorry."

Gary's mind simultaneously exploded forward and lay dormant. It was as if two independent mindsets were jousting in his brain. One thought process sped ahead with panic, thoughts darting in and out. The other half of his mind wasn't functioning at all, a flat line of absent brain wave activity—the paralysis of disbelief. "I thought at the time of surgery the liver was benign. Now it's cancer?"

"The original pathology at surgery was read as negative. Closer inspections by several experts now feel it is metastatic cancer."

Gary buried his head into his free hand. "There's metastasis to the lymph nodes too?"

Dr. Carpenter paused to realign his own somewhat scattered thought process. "Yes, four of ten."

Gary's voice crawled forward, inching its way out of his body. "That makes Lauri stage four, the most advanced stage."

"Yes. Stage four."

Gary took another deep, drawn out breath. His body cried out to surrender, but he knew more needed to be done. He pushed against the wall, straightening his defeated posture. "Dr. Carpenter, I want to thank you for all you've done. What oncologist would you use if this were your wife?"

"I already set up an appointment for you and Lauri with Dr. Benton on Monday. He is the best around. However, if there is someone else you would rather see, that's fine."

"No. Lauri and I will be there on Monday."

A strained and somber tone was evident in Dr. Carpenter's voice. "Gary, my best to you and Lauri. Good luck with all that is ahead of you. Call me if there is anything I can do. I mean that."

"Thanks Pete." Gary flipped down the metal cover on his cell phone, the snapping sound echoing in the empty hall. He leaned into the stark white wall gaining support from the sterile structure. His legs, and his spirit, were weakened by the devastating news.

Gary drove home in a mental state that mirrored the weather; gloomy with scattered snow showers. He thought about the contradiction of both being a doctor as well as Lauri's husband. His connection to the medical field brought the couple some "favors—professional courtesies." These benefits helped them navigate the sometimes stormy conditions that developed when patients confront the combined challenges of their disease, and the complexities of the medical system. However, at this time, the downside of his dual role lay before him. For the second time in several weeks, he stood alone as the messenger of ill-fated news—loved one to loved one; not a white coat in site.

The door momentarily stuck, making a rough rattling vibration, as it swung free and Gary entered the foyer. The uncompleted household chore represented but one of a many tasks that were pushed to the back burner.

"Lauri," Gary called out, "I'm home."

Gary removed his wet coat and shoes, scattering a few flakes of un-melted snow onto the floor. He climbed the stairs to find an empty living room with the afghan and pillows strewn about the couch. Looking to his left, he saw Lauri coming out of the only bedroom on the main floor. She swayed back and forth, struggling to regain her balance. He walked the few steps that separated them.

While still dazed from her nap, Lauri was acutely aware of the ashen expression on Gary's face. "Did something happen to my dad?" Lauri asked.

Gary reached out placing both hands on her shoulders. "No, your dad is fine."

"You heard from Dr. Marks." Lauri stood straight up and her eyes were wide open.

"Dr. Carpenter called."

"I have cancer, don't I?"

"Lauri...I'm so sorry."

Gary was unable to shift his hands quickly enough to prevent her from collapsing in a heap onto the floor. He followed her down, wrapping his arms around Lauri as her body convulsed. Tears filled their eyes as he attempted to squeeze some degree of comfort into her. It felt as though they had spent the past six weeks climbing up a steep mountain. Each time they made a little progress, the specter of cancer was raised, causing the ground below them to give way, preventing them from reaching the summit. At times, hope reached out and grasped their hands, pulling them up. At other times, fear and despair grabbed their ankles, pulling them back down. There was no longer any solid base on which to gain traction. The avalanche of cancer buried the couple under it ominous weight.

After several minutes, Lauri raised her head from Gary's tear soaked shirt. "I can't believe it. I'm so sorry for you. You don't deserve this." Her head fell back to his body and was pushed away as Gary's chest heaved with a staccato inspiration.

Gary kissed the top of Lauri's head. He gently rubbed his face into her thick blonde hair. He thought, *What are we going to do?* He said, "Don't worry about me. Neither of us deserves this. We'll fight this together."

Lauri and Gary sat huddled on the floor, locked in an embrace of desperation and fear. They were stone silent as words no longer possessed enough emotion to convey their feelings. The world had fallen in upon them, limiting their ability to breathe and to dream. They were in a deep abyss, secluded from hope and devoid of a future. Wrapped in their own trembling arms was their only remaining comfort.

chapter 27

LAURI SPENT THE next three days attempting to adjust to her new role as a "victim of cancer." A friend used the term and it stuck in Lauri's mind with the permanence of a song repeating itself over and over again. Try as she might, she couldn't silence the chorus.

Lauri rarely assumed the role of a victim in the past, preferring to actively engaged the challenges in her life rather than passively react to their menacing attack. It was a philosophy she instilled in her children as evidenced by a self-defense course she and Paige took together this past summer at Lauri's insistence. Lauri didn't want her daughter to be a victim, and Lauri wasn't going to be one either.

Philosophy is one thing; practicality is another. Only seventy-two hours into her battle with pancreatic cancer, Lauri knew the fight would consume every ounce of her physical and mental energy. She was determined to investigate all weapons at her disposal, both conventional and alternative. During one of her searches on the Internet, she came upon a cancer awareness web site dedicated to the importance of maintaining your sanity and drive while in the midst of a fight for your life. There were details of all the ways the cancer will try to beat you down, and suggestions for combating the onslaught. There was even a sarcastic reference to, "Cancer, the gift that keeps on giving."

Gary and Lauri made the familiar drive south to Boston for their latest, and most ominous, encounter with the best and brightest of the medical profession. Optimism and energy were scarce commodities during the tense and silent journey. They were depleted from three days of focusing on cancer. Mind and body were as joyless as the desert is arid.

Gary had spent his adult life combing the medical literature expanding his professional knowledge base. The search, over the past few days, was a grim reminder of the facts he already knew. Pancreatic cancer is incurable. The mean survival for patients initially diagnosed as stage 4, the most advanced stage, is eight months. In the Internet age with information, statistics, and advice easily, almost too casually, available at anyone's fingertips, Lauri was also depressingly aware of her projected fate. However, she held out hope of a medical advance that would improve her odds. In her mind, she was willing to accept ten years of life as the alternative to living into her eighties. Ten years instead of the previously expected thirty-five or so seemed like a fair tradeoff. Now, all she had to figure out was how to negotiate the details of this gallows bargain.

To know what she was up against, Lauri went to her most trusted source of information—Gary. He explained that a normal cell in your body exists in harmony as a cooperative member of your entire being. Your normal cells live by the rule of a common goal for the common good, the contented survival of the individual. Cancer cells represent your own cells, which have mutated. They no longer want to live in harmony with the rest of your body. They want to take over your body. They begin in a single location and eagerly attempt to spread to every part of the victim's body. The cancer cells multiply wildly, as there is no checking their growth. The spread of the cancer beyond its initial germination site represents metastasis of the tumor. Metastasis—the word alone was nearly synonymous with impending death. These "mutant cells" with unregulated growth strive to foster the demise of the body they inhabit. Your own deranged cells are conspiring to kill you.

While they had been to the expansive grounds of the hospital campus many times before, this would be their first visit to the medical building dedicated to cancer treatment. Two weeks had past since her extensive abdominal surgery, and the frigid biting midwinter wind penetrated her clothing with the ease and precision of a surgeons' scalpel. With Gary's arm around her shoulder, Lauri slowly walked from the grey cement parking garage toward the shimmering metal façade of the medical building that one of her friends would later tag with the moniker Chemo Central—CC for short. The mammoth building required six high-speed elevators to transport the volume of afflicted patients to the appropriate floors designated for the particular cancer they were battling.

The large waiting room, while initially colorful and inviting, would over time, become a mundane and progressively more unwelcome destination for the couple. The room was almost always filled with patients in varying stages of response to their confrontation between cancer and chemicals. The victims spanned the continuum from the ones who were difficult to recognize as being sick, to the ones who were difficult to recognize as being alive. Lauri wondered how she appeared to their judgmental gaze.

Lauri's vibrant red blouse was in stark contrast to her drawn and ashen face. Her shoulders strained to keep the fabric from slipping down her steep chiseled shoulders that lacked the former tissue volume to provide a secure anchor for the tasteful apparel. She repeatedly tugged at the material to recover her exposed skin. The loss of thirty-eight pounds since November had transformed her body. Rather than a person, the frame of her torso resembled a wire clothes hanger on which to drape a garment. Her displeasure and frustration with her appearance was an early repulsive "gift" from her cancer. Unfortunately, there would be many more "gifts" to come.

"Would you like your coat back?" Gary asked. "You look cold." He lifted the tan wool coat that was draped across his lap.

"Thanks. It's freezing in here." Lauri leaned forward and Gary covered her back and shoulders, pulling the coat around front to cover her folded arms.

As Gary scanned the waiting room, he thought he could distinguish the patients from friends and family members purely by the layers of clothing shielding their bodies. The second "gift" of Lauri's cancer was to heighten her susceptibility to the elements.

A young female medical assistant in navy blue scrubs guided the couple through a maze of hallways to the individual waiting room in anticipation of Dr. Benton's arrival. Lauri remained in her street clothes while the nurse took her vital signs. Vitality was a term no longer coined to refer to Lauri's physical condition. The office seemed eerily quiet given the large number of patients and medical personnel milling around. Gary wondered if it was a silence of respect or gloom; the quiet and isolation of cancer, "gift" number three.

Dr. Benton moved from patient room to patient room at a rapid pace. Gary and Lauri would come to recognize, respect, and admire, that his throttle had only two settings. Fast, for any activity between patient visits, and a speed setting of however much time a patient required, when they had his undivided attention. Time became a superfluous consideration to Dr. Benton when his patients needed him. His level of expertise related to cancer treatment, coupled with his uncompromising dedication to his patients, made Dr. Benton worth waiting for.

Dr. Benton breezed through the doorway creating a gentle wind drifting about the small but efficient space of the exam room. He stopped abruptly in front of Lauri, extending his right hand. "Hi, Mrs. Confer. I am Dr. Randall Benton. I'm sorry for the wait." A subtle, lip tight, smile accented his pleasant face. His lab coat settled in against the body contours of someone who focused on his own health, as well as the health of others.

Lauri stretched out her thinned right arm causing her red blouse to slip down off her shoulder. Her grip, reflecting her general state of being, was weak but determined. "Hi, Dr. Benton. Please call me Lauri."

"Okay, Lauri." Dr. Benton brought in his left hand and gently, but completely, surround Lauri's right hand with both of his own. There was an immediate intimacy established between practitioner and patient. Lauri felt an instantaneous transfer of warmth, compassion, and concern. She would repeatedly reach for, and cling to, this secure pair of hands as she traveled the traumatic path before her.

"We have a great deal to discuss," Dr. Benton said, "but you feel free to stop me at any time with any and all questions. I am here to help you in any way I can."

The tight smile on Dr. Benton's face further strengthened Lauri's bond to the first, and ultimately the only, oncologist she would ever know. Dr. Benton released his comforting grip and turned toward Gary. Gary had risen from his chair when Dr. Benton entered the exam room. The two men firmly grasped hands. "Hi, Dr. Confer."

"Hi, Dr. Benton. Call me Gary."

"All right. Both of you are welcome to call me Randall. My mother, God rest her soul, would never let anyone call me Randy." Randall and Gary took their seats.

"Lauri, I reviewed your records and discussed your case with Drs. Carpenter and Marks. Like many patients with pancreatic cancer, you have been through quite an ordeal just coming to a diagnosis. How are you feeling today?"

The tone and delivery indicated to both Lauri and Gary that Dr. Benton wanted to know how she was feeling on this day relative to the early stages of her battle with pancreatic cancer. Life, from this point forward, would pit her mental and physical stamina against her adversary, pancreatic cancer. Dr. Benton would be one of her many lifelines. She was now in a fight for her life, requiring a variety of lifelines for survival; cancer "gift" number four.

Lauri leaned forward in her chair and repositioned her blouse. "I'm okay...scared, really. Both of us did a lot of reading and it didn't sound promising. What do you think? What are my chances?"

Dr. Benton peered into Lauri's eyes; his facial expression was a blend of determination and realism. It was a look that Lauri and Gary would encounter repeatedly in the many challenging months ahead. They would always be able to count on Dr. Benton to be as forthright as they wanted him to be. He would never lie to his patients, but his experience taught him to flavor his response to meet the physical and emotional needs of those under his care. He correctly sensed that Lauri wanted concrete answers to her uncompromising questions.

"Pancreatic cancer represents one of the most difficult cancers to fight. We in the medial profession wish we had more to offer our patients. That is the reason I am involved with research, to find better treatment options for patients suffering from this type of cancer. Before I give you a direct answer, and I will give you one, let me first discuss your options for treatment." Dr. Benton reached over and again grasped Lauri's hand. "Are you okay with that?"

"Yes, but I do want an honest answer." Lauri smiled at Dr. Benton. Her expression was beautifully revealing, one of hopeful innocence tempered with fearful realism. Dr. Benton would cherish that smile each time he saw it grace the face of a woman for whom he knew there were to be many more harrowing experiences in her abbreviated future. The ultimate loss of Lauri's innocence, coupled with a projected length of survival—cancer "gifts" number five and six.

"I sense that you do, and you shall get an honest answer." Dr. Benton released his grip without leaning back or diverting his fixed but comforting gaze from Lauri's eyes. "Lauri, I will always be as open and honest with you as you want me to be. I respect the right of my patients to know the truth. However, medicine is not an exact science. None of us have a crystal ball. I will tell you what I think based on my experience with patients I have treated with circumstances similar to your own."

"Thank you, Dr. Benton."

Lauri looked toward Gary and cast a forced smile in his direction. Gary returned the visual connection and slid his chair next to Lauri. He reached out and grasped her hand. It was a gesture as much for his own support, as well as for hers.

Dr. Benton spent forty-five minutes with the middle-aged newlyweds discussing the range of treatment options, both standard and experimental, available to Lauri. His recommendation was to start treatment in three weeks, as Lauri needed the time to fully recover from her recent surgery. "Chemotherapy puts a tremendous strain on the body. We need you healed from surgery before we hit you hard again." Dr. Benton concisely and clearly covered all available options. He turned toward Gary. "Does my discussion parallel what you read or talked about with the oncologists at your hospital?"

"Yes it does," Gary said. "Based on Lauri being stage four and already having the Whipple Surgery, I assume there is no role for radiation therapy."

"Not at this time. Rarely, it is used to combat local recurrence." Dr. Benton turned toward Lauri. "Do you understand what Gary and I are saying?"

"Yes." Lauri gently laughed. "Living with a doctor, I consider medical jargon to be my second language."

Gary slyly chuckled. "Dr. Benton, you have to understand that Lauri often thinks she is a doctor. She's not intimidated by medical concepts or terminology."

All three inhabitants of the room laughed. This exchange set the tone for the fated interaction of this trio. Despite the gravity of their shared situation, there would always be some humor to elevate their spirits. Most often, it was Lauri who provided the comedy as a way of relieving the tension for everyone.

While given the choice to take some time to consider her options before making a decision, Lauri didn't want to think, she wanted to act, or more accurately, attack. She was not timid about doing battle with her cancer. Lauri looked intently at her oncologist. "Hit me as hard as you can, Dr. Benton. I want to fight this thing all the way."

"Okay, Lauri. I will be as aggressive as your body will tolerate. I feel a two drug approach would be appropriate given that the cancer has already spread to your liver and lymph nodes. I want you to know that you are in control of your treatment, and you decide how much and when. You will always have three options, and you can be assured I will always respect your choice." Dr. Benton reached out and grasped Lauri's hands for the third time during this visit. "You can continue taking the chemotherapy you are on, you can choose to try something different, or you can choose to stop treatment all together. Sometimes, patients get to a point where they have had enough."

Lauri found it hard to imagine she might choose to stop treatment, unless of course, she was cured. Despite all she had read and all she and Gary discussed, Lauri was not ready to give up the hope of a miracle.

Dr. Benton released the physical bond with his patient and eased his chair back in front of his computer screen. "Let me look at the chemo schedule." After a brief silence, he said, "We will set you up for your first treatment in three weeks. The plan is once a week for three weeks and then one week off for the IV chemo, and one pill everyday for the oral medication. This treatment will run for six months, if you can tolerate it. If you can't, we will stop for a period of time. We call that a Chemo Holiday."

Dr. Benton swiveled his chair back around and faced Lauri and Gary. His posture stiffened. An ominous and palpable period of silence punctuated Lauri's first visit with her oncologist. It wasn't a pause of uncertainty or hesitation. Dr. Benton had delivered this speech far too many times to the multitude of pancreatic cancer patients he had treated. It was a pause of respect and humility. Respect for the patient before him and the supreme challenges they and their family faced. And, humility; a humbleness born of knowing there was only so much hope and treatment he and the medical profession had to offer. "Now, as you requested, we can discuss longer term issues."

"Thank you, Dr. Benton," Lauri said. "I need to know. I have five children and a husband to think about."

"Lauri, stage four pancreatic cancer, in all honesty, is very resistive to treatment." Dr. Benton's tone was serious and direct, just what his patient had requested. "In the oncology profession, we don't talk about the possibility of curing such an advanced stage of pancreatic cancer. We like to look at survival in six-month intervals. In my experience, you will do okay over the next six months. Beyond six months, it will depend on your response to chemotherapy."

Lauri sat motionless. While she knew the statistics were grim, the bleak depiction of her fate momentarily took her hope and breath away. Gary put his arm around Lauri's shoulders. He too was without the breath to respond. While Dr. Benton's comments were not unexpected, the cold reality of an expert in the field telling you there was no hope of survival, demanded, and received, your full attention.

Gary focused on the purpose of their visit...information. There would be time later to crumble in private. He knew what Lauri's next question was, but he also realized she was unable to ask it. "If Lauri can tolerate the six months of chemo and if the cancer responds to the chemotherapy, what do we do after that?"

Dr. Benton shifted in his chair. There were no easy or comforting answers for him to give. Despite his years of experience and the number of patients he had seen come and go from his care, he was never able, or even willing, to emotionally separate himself from his patients. In fact, his salvation came from establishing a bond with his patients. That bond enabled him to better deal with the eventual loss of the person he was doing his best to care for. Dr. Benton swallowed hard. "Most often, at the end of six months of treatment, if we get a good response, we stop the chemotherapy. We then wait for the cancer to return before we consider alternative treatments. It has been our experience that even if we get a good response from the chemo, it tends to stop working after six months, and there is no benefit to continuing. Unfortunately, ultimately, the cancer will return."

Neither Lauri nor Gary had any more questions. Each hopeful inquiry generated a realistic but demoralizing response. They were not upset with their doctor, they were devastated by her cancer.

"I know this is always a very emotional time," Dr. Benton said. "I am going to give you some time alone in the exam room. When you are ready, stop by the desk to pick a day in three weeks to begin chemotherapy. I'll check with you in a few days. Call me with any question. I mean that, don't hesitate to call."

As Dr. Benton exited the room, tears flowed from Lauri's eyes. Her head collapsed onto Gary's shoulder. He turned toward her, wrapping his arms around her frail torso. There were no words that either could offer; there was only the comfort of the one you love. Now, that love was in peril. Not because of anything either of them had done or not done. They were being torn apart by a cancer that was destined to take control of their life, and ultimately create a gulf between them on the scale of heaven and earth. The finality of love lost and life lost, cancer's terminal "gift."

chapter 28

WHILE LAURI AND Gary had told the children of her diagnosis of pancreatic cancer, they decided to wait to have another family meeting until after their first discussion with Dr. Benton. Once again, the four living away at college made the trip home. The entire family gathered in the living room on Saturday evening, which eliminated the need for any of them to make their respective drives back to school until the next afternoon. Gary didn't want any of them behind the wheel after hearing the somber news.

Paige sat nestled in her mother's arms with Nick R seated at his mother's side, his right arm around her shoulder. Jack and Ben shared the small couch with both young men clutching a pillow under one arm. Nick C sat in the lone high back chair, its patterned fabric matching the pillows his brother and stepbrother had in a headlock. Gary was standing. A large glass coffee table separated Gary from his suffering family.

His eyes scanned his children, taking a visual assessment of their respective moods. Their blended facial expressions depicted a combination of fear and sorrow. While in age they were all adults, in his mind, they were, and would always be, his children. He wanted to shield them from pain, but there wasn't a weapon at his disposal to fend off the inevitable suffering that lay before them. This most fundamental and unalterable parental conviction, protect your children at any cost, was ripping his heart right out of his chest.

He thought back to happier times. For all intents and purposes, the kids grew up together. When the couple met, Jack and Paige were twelve, Ben and Nick C were fourteen, and Nick R was eighteen. There were plenty of overlapping, nauseatingly similar adolescent challenges. These traumas were successfully resolved with the understanding and cooperation of their parents. While the children didn't share a bloodline with both Lauri and Gary, their love and respect for their stepparents paralleled the love and respect the couple felt and demonstrated toward each other. Both Lauri and Gary believed in parenting by example. When this approach didn't achieve the desired result, there was always the fall back position of consequential parental persuasion—do it, or else. Neither Lauri nor Gary was squeamish about exercising their authority to alternate between sugar and a stick.

Now, five years of sand had passed through the hourglass, and they were kids no more. Gary made individual eye contact moving from left to right around the semicircle. "As you all know, your mother and I met with Dr. Benton, the oncologist, this week. He gave us several options for treatment, all involving different types of chemotherapy. It is going to be a really tough battle. We will do everything possible to fight as hard as we can."

There was no need to be explicit about Lauri's poor chance for survival. All the children had already solicited predictions from the various pancreatic cancer websites. Unfortunately, there was no blind optimism in this era of instantaneous and limitless information retrieval. They might be sheepish about steadfastly believing what they had read, but there was no way to pull the wool completely over their eyes.

Paige strained forward to gain some separation from her mother and ask a question. It was a wasted effort as she collapsed back, nearly assuming a fetal position. Lauri more firmly wrapped her arms around her only daughter as her last born gently whimpered.

"How long will the chemo go on?" Nick R asked.

Gary chose his words carefully. "Six months, as long as your mom can tolerate it."

Lauri squeezed Paige a little tighter. "I'm going to fight this thing with all I have. I believe we can beat this. I am not giving up."

Nick R gently pulled his mother towards himself. "I know you won't, Mom." He kissed his mother on the cheek and then turned back toward Gary. "How will they know if it's working?"

Gary walked over beside Nick C as he could tell his first born was struggling to maintain his fragile composure. Gary rested his right hand on Nick's shoulder trying to impart both fortitude and comfort. "They will do follow-up CAT scans every two months." Gary gently squeezed his son's shoulder. "If the tumor improves, or even if it stays the same, they will continue with the chemo. If the tumor grows, they will move on to a different drug."

Ben, Lauri's quiet child, surprised Gary by speaking up. "How many different drugs do they have?" Ben shifted the pillow from under his right arm to his left, applying enough pressure to nearly rupture the foam through the fabric.

Gary knew they were all wishing for an endless supply of chemicals to give to Lauri in hopes of destroying the alien cells that were invading her body. However, he also knew that in a small way, he needed to begin preparing everyone for the reality of the challenges they jointly faced. "A few meds are approved for treating pancreatic cancer. And, there are some experimental chemo agents. For now, it was decided to wait on experimental ones to see how the cancer responds."

Gary noticed that Paige was getting progressively more uncomfortable. She kept shifting her position against her mother. Paige reached her limit of control and composure. Her previous subtle sounds of grief were now magnified into a full-blown effervescence of emotion, and her body began to convulse. The earlier trickle of tears blossomed into a torrential downpour. Lauri squeezed her little girl tighter.

Paige's individual release was contagious, inciting a communal catharsis. Each member of the family was humbled into submission. No one was able to withstand the devastation of their shared fear and sorrow. It was a time when stoic resistance was as futile as an umbrella in a hurricane.

The precipitous crescendo/decrescendo emotions of three hours ago had settled into more manageable fluctuation above and below the baseline. The boys moved to the basement to watch hockey. The familiar sibling banter echoed up the stairwell. Lauri and Paige remained locked in an embrace watching one of the many "chick flicks" they loved. They had seen the movie so many times that they could recite the dialogue verbatim. While mother and daughter remained silent, Lauri smiled as she resurrected memories of the many times Paige and her girlfriends could be heard screaming the lines as they watched the movie while sharing their friendship and popcorn. Lauri knew that these unbreakable bonds of commitment, which were forged over time through linked adolescent joys and traumas, would help to sustain her little lamb for the very adult challenges she would face in the near future.

Gary sat at his desk in the den. The prior weeks represented the most demanding period of his entire life. His professional life focused on illness; his home life now revolved around illness; his sleep was fragmented by thoughts of illness—a 24-hour preoccupation with disease and possible death. However, the greatest challenges were yet to come as Lauri fought for her life, and Gary stood guard at her side.

There was so much to think about doing, and yet, at this very moment, there was nothing specific to do. Friends and family had already contacted him with offers of help. Lauri, having left Massachusetts for the first time in her life only eight months ago, had a huge local and loyal contingent of people ready and wanting to lend a hand. All Gary and Lauri had to do was ask. Not an easy task for two individuals who had lived a life committed to self-sufficiency.

Gary smiled as he reflected on the five years leading up to Lauri's illness. The walls of the den were covered with over fifty similarly framed photos that chronicled the family's adventures. The couple's bonding was gradual with a very slow descent of the protective walls they had both built around themselves. They shared the pleasures and disappointments of not only their lives, but also the lives of their children. As their love and trust grew, the self fabricated emotional barriers toppled, their independence evolving into interdependence. It was a joyously shared security and intimacy; the comfort of knowing you had the love of your life to watch your back, and wash it.

The bond the couple forged from both commonality and compromise was now threatened, and being eroded by a demon from within…Lauri's cancer. For Gary with his medical knowledge, there was no amount of wishing it weren't so that could cloud his intellectual clarity of the fact that the woman he loved was going to die, long before he had ever expected. What was in doubt was the process. How long would they have together? How much would Lauri suffer? How could he help the kids to live with, and deal with, the tragedy? These, and so many other distressing questions, would plague him for their remaining time together.

Despite the sadness of the day, or maybe because of it, Gary knew the family needed some comfort, pleasure, and distraction. Lauri always impressed Gary with her ability to accept life's circumstances, and make the best of them. Lauri worked her way through life's obstacles with strength and determination, but did so without ever relinquishing her zest for life or the smile on her face. Gary left the den and headed into the living room where mother and daughter remained eerily silent. "Hey girls, how about some ice cream with chocolate sprinkles?"

Paige shifted slightly in her mother's embrace. Their clothes were densely wrinkled from the hours they were locked in each other's arms. She raised her head, tilted it to the right, smiled up at her stepfather and said, "Gary, you know they're called jimmies."

A broad but tired smile came over Lauri's face. "Yes Gary, you know jimmies are my favorite."

Gary chuckled. "Oh that's right, if you come from New England. Out west they are still sprinkles. How about it, ice cream with jimmies?"

"Yes. Most definitely," Lauri said, in a weak but playful voice.

Paige stood up. "I'll help. Should I ask the boys?"

"Sure. Go downstairs and ask them," Gary said, as he took her place on the couch next to Lauri.

As Paige descended the stairs to the walk-out basement, Gary put his arms around Lauri and kissed her lips. She looked so frail and helpless that he wished he could cradle her in his arms and somehow carry her away from all this insanity. It truly was insane. How could this beautiful and previously healthy forty-seven year old woman now be dying of pancreatic cancer? It was sheer insanity laced with unfathomable sorrow. Unfortunately, it was also the stark reality of their new life together.

Gary starred into Lauri's crystal blue eyes. "How are you holding up? It's been a tough day."

Lauri leaned in. "I don't know...not good. It's great to have the kids home. But, it makes me realize how much I am going to miss them...when I'm gone." Tears aimlessly rolled down Lauri's puffy face as she choked on her final words before collapsing forward into Gary's arms.

Gary held on as tight as he dared. Before her illness and weight loss, he could have squeezed her as much as he wanted. Now, he had to comfort her with an element of care. He felt her bones beneath her thinned exterior. It was a tactile confirmation of the cancer's persistent attack on her body. The cancer was relentlessly consuming his wife one pound at a time, and there was little he could do about it.

Gary timidly released his embrace. Lauri gently fell away from him. He laid her down on the couch, placing pillows beneath her head and feet. She was completely exhausted. "Why don't you rest a bit? I'll help Paige in the kitchen and then we'll sit out here with you and watch the rest of the movie."

"That would be nice. Sorry I don't have more energy." A subtle smile creased Lauri's lips.

Gary bent and gently kissed those perfect but slightly trembling lips. "Don't worry. Get some rest." Gary covered Lauri with her favorite gold and brown afghan.

He quietly walked into the kitchen and was joined by Paige. Father and stepdaughter prepared the desserts and carried the heaping bowls down to the sports fans in the basement. They returned to the kitchen to clean up.

Gary walked over to Paige and wrapped her in his arms. Her head settled down onto his shoulder. Still upset, but lacking the energy to generate any more emotion or tears, she silently absorbed comfort and strength from their embrace. While not linked by genetics, their bond was strong, the result of shared history rather than blood. And though Gary wished he was her biological father, for her sake and the sake of her brothers, he knew that was another reality they all had to accept and deal with. They built a supportive and loving bond, and that connection would help sustain them during the rough times ahead.

Paige was only eighteen years old and facing a trauma no child should have to endure. She, like her mother, had radiant beauty, both on the skin surface as well as burning deep within the soul of her being. Gary always smiled when he noticed the common features and feelings that passed between generations. In particular, they possessed the same twinkle in their eyes. Mother and daughter also shared a deep concern and compassion for others, and now, those emotions were more intimate.

Their embrace slackened and they stood side by side at the grey kitchen counter. Gary meticulously corralled the stray jimmies, which always seemed to hide themselves between the relatively few functional items on the counter. Lauri and Gary kept the spartanly appointed kitchen white glove clean. Paige replaced the cardboard covers to the several half-gallons of ice cream they had opened. The size of the family, and their individual preferences when it came to dairy delights, routinely necessitated the utter contribution of more than one cow.

Before returning to the living room, Gary whispered to Paige, "Would you like to sleep with your Mom tonight? I can sleep in your room. I think she would really like that."

"I would too." Paige wanted to say more, but the words were locked inside.

Gary wrapped his arms around his only daughter. His heart was breaking for the entire family, but most profoundly for the mother and child who shared the same golden hair and glistening smile. "Go ask your mom like it was your idea," he said.

The dramatic deep red walls of the kitchen were an appropriate backdrop for the intense emotion of the day. Paige softly stepped into the quiet living room with its soothing gold walls. Lauri had spent months picking the perfect furniture and accessories to reflect her traditional but stylish tastes. Paige knelt on the gloss finish hardwood floor next to the red couch where Lauri rested with her heavy eyes barely open. Paige gently laid her head next to her mother's and sweetly looked into the eyes of the most comforting and influential person in her life. "Mom, can I sleep with you tonight?"

While Lauri wanted to break down and cry, she knew her little girl needed her to be strong. Gathering every ounce of control she had, Lauri replied in a soothing maternal tone, "Sure, Dolly. I would love that."

chapter 29

THE WORDS "START Chemo" were highlighted on both Lauri's and Gary's pocket calendars, as well as indicated in red felt pen on the family calendar inside the tall white kitchen pantry cabinet. Three long weeks had past since their first appointment with Dr. Benton. As promised, he had made follow-up calls to the couple. Each morning, Lauri placed an X through the square of the prior day, which brought her one day closer to beginning in earnest her fight against cancer. She spent the time struggling to remain positive about her prospects for survival, despite overwhelming odds to the contrary. Lauri viewed her cancer in very personal terms, and was damned if she would be bullied about by "mutant cells" as Gary had called them.

Gary's Valentine's Day card proclaiming love, support, and encouragement sat on the corner of Lauri's nightstand. She read it every morning. It rested atop a box of her favorite chocolates; unopened, as Lauri's nausea prevented her from enjoying the treats. Many items now crowded her nightstand, some teetering on the edge. She considered all of them essential in the fight against her cancer: medications, self help books focusing on cancer, religious medals and statues given to her by loved ones, copy of the bible, and pictures of her children.

Lauri understood that chemotherapy represented an attempt to stop the growth and spread of the cancer cells. The challenge came from the fact that the cancer was actually a mutant version of oneself, and thus, the chemicals designed to kill the cancer, also destroyed some of your own normal cells. This death of your own good cells resulted in the side effects of the chemo. Lauri didn't look forward to poisoning herself in hopes of saving her own life. However, the alternative was to give up without a fight, and that just wasn't a plan she could live with.

Over the past months there were so many "firsts": new husband, second family, living in a new state. Like many of the others, the first day of chemotherapy evoked a mixture of emotions, pulling her thoughts in every conceivable direction. The physical act of recording another passing day on the calendar produced the competing emotions of either being one day closer to freedom and a renewed lease on life, or one day closer to death because of the lack of a stay of execution. She wished the oppressive weight of her dilemma could be converted into pounds to replenish her withering body.

Four weeks had passed since the diagnosis of pancreatic cancer entered Lauri's life. It had the feeling of an uninvited guest in her home, an unpleasant visitor who quickly wore out their welcome, but unfortunately, was in no hurry to leave. The family calendar became the focal point in her battle to expel the intruder; command central. The oversized daily squares on the calendar were rapidly filled with Lauri's plan of attack: conventional medical appointments, unconventional alternative methods of treatment, gatherings with family and friends when she was able, religious support. Atop the schedule of combat was her greatest motivation to survive, pictures of her family.

The picture for the month of March 2007 dated back to late summer 2001, and the first time the two families got together. It was a spontaneous photo Gary had taken during a BBQ at Lauri's house. In the foreground, Nick R and Nick C were tending to the grill, likely talking sports, as swirls of smoke floated in the air. In the back-ground, Paige, Ben and Jack were in the pool, tossing around a Frisbee. The screams and shrills typical of young teenagers leapt from the glossy surface. Lauri was off to the side, carrying a tray of drinks to satisfy the thirst of the family and friends lounging on the pool deck.

Now, when Lauri looked at calendar, it served the duel purpose of reminding her of happier times, and inspiring her to be
around long into the future for all the other milestones which lay
before the feet of her new family. She had the eerie feeling that her
calendar picture was like a worn family photo wedged into the helmet of a solider in battle. As bombs exploded around the foxhole,
the terrified young man momentarily removed his helmet. The
flash of the explosion illuminated the photo of his wife and three
year old daughter, as a mixture of dirt and tears rained down upon
it. He thrust the helmet back on his head, determined to make it
home at all costs. Lauri searched for the same drive in her fight
with cancer.

Two nights before beginning chemotherapy, family and
friends gathered with Lauri and Gary as a communal show of
support. They also wanted to map out a simple way to cover the
needs the couple wouldn't be able to handle on their own. Loved
ones, with either a genetic or historical link, were yearning to be
involved, and the couple was grateful for the help. There was also a
selfish benefit to volunteering. It allowed them to spend time with
Lauri, whom they all sorely missed. Tears of joy laced with sorrow
were plentiful, and after ninety minutes, Lauri needed to leave.
The others continued on without the couple that would dominate
their collective thoughts and prayers.

As agreed upon at the meeting, Lauri and Gary would communicate via email with the large group. The next morning, Lauri
sent off her first group-wide communication. The following morning, Gary sent off his own message.

LAURI
MARCH 1, 2007 8:57 a.m. LOVING THOUGHTS
*I want to thank all my family and friends that went out of their way
to attend the get together last night. We were touched by the amount of love,
concern, and positive attitude you extended to us. Nobody could feel more
love than I do at this very moment. Thank you all so much. With this support I know I will get better and be able to spend years and years with*

all of you doing what we do best…laughing, crying, being silly, drinking martinis, and just loving each other from the bottom of our hearts. Looking forward to seeing you again soon.

All my love, Lauri oxoxox

GARY
March 2, 2007 5:45 a.m. FRIENDS
Lauri and I wanted to thank everyone for attending the meeting and lending their support for the journey ahead of us. While our physical needs are not great at this time, the powerful emotional support and positive healing influence of this group will provide immeasurable benefit not only for the two of us, but also, and equally as important, for every member of the group.

It was nice for me to get to meet some of Lauri's friends for the first time, and to reconnect with her friends and family whom I don't get to see as often as I would like. Many weeks ago, Lauri and I were talking about friendship and her many different circles of friends. As she has done many times before, Lauri amazed and impressed me when she commented that she could remember back to her childhood when she used to think about friendship, and how important it was to be a good friend. It was obvious to me that her lifelong endeavor to be a good friend has served to expand many small circles into a single larger union for the benefit of all.

Gary

The patchy ivory cloud cover allowed intermittent sunshine to pierce the windows of the SUV, causing enough glare to blind any driver. Gary turned down the visor to improve visibility. Lauri extended her neck, allowing her blonde hair to drape over the headrest as she basked in the rays emanating from the only star close enough to feel, as well as see. The couple slept soundly the night before; a result of shared and pure exhaustion. There was little discussion along the route to their first encounter with chemicals at Chemo Central.

Before getting into the car, Lauri reread some of the many emails of support and encouragement she received from family and friends over the past weeks. She lacked the stamina to converse individually with the substantial number of concerned well-wishers.

The drive to Boston to begin the battle for her life passed quickly as Lauri dozed. The couple was well schooled in the process of negotiating the challenges of traffic and parking at the well-known mega medical center in Boston, a city that would always hold a special place in Lauri's heart. During the disco era, while in her late teens, she danced the night away with friends in the many clubs on Tremont Street. She worked for years at Logan Airport and still had a large group of friends from her airline days. A back injury had forced her to give up the work she loved. Prior to cancer taking over her life, she worked for her father, and then her brother, in the center of downtown for over ten years. While the family would always joke about the challenges of employing relatives, Lauri's work ethic and dedication to the job were no laughing matter.

The sterile white walls of the individual chemotherapy room were covered with several beautiful landscape photos and posters. Lauri was sure the inference was for the patient to attempt to transport themselves to their respective "happy place" during the unwelcomed, but hopefully effective, dose of liquid hell. She thought, *Why not just move the entire set up to the lake, complete with margaritas, chips and salsa for everyone?* She would prefer a party with friends to an encounter with chemical weapons of personal mass destruction any day.

Dr. Benton breezed through the doorway. The sides of his white coat lifted away from his body and skimmed the doorframe as he entered. He wore a meticulously pressed blue button down collar shirt with a matching paisley tie, knotted to the same exacting standards as the unblemished cotton it draped in front of. He was a handsome man with gentle facial contours which portrayed a slightly adolescence innocence. Wire rim glasses were securely perched on his chiseled nose. He was trim, but not thin, and stood average in height at 5'9".

The nursing staff, as they became friends with Lauri and Gary over the course follow-up visits, depicted him as the quintessential family man. Dr. Benton had three children that he loved to talk about, and a "very understanding wife" he obviously adored. Sometimes physicians' families can be neglected as an unintentional, but unavoidable, consequence of professional obligations. Dr. Benton's family was no exception.

Lauri's friends, after accompanying her to some of her subsequent office visits and chemo appointments, were so taken with her oncologist that they took to referring to him as Dr. Gorgeous, when not in his presence. Lauri could always count on her large and close-knit group of friends to provide humorous interludes to elevate her spirit. Their love for each other fostered an interdependence born of communal triumphs and tribulations. These cemented bonds were impenetrable to external influences. They were peas in a very secure and very large pod.

"Ready to get started, Lauri?" Dr. Benton said. His comforting smile complemented his pleasant and reassuring tone.

"You bet." Lauri's smile and tone were strained as she was frail in body and spirit. She was petrified of what was ahead, and yet, she resisted showing fearful emotion. Lauri lacked comfort with her own frailty, and most times refused to acknowledge it. This combination inflicted its own carnage on her being. "We are going to lick this thing...right?"

Gary reached across the over-sized tan vinyl armrest and grasped Lauri's slightly trembling hand. His moist hand brought a slight chill to Lauri when their skin touched. "Dr. Benton will give it everything he has," Gary said.

Dr. Benton grasped Lauri's other hand. Her hands were held by the two most important doctors in her life. Gary had rescued her emotional being years ago, and now, Dr. Benton was charged with saving her physical being. They were a trio fighting for Lauri's life, and desperately striving to avoid becoming a duo.

"Lauri," Dr. Benton said, "I will finalize the instructions to the nursing staff on your chemo. They will be in shortly with your dose, which should take about an hour to administer. When it's over, you can go home and rest. You will be exhausted and we will get Gary a wheelchair to take you to the car." Dr. Benton gently squeezed his patient's hand. "We will fight this cancer together. We will use everything we have for as long as your body can tolerate it."

Lauri made a futile attempt to firmly grip her oncologists' hand. "Thanks."

Dr. Benton released his grip and reassuringly stroked Lauri's forearm which was covered by a blue thin nap sweater. The fabric stood on end from the static electricity of his touch. "Mary will be right in," he said. "She's a gem of a nurse. You'll love her—just like the rest of us do. I'll see you before you leave." Dr. Benton spun to his left, cast a brief nod in Gary's direction, and hurried for the door. As his pace quickened, his white coat separated from his frame, again brushing the door jam on his way out. The vision made Lauri think of the white caped version of a super hero, her doctor super hero. They were thrown together by fate; ready to fight her arch nemesis, pancreatic cancer. Unfortunately, this was no comic book fantasy. *Reality bites*, she thought, as she drifted off.

Lauri awoke to a firm but comforting hand on her shoulder. "Lauri, my name is Mary. I will be your chemo nurse."

As her eyes focused, Lauri was greeted with the most inviting glistening white smile. She immediately felt a special connection. Mary grasped both of Lauri's hands with her own and gently shook them, applying reassuring pressure which implied, *you and me girl, we are gong to fight this cancer together.* There was no need to make any verbal declaration. Their mutual commitment was as obvious as the contrast of their skin color. Mary became a fixture in Lauri's life, a beacon of illumination and warmth to guide and comfort her through the physical and emotional maze of chemotherapy.

"Thanks, Mary." Lauri released her nurse's grip and extended both her slender arms. Mary leaned in and wrapped her ample arms around her patient's shoulders, attempting to transfer comfort and strength in equal measure. Mary understood that all patients, and in particular cancer patients, need love and understanding along with treatment.

Being born and bred in Boston, and having risen from a financially impoverished upbringing, Mary roots were anchored in New England. Her strengths were home grown indoctrinated beliefs preached to her seven days of the week by her janitor father and housekeeper mother. The three shared a subway ride to work for years, before Mary exchanged vows and moved out, but not on. They still met for lunch in the hospital cafeteria when their work schedules permitted. As was true for every meal at home growing up with her two brothers and one sister, each meal at the hospital began with the clasping of hands around the table, forming a continuous family circle to jointly give thanks for the many blessings in their life.

Mary knew the challenges of life were hard enough at the extremes: pro or con, black or white, life or death. At the end points, you were forced to adjust to the facts. It wasn't easy, and often it wasn't pretty, but the defined choices ultimately commanded a finality of adjustment. You had to deal with the options before you, and make a decision. "Like it or not, that's the way it is," Mary's mother used to say.

It was often the shades of gray that made many experiences more difficult than the defined choices at the extremes. You had to constantly adjust to attempt to smooth the path. That was Mary's conviction when it came to her cancer patients, many of whom were terminal. Mary wasn't there when they came into the world, and only once was she present when they met their maker, but she was always there for the battle in between, the shades of gray between the beginning and the end.

The conflicting emotions of life in general were stressful enough. The trauma of adjusting to living a life, while dying of cancer, was an unimaginable and often times unsustainable compromise. The patient's emotions swung back and forth like a heavy pendulum, experiencing the crushing gravitational forces of the endpoints, life versus death, as well as every tortuous increment in between. It was Mary's role to slow the swing of the pendulum, giving her patients time and strength to cope. Because, like it or not, that was the way it was.

Mary didn't like it, not one little bit. Mary knew mortal intervention could influence the shades of gray of Lauri's cancer, but her experience told her it would take a miracle to alter the end point.

With some of her patients, it took time for Mary to connect. Not this time. She already felt a unique union with her newest chemotherapy patient, a special bond that would make Mary's endpoint loss of Lauri more profound and everlasting than many. Their skin color reflected the extremes, but the ultimate depth of their friendship and love would smooth the many shades of gray they encountered together.

Mary released her embrace of Lauri and turned toward Gary. "Hello Dr. Confer."

Gary rose from his chair. "Please call me Gary."

"Now you know I can't do that. Well, Dr. Confer, just let me know if you need anything. You and I will work together to get Lauri through her first round of chemo. This will be a challenge for Lauri and you. Can I give you a hug to get you started off right?"

"Sure, Mary." Gary stepped forward and they embraced. "Thanks for helping us through this."

"I will be here for both of you, as will Dr. Benton. We are a team."

Mary released Gary and went back to her patient. "Lauri, I am going to connect your chemo to the IV line. I will sit with you and hold your hand during the infusion. You will do fine. Don't worry, I'm here."

chapter 30

THE CIRCUMSTANCES SINCE the beginning of the New Year represented extreme adjustments for couple only sixty days into "marital bliss." While nothing had gone as planned, and while their current circumstances couldn't be further from their wildest morbid imagination, Gary and Lauri were still in love. However, that love had already started to evolve. It was a metamorphosis of necessity as mutual independence progressed toward unilateral dependence. Lauri's physical energy and emotional strengths needed to be directed to fight her cancer. She was determined to fight and win, despite the undercurrent of knowing that when you have to motivate yourself to believe you are going to live, it is more likely that you are going to die.

Lauri's fears were locked deep inside, in that personal and private vault which protects the soul of our existence. Her fear of death was most intimately tied to the loss of a future, rather than concern over method and degree of suffering. She had endured many painful challenges in her life without burdening others by sharing her sorrows. Her relationship with Gary was different. They shared a comfort with each other unlike any thing either had ever experienced. The joining of their lives was like the confluence of two rivers. Once combined, there was no way to distinguish the separate components which now comprised a mightier force of nature and nurture. They were in this together, hand in hand and heart to heart, as long as mortally possible.

174

GARY

MARCH 2, 2007 9:43 p.m. CHEMO DAY 1

Lauri had her first session of chemotherapy today. Lauri and Mary, her chemo nurse, immediately connected. Her chemotherapy consists of a once a week IV infusion of Gemzar and a once a day pill, Tarceva. If you are interested in knowing more about these or any other medications, try an Internet search. Lauri is quite fatigued but otherwise is doing well. She felt the staff was excellent and she was able to coax a smile out of Dr. Benton, which pleased her. She will be on a schedule of once a week IV infusion for 3 weeks followed by 1 week off. She will continue the oral medication on the off weeks. She asked me to thank everyone for the prayers and well wishes.

Gary

Lauri, exhausted from her first day of chemotherapy, struggled with the layout of the condo. Gary suggested she sleep in the bedroom on the main floor, but she insisted on climbing the steep stairway up to the master bedroom. With her weight loss, Gary could have carried her up the incline. Lauri refused to give pancreatic cancer the satisfaction of turning her into an invalid. Gary supported her as she ascended one step at a time, grasping the oak handrail with her lean right hand. Her absence of body fat allowed the individual muscles in her arms and hands to be visible beneath her skin, as they contracted in an all out effort to propel herself to greater heights, both physical and emotional. While she would tell you that she was a lover and not a fighter, Gary knew Lauri to be capable of amazing feats of stamina and perseverance. If pancreatic cancer was thinking about taking her life, it had better be ready to do battle to the bitter end. Unfortunately, Gary knew that it was.

He helped Lauri into bed, pulling the thick comforter up to her chin. The soft green tones of the bedding perfectly accented the wall paint. Two large, tastefully framed Monet prints on the walls, depicted lush gardens overflowing with muted yet captivating flowers. The larger of the two was centered over the headboard. Lauri cherished the depth of serenity and security this room held for her, and she would spend every possible night in this room with the man she loved.

"Do you have time to lay down with me?" Lauri asked.

"Sure." Gary moved around the foot of the bed and lay on top of the comforter. He wrapped his arm around Lauri as she slowly rolled toward him and nestled her head on his chest. Lauri's blonde hair caressed his face and the familiar scent of her shampoo brought back memories of happier times.

Several quiet minutes passed and Gary thought Lauri had fallen asleep. He was slightly startled when she twisted up on her left elbow and looked him straight in the eyes with their faces only a few inches apart. She looked serious but relaxed. Her faced slowly approached his and she gently kissed him. She eased back and said, "I know it doesn't look good—I won't stop fighting, but I'm really scared."

Gary struggled to respond as the lump in his throat expanded with each passing second. His face slightly quivered and he bit his lip as he fought back the tears. "I know." Gary kissed her on the forehead. "I'm scared for the both of us."

"Promise me, if there's no hope, you won't let me suffer. I don't want to lose control and become a vegetable."

Gary swallowed hard without relief of the mass of tension now nearly blocking his airway. "I promise."

The dramatic change in their lifestyle necessitated that the couple split their emotions between practical realism and unfettered optimism. They would appropriately prepare for the care and support of Lauri's children should she lose her battle with pancreatic cancer. Simultaneously, they believed she could be cured, to maintain their sanity, and Lauri's drive to survive. They would swing back and forth depending on the issue under discussion. It was a two-faced discourse which neither saw as unreal or inappropriate. At times, they would float downstream buoyed by a current of hope and joy. At other times, they would struggle upstream, drowning in the rapids of fear and despair.

Lauri looked deep into Gary's eyes. He felt like she was looking through him. He sensed that the wheels of thought were rapidly rotating in her mind. "Something you want to talk about?" he said.

Lauri smiled while gently sighing. It was a subtle smile of recognition. She knew Gary appreciated the swirl of thoughts circling around in her head, familiarity born from the five and one half years gestation of their relationship. "I'm afraid of all I am going to miss: graduations, weddings…grandchildren. Everything we've talked about and looked forward to. Thinking about it is killing me more than the cancer."

Gary swallowed again without relief. Realistically, it was unlikely Lauri would survive to decorate another Christmas tree. He had already been thinking about what he could do to stuff as much life and happiness into whatever time she had left. Now, he also recognized that he needed to find some way for her to believe in a future. If Lauri's prospects of a terrestrial future were grim, perhaps a spiritual future was a viable option. "Lauri," Gary said, "I believe that some way or another you will see all of the things you think you will miss. If not on this Earth, then from heaven. You won't miss anything. The kids will always know you are with them."

Lauri's expression now shifted to quizzical. "Do you really believe that? I'm not sure you believe in God, and now you're talking about heaven."

Gary tenderly brushed Lauri's hair away from her face. "What's important is what you believe, and what I can help you to believe. We are in this together. I believe there is something for you beyond earth…you can count on it."

"I hope so. I want you around forever." Lauri's eyelids closed and her head settled back onto Gary's chest.

Gary wrapped both arms around Lauri. For now, she was at his side. He would cherish each and every moment they had left. "Get some rest. I'll hold you till morning."

Lauri drifted off into that transition world between the sunset of her consciousness and the dawning of a new day. A world where reality surrenders to our wishes, and freedom is absolute. Her body flowed into Gary's like the melting wax of two flaming candles that combine into a united solitary silhouette. They were one, just like the ten-inch white alabaster statue on Lauri's night-stand. The keepsake depicted a man and woman embracing, faces caressed together, arms intertwined, and their indistinguishable bodies blending in singular union looking like the soft undulating folds of a satin curtain. The delicate cursive inscription on the statue read, "To have and to hold."

chapter 31

GARY
MARCH 9, 2007 8:08 p.m. 2nd IV CHEMO COMPLETE
LAURI COMPLETED HER *second IV chemo today with Gemzar and has been taking the daily dose of Tarceva. She is quite tired afterward and is resting comfortably tonight. The Tarceva is causing a rash, one of the known side effects. Otherwise, so far she is tolerating the chemo well.*

She asked me to thank everyone for their concern, and she wanted everyone to know she wished she had the energy to talk to you individually. Eating remains a challenge. She asked me to ask everyone (myself included), not to ask her about her eating and nausea. She finds it is enough of a challenge just to get herself to eat. It would be easier if it weren't a topic of conversation.

We are excited to be going away next Saturday. Thanks again to everyone.
Gary

GARY
MARCH 13, 2007 7:22 p.m. CANCUN ON HOLD
Lauri and I are putting our trip to Cancun on hold. She is having some difficulty with the combination of her second IV chemo treatment and her generally poor stamina from her disease. The combination of these two, coupled with the sedative effects of the other meds, is really draining her energy. She is finding it difficult to be up and about for any length of time. Her nausea remains an additional problem, limiting her food intake, which also saps her energy. We will postpone the trip until better days.

Lauri did want me to apologize to everyone for her inability to communicate with everyone. She really wishes she had the strength to answer the calls and emails, but she is just unable to at this time. She does however enjoy listening to the phone messages and reading the emails as it provides a reminder of the active life she used to lead. I also feel it is very good for her to know that all of you are thinking of her.

We send our best to all.

Gary and Lauri

GARY

MARCH 15, 2007 9:40 p.m. A BETTER DAY

Lauri is feeling better today. The hydration has helped significantly. A decision was made to take her off the Tarceva (the oral chemo) for a few days to let the rash calm down. She is also off the antibiotic, which may have contributed to her nausea. We have also cut back to a clear liquid diet. All of this is helping keep the nausea at a manageable level. It is a symptom that may never resolve completely. Her spirits are also on the rebound. We talked about taking some drives next week to get her out of the house. She suggested we take a drive to Virginia, seriously…Virginia. She always surprises me and makes me laugh. I told her we might start a little closer to home and expand the radius as she improves.

Denise and Liz are taking her to chemo tomorrow. She will also be getting a chemo-port catheter placed next week. This is a large IV catheter placed in the upper chest with a port that can be accessed through the skin for chemo and any other fluids she needs. This is common in chemo patients as it becomes more difficult to get peripheral IV access, as their arm veins become more difficult to puncture.

We both send our best to everyone and thank them for their support.

Gary

GARY

MARCH 16, 2007 10:45 p.m. CHEMOTHERAPY POSTPONED

Denise and Liz took Lauri to chemo today. However, because of Lauri's fatigue coupled with some dehydration and some ongoing gastrointestinal symptoms, Dr. Benton elected to give her a week off of her chemotherapy. They did give her some additional hydration and additional meds for the

weekend to attempt to improve her baseline. She will be getting her chemo-
port catheter on Wednesday. Her chemotherapy will restart next Friday. As
I am off this coming week, I will take her for the port and chemo.

She is doing better this evening. She sends her thanks to everyone for
their concern.
Gary

LAURI
MARCH 17, 2007 10:47 a.m. THANKS
I must have the most wonderful family and friends. No matter what,
they keep going, sending me hugs, love, support, and the strength I need. I
am truly blessed. I wish I was more up and about for visits, but I'm work-
ing on it.

I am hoping my wonderful docs are starting to get me leveled off and
the good lord is hearing all our prayers, so I can shortly see all the people I
love so much.

Please know I am fighting my hardest to be with all of you again.
I love all of you and again thanks for the notes and messages.
Love, Lauri

Gary's life consisted of going to work and then coming home
and taking care of Lauri. When she was resting, he completed the
household tasks or spent time researching her illness and possible
treatments, both conventional and alternative. He wanted desperately to instill some joy and pleasure into her life, which now consisted of getting treatment and then attempting to recover from
the side effects. She often rested on the couch watching TV. The
couple spent hours huddled together watching wedding shows and
"chick flicks." There was nothing he would deny her, and yet, there
was little true fun and happiness he could instill into their life.

Gary took numerous pictures of Lauri and her friends that
visited over the weekend. When he looked at them, it broke his
heart. Her face was completely covered with a severe acne type
rash, a side effect of her chemotherapy. The only part of her face
devoid of red blistering eruptions were her pearly white teeth. The
extreme physical disfigurement would have caused most individu-

als to shun contact with others. However, Lauri was never one to let adversity get her down. She desperately wanted to reconnect with her friends. Beyond her own needs, she knew her friends yearned to be with her as well. She was determined to live life to the fullest measure possible. Lauri wore a genuine and beautiful smile on her face in every single picture. There were several group pictures, as well as individual ones with Lauri and each of her friends. It was the happiest Gary had seen her in months.

Gary sank back into the deep red fabric couch. Lauri's head was nestled on a pillow, supported by his legs, which were extended and perched on the ornate glass coffee table. For his internal thermostat, the prevailing conditions were nearly sweltering as he now kept the temperature high enough for Lauri to be constantly comfortable. Their previous Mars/Venus meteorological compromise was cast aside for a lifestyle that gave preference to the needs of the goddess planet.

Gary ran his fingers through Lauri's hair. "Hey, I'm glad you are having a good day."

Lauri twisted around, resting the back of her head in Gary's lap so she could gaze up at his face. "It's nice to have some energy back."

Gary smiled and then bent down to kiss the woman that had brought so much pleasure to his life. She wrapped her arms around his neck and firmly pressed their lips together. "You are feeling better, aren't you?" he said.

"This is the best I've felt in quite a while."

"How about we go buy you that convertible you always wanted?"

Lauri face beamed with joy. "You really mean it?"

"Yes. Let's do it. I really want you to have it."

"Gary, you are so good to me. Thanks for being there through all of this."

"I will never let you face any of this alone." The couple hugged for a long time, each shedding a few tears. "Now, let's get you that hot car."

Despite the frigid conditions of late winter in New England, the couple purchased a metallic gray, hard top, retractable roof convertible coup while the ground was still covered with snow. While it might have been more practical to wait until the weather conditions improved, the couple was keenly aware that time and health were not circumstances under their control. *Live for today,* Gary thought.

At the slightest break in the weather, Gary would chauffer Lauri around town with the roof down so she could feel the wind and sun caressing her body. It was a simple but treasured pleasure, at a time when life was anything but simple, and pleasure was nearly as rare as surviving stage 4 pancreatic cancer.

chapter 32

GARY SPENT HIS time driving to and from work in quiet yet frenzied reflection; his thoughts sometimes as disjointed as an improvisational jazz ensemble. When he felt like things were finally under control, an unexpected intrusion pierced the calm with the subtlety of a dissonant piano chord. Gary did his best to keep the melody of the family within an octave of their former baseline.

Communication with the kids was the key. Gary talked to each of them every few days on the phone. Nick R, the only one beyond school, dropped in more often to check on his mom. While Lauri rested, Gary and Nick R often talked over a couple of beers. The four college kids made more frequent weekend trips home to both lend a hand, and hold Lauri's.

GARY
MARCH 21, 2007 2:13 p.m. CHEMO PORT
Lauri and I just returned from the hospital where she had a chemo port catheter placed. It went very well. This will make the process of chemo and blood draws easier. Lauri won't have to be stuck with needles nearly as often. She is exhausted.
Gary

GARY
MARCH 23, 2007 3:23 p.m. CHEMO POSTPONED
Lauri and I went to the hospital today expecting chemo to restart. Because of her continued nausea, which remains a bit of a mystery, as

well as her continued fatigue and weight loss (two additional pounds this last week) it was decided to give her one more week off chemo, as well as to change some meds and perform some additional tests next week. On the positive side, the new port worked well. We are both feeling somewhat frustrated but have learned to roll with the punches over the last couple of months.

Gary

LAURI
MARCH 29, 2007 7:37 a.m. HELLO
Hi everyone,

I'm having a pretty good week. My tests on Tuesday came back normal and I have minimal nausea. Thanks for all the notes and support. It means a lot.

I am scheduled to resume my chemo tomorrow (not looking forward to it) but hoping some of the side effects will be lessened.

Anticipating I have no side effects, I would love to have some short visits over the weekend from some people I haven't gotten a chance to visit with in awhile. Please let me know. Gary is on call at the hospital all weekend during the day and gets home around 4 p.m. so I will probably be alone.

Thanks again for all the notes and love you are sending...I am a very lucky person to have so many wonderful people in my life caring about me.

I love you.
Lauri

GARY
APRIL 1, 2007 7:13 a.m. POST CHEMO
Lauri had a bit of a rough day post chemo on Saturday. By the end of the evening, she was improving. When I left for work this morning, she was feeling better. The day or two after treatment always seems to be a challenge. She is back on both the Gemzar (IV once a week) and the Tarceva (pill everyday). Nausea continues to be her major symptom. It has been resistive to any and all legal and illegal remedies. It is an ongoing battle that has resulted in further weight loss. Lauri is doing everything in her power to improve her food intake.

She is considering switching her chemo day to Tuesdays with the hope that she would feel better on the weekends and be able to enjoy more time with family and friends. She is really looking forward to getting outside and planting her flowers.

Gary

Five weeks had passed since Lauri's treatment began, eight weeks since her diagnosis. "Chemo" and "side effects" became the most frequently uttered words in conversation. Chemotherapy, now there is a remarkable term. Patients, health care workers, family members, and friends often shortened the word to just "chemo." You would hear them fling out the word "chemo", and the intonation had an eerie and yet somewhat frivolous quality. It was as though they were replacing a term shrouded with anxiety and loathing, with a shortened, less menacing adaptation to make it easier to accept, much like coating a pill in honey makes it easier to swallow.

Lauri felt that having the words chemo and therapy linked in expression and action was a stark contradiction. From her perspective, the ravages of the treatment were as far removed from therapy, as was a scorching sun drenched day at the beach from a cloudy frigid day at the top of Mt. Everest.

Therapy implies healing and comfort. Cancer relentlessly invaded her body, and the term therapy seemed to lack the brutality required to fight such an adversary. As Gary had explained to her, cancer represented a particularly challenging disease for the medical profession to battle. With illness like infection, it is a foreign or external invader taking up residence in your body, and medicine can be administered to rid your body of this unwelcome intruder. Often, the therapy was successful with little side effect to the remainder of the patient.

Cancer, representing a defect in your own cells, was an internal invader. The cancerous cells were your very own cells that now lacked the ability to control their own growth. Chemotherapy attempted to stop the uncontrolled grow of the cancer cells. As a consequence, the medication produced side effects.

The ill effects of the drugs are varied, but in Lauri's case included increased nausea, intermittent vomiting, reduction in blood cell counts, and relentless, cloistering fatigue. At times, Lauri lacked the energy to lift her head from a pillow. There were times when she yearned for death over life, as the attempted cure seemed to be worse than the disease. Cancer, with its criminal attack on her body and mind, depleted her of hope for a future while simultaneously stripping away the energy to enjoy life in the present. Ironically, in the terminal set of circumstances, the only way to kill the cancer is for the cancer to kill its reluctant host. The cancer dies along with the patient.

LAURI
APRIL 3, 2007 9:43 a.m. HEALING SERVICE
Gary and I are planning on attending the healing service this Wednesday. If you would care to join us, we would love to see you there. It runs from 7 to about 8:30 p.m.

Thanks for all the love and prayers, especially this very holy week. Happy Easter to all my wonderful family and friends.
I Love You,
Lauri

LAURI
APRIL 7, 2007 9:37 a.m. HAPPY EASTER
Thank you to everyone for your continued thoughts and prayers. My Chemo treatment went well yesterday. Dr. Benton reduced my therapy 25%, trying to reduce my side effects because my white cell count was low. I got to visit with a few of my special friends—Estelle, Amy, Claire and Charlotte—during my treatment. It was so nice to see all of them. I received a beautiful quilt from some of my friends at the Healing Service on Wednesday. I wrapped myself in the quilt during my treatment, and my friends got to read all the messages that were written on the quilt. It brought back a lot of wonderful memories.

I am looking forward to spending Easter with my family at my brother brother's home. All the kids are home from school so it should be a wonderful day.

I continue to believe that with all my friends and family's support and prayers I will be healthy again soon. We are going to receive this miracle. Thank you. I wish all of you a Blessed and Happy Easter and know I love you all.

Love, Lauri

GARY
APRIL 14, 2007 10:12 a.m. ALTERNATIVE METHODS
Lauri started acupuncture last week (her third visit will be today) as well as some Chinese herbs. We also just received a wrist stimulation band. These are all attempts to reduce the nausea to allow Lauri to lead a more active life. Friday was a good day. Lauri is feeling poorly this a.m.

Gary

LAURI
APRIL 20, 2007 2:12 p.m. A GOOD WEEK
Hi family and friends,

I returned from my visit with my mom in Florida last night. We had a great time. It was so nice to be in the warm weather and get some fresh air.

I have been feeling a lot less nauseated and fatigued this week. Hopefully things are starting to level out. I also have been able to eat more. I hope this continues and I am looking forward to being more social with these improvements.

Thanks for the continued love and prayers.

Love, Lauri

GARY
APRIL 24, 2007 2:32 p.m. CHEMO RESTART
Lauri restarted chemo today. She is resting after a long day at the hospital. Lauri is doing better with only a couple episodes of significant nausea this past week. Her appetite is improved, as is her energy level. For the first time since November, her weight stabilized, without any weight loss over the past 11 days since her last chemo treatment. We are very thankful for that progress.

Gary

GARY

APRIL 30, 2007 9:24 p.m. CHEMO UPDATE

Lauri's chemo was postponed today. She had a difficult week and lost 5 additional pounds. She will be switching to a one week on, one week off plan to see if she can better tolerate the treatments. It goes without saying that she is making every effort to battle through the nausea, and to that end, she will be trying a new nausea medication. It is hoped that the new chemo plan and the new nausea medication will improve both her ability to consume more calories and well as improve her quality of life. Thanks to everyone for their support.

Gary

Two very long and draining months of chemotherapy had passed. Lauri was fatigued and consumed beyond recognition, being a sliver of her former self. Gary represented the collateral damage of Lauri's cancer, and he was worn out physically and emotionally. His profession was nearly impotent against the perpetual attack of her cancer.

Lauri supplemented standard medical practice with alternative approaches, grasping at any method of longevity enhancement. She took a mixture of vitamins, herbs, apricot pits and off label medications. She cleared all of these with Dr. Benton who always responded with his patented reply, "As long as it won't hurt you, go ahead."

The couple sat in the empty waiting room of the acupuncture clinic they found with the help of a friend. Gary tried to arrange Lauri's appointments on his day off, following a night of call. His arm curved around her shoulder. He could feel the pressure of her bones digging into his arm. The fabric of the white sweat suit with yellow piping hung limply on her angular frame.

Gary turned toward Lauri and she smiled. It was a faded smile, a facsimile of its former happiness and brilliance. Her cancer acted like a relentless sandstorm, destined to erode Lauri's former luster. However, she wouldn't surrender without continuing to fight. She was relentless too.

"How was your call?" Lauri asked, as she moved her arm from her lap and rested it on Gary's leg.

"Fun as always." Gary yawned. "A guy was brought into the ER who had been stabbed a few times. He was a mess. We did several CAT scans on him."

Lauri's smile faded into a serious expression. "I'll bet his wife did it," she said, her eyebrows arching skyward. "I'm sure he deserved it." Lauri poked Gary in the side.

The couple began to laugh uncontrollably. Their bodies convulsed against one another, enjoying a rare moment of pleasure. It was a spontaneous resurrection of their former life, and it felt good to shed a few happy tears.

Gary kissed Lauri on her forehead. "Thanks. We needed that."

chapter 33

LAURI
MAY 4, 2007 8:45 *a.m. A GOOD WEEK*

I AM HAPPY TO SAY *that being off chemo this week has given me a chance to enjoy some activities with my family and friends.*

My son Nick is in the process of moving into his new condo so I have lent a hand picking out things for him. He might just be being nice, but he says he appreciates it. And I love decorating!!

I attended the healing service on Wednesday and was so happy and delighted to see Sarah, Melinda, Julie, and Mia there. I received lots of hugs! Thanks to all for the continued prayers and support. Keep believing in miracles because I know I am about to receive one. The power of prayer is working.

I also enjoyed lunch with my brother and my former fellow workers in Boston. I drove myself in my convertible. It was great. Thanks to everyone for helping me to stay strong and keep my spirits up. You are the most amazing friends and family anyone could ask for and I am the luckiest person to have all of you in my life.

I hope to be able to see more of you as my chemo sessions will be every other week, which should give me a good week in between.

Love, Lauri

LAURI
MAY 23, 2007 7:42 a.m. CHEMO UPDATE
Hi everyone,

Elaine drove me into Boston for my chemo treatment yesterday. As usual, the company and conversation was wonderful and relaxing.

I maintained my same weight as two weeks ago, which I consider very positive news! Dr. Benton thought I looked wonderful and strong and we discussed my going back on the daily oral chemo medication, which I started last night. It knocked my down last time I was on it but I want to keep fighting as hard as I can. I received my chemo infusion without any hitches and we headed home. I will stay on the steroids for the next three days to help the nausea medication to work better. Dr. Benton has scheduled a CAT scan for next Wednesday, May 30. Gary will be off that day and will be able to take me. I would like to ask all my friends and family to continue to pray for me and to include a prayer for clean results on the CAT scan. I believe the power of prayer is working and I will get through this "bump" in the road. I will be the Miracle we have all been asking for. Thank you so very much for all your love and support. You have all made such a difference in my life.

Love, Lauri XO

LAURI
JUNE 8, 2007 10:45 a.m. HELLO
It has been four months since starting chemo. I couldn't be doing as well as l am without all of your love, support and prayers. Even Dr. Benton seems impressed! My visit went well. I put on eight tenths of a pound in 2 weeks. I will try to make it a full pound for next time! Paige spent the day with me and got to be involved with the positive communication between Dr. Benton and myself. I am so proud and amazed of how mature and strong she is through all this. I was feeling well over the last week and was able to spend some time with friends and family.

My niece graduated high school this past weekend and I was able to make the Baccalaureate Mass on Friday and hear her sing. What a beautiful, moving voice she has. Many in the audience were in tears when she sang solo the Lord's Prayer.

I went in to work on Monday. I golfed 8 holes on Tuesday with Sarah. We would have made nine holes if the sky hadn't opened up. We were in the middle of a major thunder and lightning storm. I guess it was God's way of keeping me laughing! By the time we got to our car we were dripping wet!

Wednesday night I attended the healing service and was accompanied by several friends and cousins. We had a wonderful night. We were all blessed and reassured that God is a loving and healing God and I will be a miracle.

Again, thank you for all your love and support. I hope to see more of you very soon.

All my love, Lauri

LAURI
JUNE 17, 2007 8:45 a.m. HELLO
Hi everyone,
I love reading all the encouraging and loving comments. Thanks so much. I think the daily Tarceva pill finally kicked in this week. It kept me pretty grounded most of the week. I was able to have my cousins visit on Monday and we had our final meeting for our family reunion in July. Total coming...108! I hope my cousin's house is still standing when we all leave.

Tonight Gary and I leave for Martha's Vineyard to visit with Ben. It is his 21st birthday next week so we are bringing gifts. We will return on Tuesday. Chemo is on Friday.

Thanks again for your prayers and love.
Love, Lauri

Seeing Lauri enjoying life again made Gary smile. They were four months into their battle with cancer and experiencing a brief reprieve. However, his medical knowledge and experience gave him significant pause, as he knew in his heart that despite the calm, a storm loomed in the distance. And, it would be the storm of the century.

His job became an increasing burden. He read the studies of cancer patients on a daily basis, beating home his own familial challenges. With every CAT scan of the pancreas he looked at, he scrutinized the tissue looking for signs of the cancer that was bent on taking the life of his better half. Several times, he thought he had found an early pancreatic cancer. On further workup, mercifully, for this patient and their family, there was no cancer. As a colleague told him, "Sometimes, when you have a hammer in your hand, everything looks like a nail." Work provided a physical escape, but not an emotional one.

The couple spent time discussing their future, months versus years. Lauri let her guard down with Gary; her fear and sorrow replaced the picture of hope and happiness she constantly tried to portray. When Lauri was really down and wanted to talk about life after death, Gary held her in bed and recounted what he thought heaven would be like for her. He formulated the perfect heaven for Lauri. He knew mortals offered only limited hope, and he desperately wanted to do all he could to minimize her spiritual uncertainty and its associated suffering.

✳ ✳ ✳

The blazing sun and humid air of July 4th heralded a beautiful day for the women of Venus and a sweaty hell-hole for the men of Mars. The couple spent the day at the lake enjoying the company of family and friends. Lauri's nausea, her initial presenting symptom and an unwelcome constant companion in her life, was manageable on this day. She lay down only twice to allow the tsunamic waves of disgust to dissipate into more tolerable breakers on the shore of her being. The cancer that invaded her body, in concert with the chemotherapy attempting to scare the demon away, conspired to rob her of feeling good—any time or any place. Now, as the icing on the devilish cake, it had also taken away any memory of feeling "completely normal."

Lauri battled through her symptoms, scratching and scraping out remnants of her former life. Even the not so casual observer was often oblivious to her plight. She had the fortitude of Hercules and was able to absorb all the pain her adversary dished out. Lauri rarely surrendered to the constant onslaught. She and even less frequently wore the consequences on the sleeve of her modern day garment.

Lauri loved to entertain and was intimately and joyously involved in the day's culinary preparations. What a beautiful day, she thought. She wore a mid-thigh length light fabric dress with a US flag pattern commemorating the holiday. Gary called it her "Betsy

Ross dress", and slyly commented, "Now there's a flag I'd love to unfurl." His quick wit and continued interest made Lauri smile.

As the afternoon meandered toward evening, the guests scattered. The kids were in the living room and the muffled banter filtered through the walls and crept beneath the door. Lauri reclined in bed while Gary showered, his third of the day. She clutched her calendar, now as essential as her cell phone, and looked ahead to next week's schedule. Five months had past since her diagnosis, seven months since she started feeling ill. She shook her head in wonder—had it really been that long?

Lauri grinned as she looked at the family picture for July. It was a snap shot of the five kids from last summer at the lake, sitting at the kitchen table playing cards—five hundred rummy. Gary had interrupted the contest and insisted that they all turn toward the camera. Five pairs of white teeth gleamed in the flash. There was a scattering of baseball caps, some reversed in hope of turning their luck around. The table was covered with chips, cookies, brownies and drinks. There was hardly room for the cards which were stained with ten pairs of greasy fingerprints.

Lauri set the calendar on the nightstand. The bedroom was warm, but tolerable. A gentle easterly on-shore breeze filtered through the continuous bank of open lake view windows and swirled around the room. The orange hue of the setting sun temporarily set the horizon on fire.

Gary settled onto the bed. Lauri felt free to bare her soul and search for spiritual comfort as she lay securely wrapped in the arms of the man she would love for eternity. When the fear of death becomes an uninvited daily companion in your life, rather than a distant acquaintance, you are propelled to seek solace beyond your gravity-bound thoughts.

"What's heaven going to be like?" Lauri asked, basking in the residual warmth of the day and the heat emanating from Gary's body.

Gary squeezed Lauri as tight as he dared. "In heaven, there is no pain or sorrow. And, especially for you…" Gary kissed the top of Lauri's head, "…there is no nausea."

"Wouldn't that be nice!" Lauri shifted her body and brought her arm up, placing it across Gary's chest. She nestled her head between his shoulder and face and watched as the sun disappeared. She silently mourned the loss of another summer's day, wondering how many more she had left on her personal calendar. "Tell me more."

"Heaven is free of all the negative things we have on Earth. Negative thoughts, negative actions, and negative people. It is calmness...a perpetual happiness. And for you, it is always warm."

Lauri shifted her head and kissed Gary's cheek. "And for you, it is always air-conditioned."

Gary chuckled. "That would be great."

"So in our heaven," Lauri said, "we both get to be comfortable. I love it hot and you love it cool. How does that work?"

Lauri slid her body on top of the man she loved. They were flesh to flesh with the pounding of their hearts inches apart and resonating as one.

"You know Baby, that's the beauty and mystery of heaven. You get to be warm, I get to be cool, and we get to be together."

chapter 34

Gary sat at the kitchen counter surveying the state of chaos that was now the norm for their home. With Lauri's extreme fatigue and increasing medical needs, concern over the organization and cleanliness of the home was not only down on the priority list, it was off the list.

Gary shook his head as he scanned the home: his own unwashed dishes in the sink, scattered crumbs on the kitchen counter, pill bottles and weekly pill organizers spread about the kitchen and living room, blankets and pillows haphazardly thrown on the couches, and a few stray M and M peanut candies, Lauri's favorite, on the floor where she had dropped them, unable to bend over and pick them up. The kids had stopped referring to their parents as "clean freaks."

This foreign life-style became a tolerated part of their existence as more pressing issues were forefront in their minds. When time and energy permitted, the couple reassembled the physical trappings of their former life. The emotional stretch-marks couldn't be smoothed with a fifteen minute facelift.

LAURI
JULY 6, 2007 3:07 p.m. HELLO
Hi everyone,
Wanted to send you an update. Had my chemo treatment yesterday. I was escorted by Sue, April and Celia. They were great company and support for me. Dr. Benton made a comment about the large amount of friends

I have and he is amazed to see new friends each visit. I am very lucky to have all of you in my life.

Good news. I gained a total of 2 pounds over the last 2 weeks. How many women do you know that are thrilled to hear they gained weight????? I wish the hair on my legs would fall out as fast as the hair on my head. I asked Dr. Benton about this, he smiled and commented that it probably is, but I don't notice it as much as I notice the hair on my head. Not sure he is correct. Think he was just trying to make me feel good.

The last few weeks have been very good for me. Gary and I have been able to go to the lake a few times and do some boating, which we both love. I also have had lots of visitors come to Nashua. Some have brought food and wine. We spent hours laughing and talking. Others and I have gone out to restaurants. We all love to ride in my hot little convertible!!!! I look forward to seeing more of you. I feel like the old me again. It is great seeing everyone I love so much. Thanks to you all for making me feel so loved.

Unfortunately, chemo hit me a bit harder this time and it seems to be taking me a little longer to get back on my feet. I am hoping we can figure out what to do so this will not happen again.

I am planning on attending the healing service this Wednesday, July 11th at 7 to 9 p.m. If anyone is interested I would love to see you there.

Thanks again for your love and support.

Love, Lauri

LAURI
JULY 24, 2007 9:00 a.m. HELLO
Hi everyone.

Well it's Tuesday and things are improving daily. Thanks for keeping me in your thoughts and prayers.

My big family reunion is coming up this weekend. I am really looking forward to it. We are expecting 108.

I am planning on attending the healing service on Wednesday at 630 p.m. A few of my cousins from out of state hope to join me. In fact, my cousin Kate from Chicago, who is currently in training for the Pancreatic Cancer Road race in September, running in my name, will also be attending. Would love to have any of my local friends and family join the service if they are free. I know she would love to meet my local friends and family that give me so much support and positive attitude through this whole "bump."

I feel extremely fortunate that I am feeling so well and will continue to do so with all your love, support and prayers. They will find a cure for me!!!! Thanks for everything! I love you.
Lauri

GARY
AUGUST 3, 2007 8:43 a.m. LAURI ADMITTED TO THE HOSPITAL
Lauri had a great time at the family reunion this past weekend. She was scheduled for chemo today. However, she had a very rough night and her medical workup showed pancreatitis—inflammation of the remaining pancreatic tissue left from her surgery. This requires hospitalization and medication. If all goes well, she will be out by Monday. Chemo is postponed.
Gary

Gary and Lauri had many private discussions about her wishes, should her miracle never come. She never lost hope, but she was never so naïve as to lose perspective. Her children were the cornerstones of the purpose of her life. She was determined to construct a foundation for their benefit that would withstand the test of their earthly time. The couple cried their way through these necessary but painful talks, wishing with all their combined might that the implementation was far off. Lauri felt fortunate that Gary was someone she could count on now, during her struggle with cancer, and later, when that struggle was over.

Gary desperately wanted to give Lauri a belief in a future he feared she wouldn't get to experience on Earth. There were so many sentinel events in the years ahead. Prior to her cancer, Lauri casually assumed she would be an active participant in all of them. The satisfaction of seeing all her children graduate from college, the joys of being a grandmother, and the quintessential, albeit at times potentially traumatic, pleasure of experiencing the wedding of her only daughter. These were all events she had assumed she would experience.

Now, reflections on these milestones caused a dark cloud of mourning to obscure Lauri's hallmark rose-colored glasses. Gary knew there was no way to rid Lauri of the frightening uncertainty of the unknown, and the equally frightening reality of her known circumstances. However, he could attempt to paint a picture of life after death, which gave her some hope, if not relief. The canvas of Lauri's life still had room for alteration, if not some degree of restoration. Gary took an unfamiliar brush in hand, motivated by the desire to give Lauri what she had given to him, a brighter perspective on life and love. He began writing down some thoughts that might breathe life into the afterlife.

GARY
AUGUST 7, 2007 9:20 p.m. LAURI IMPROVING
Lauri is slowly improving. The plan is to release her home tomorrow morning. Her sister will be bringing her home.
Gary

LAURI
AUGUST 8, 2007 4:07 p.m. I'M HOME
Hi everyone,
I was released from the hospital today and am feeling well. Ready to get back in the swing of things.
I want to thank everyone for all your prayers and never ending support. I continue to remain strong and positive because I have so many wonderful and caring friends and family. Thank you from the bottom of my heart.
Love, Lauri

LAURI
AUGUST 14, 2007 5:14 p.m. HELLO
Hi everyone,
I had my chemo infusion on Monday and everything went as planned. I was pretty much a couch potato the rest of the day. Each day I will feel a

little better. Today I took Paige to get her hair trimmed. Tonight we are meeting friends for dinner. Not sure how I did all this when I was working!!!

Wednesday evening I am going to the healing service. If anyone wants to meet for a bite around 4 p.m., I'll be up for that. Let me know.

Thanks again for the support and love.

Love, Lauri

Over seven months had past since Lauri's diagnosis, nearly nine months since she started feeling sick. The day's heat and humidity lingered into the August evening as the couple drove south to the Wednesday night healing service. With the convertible top down, Lauri basked in the warmth as the thick, moist air blew through her thinning hair. The air conditioning blew full blast on the driver's side, straining to keep Gary from sweating. The music resonated from the speakers and the car reverberated from the crushing base tones. They had spent as much time as possible this summer cruising around in the car, holding hands and attempting, if only briefly, to resurrect their former more blissful lifestyle.

The healing services always rejuvenated Lauri. Frequently joined by family and friends, the communion of souls and positive thoughts gave her strength and hope to keep fighting the cancer. There were many others afflicted with illness who also attended in hopes of receiving their own miracle. Lauri too was looking for divine intervention.

At the end of each service, participants were invited to come forward and share their stories of faith and support.

Betsy, or "Bee", as most referred to her, slowly made her way to the podium. She was quite nimble at eighty-two years of age, balancing her plump frame between her good right leg and the metal cane in her left hand. Not even the elevation of high heels caused her to be unsteady. When her son suggested she relinquish the spikes for a more stable pair of flats, she not so delicately replied, "Maybe you should mind you own beeswax and cleanup your own untidy appearance."

Bee was a formidable force of nature, and she was not about to give up her independent mind or her cherished pumps. She was tastefully dressed in an impeccably pressed tan pantsuit with a pink blouse sporting a neatly tied bow at the collar. She passionately adhered to the belief that if you were going out, you should try to look your best. Bee never missed an opportunity to get all gussied up. She loved the attention.

Bee adjusted the microphone and began her story. "My dear Peter and I battled his cancer for three years. Like most of you here, we went through several rounds of chemotherapy. Each time, the cancer returned. And, each time, my faith was challenged. I spent more and more time praying for a miracle. To help him, I began rubbing St. Raphael's oil on him. When he went blind, I rubbed the oil on his eyes. As his health continued to fail, I began putting St. Raphael's oil into his food. I know my prayers, my faith, and the oil prolonged his life. However, the time came when there was nothing more that could be done, and my veterinarian told me we had to put Peter down."

Gary and Lauri immediately looked at each other. It was all they could do to contain themselves. The church was stone silent, the stunning quite of bewilderment and fear. Each member of this community of faith and hope was now petrified that they would be the first to bellow forth an uncontrolled and inappropriate explosion of emotion, primarily disrespectful uproarious laughter. Most sat with their heads bowed in dread, not reverence. It was a gathering of souls grasping for anonymity, as they knew the mere acknowledgment of someone else might cause a disintegration of their fragile solitary composure. A friend to Lauri's right bent toward her and whispered in her ear, "Did she say veterinarian!"

Lauri turned to her friend with a big smile on her face. "I believe she did."

chapter 35

LAURI REACHED A MILESTONE—eight months had past since her diagnosis of stage 4 pancreatic cancer. While they didn't discuss it, the significance was not lost on either Lauri or Gary. On a statistical basis, half of all those diagnosis with Lauri's advanced degree of cancer were now dead. She had beaten the odds; she was still alive. It was hard to feel lucky, but given the alternative, she was.

LAURI
SEPTEMBER 4, 2007 9:34 a.m. UPDATE
Hi friends and family. Gary and I saw Dr. Benton on Friday at my chemo appointment. He thinks everything looks great. We discussed the possibility of taking a 3 month break from receiving chemo treatments, a "chemo holiday" as they call it. He is in favor of this, as I will have had nearly eight months of treatment after finishing out the month of September. The plan would be to start up again in January. He will do a CAT scan shortly after the last treatment in September, and then another before we start again in January. I am looking forward to feeling good during these three months, and having less nausea. I hope and pray the cancer does not show up during this period and would like to ask all of you to continue with your prayers for me. I know they are working.

I am planning on attending the healing service this Wednesday at 7 p.m. I will continue to keep you all up to date of my progress. I also hope to try and see more of you during this period while I am feeling good. Thanks for your love and support. I am very blessed to have all of you in my life. Thanks for all of your prayers and please add one for my cousin Kate who will be running in Chicago in support of pancreatic cancer research. My deepest thanks to Kate for her unbelievable efforts…and to all of you for your donations. I know someday we will find a cure.

Love, Lauri

LAURI
SEPTEMBER 30, 2007 10:10 a.m. UPDATE
Hi everyone,

After a tough week at home, I returned on Friday to Boston for my final chemo treatment for the next three months. I had lost 5 pounds since my last treatment.

They decided to keep me on steroids for a week this time and taper me off them instead of all at once. This could help with the fatigue and nausea. I hope to be up and about in a couple of days, and maybe even get together with some of you this week. I will be in touch as soon as I am feeling the strength. As always, thanks for your support and love through this whole ordeal. You all give me the will I need to persevere. I love you.

Lauri

Gary
OCTOBER 1, 2007 10:17 p.m. CHICAGO RACE – WINGS AND LEGS

We would like to express our deepest appreciation to everyone who so generously opened their hearts and their wallets in support of Kate's philanthropic run with pancreatic pace setters on September 9th, in support of Lauri and continuing research related to pancreatic cancer.

When cancer attacks so close to home, the battle becomes personal. We have been blessed with incredible support, prayers, and encouragement from an ever-expanding circle of family and friends. Success in any battle requires wings to soar above the fray to devise a plan of attack, and legs on the ground in the trenches to push toward completion of the desired goal. Your contribution will provide both wings and legs to enhance pancreatic cancer research.

We would like to extend a special and heartfelt thank you to Lauri's cousin Kate whose giving soul conceived the idea to participate, and whose strong will and legs carried her to a glorious completion of the race.

Sincerely, Lauri & Gary Confer & Family

LAURI

OCTOBER 10, 2007 9:28 a.m. HI EVERYONE

As most of you know, I had a CAT scan last Friday. Good News Again!!!! There was no evidence of cancer! I see the doctor on Friday for an updated report, but currently everything looks great!

I am continuing to gain a little more strength everyday.

Thanks for the continued prayers and support. I am beating the odds!

Love you, Lauri

Lauri sat on the couch staring at her calendar, her bewildered expression as blank as the date boxes. October, November, and December—devoid of chemotherapy appointments. The preceding eight months of chemo, nine months since diagnosis, had exhausted her body, and at times her spirit. She jumped at Dr. Benton's offer of a "chemo holiday", wanting and needing a break from the endless torture. When they had originally met with Dr. Benton prior to beginning chemotherapy, he had suggested a break in chemo after six months of treatment. Lauri had refused to stop at six months, gutting it out for two additional months in hopes of a cure. Was her current decision to stop chemo a leap of faith or a potential fall from grace—only time would tell?

The family picture above October was taken three years ago. Nick R (away at college) and Gary (the photographer) were not in the photo. Nick C was at the center of the lineup. To his left were Lauri followed by his brother Jack. To his right were Paige and her brother Ben. All arms were intertwined over each other's shoulders. The group formed a full house—three blondes, Lauri, Paige and Ben, and two sporting brown hair, Nick C, cut short, and Jack, musician style shoulder length.

There were smiles across the board as the family had just finished an adventure negotiating the twists, turns, and dead ends of a cornfield maze—a New England fall tradition. Their blue jeans were dusty and there was straw scattered in their hair. Nick C and Paige won the prize—chocolate not cheese—as they teamed up and completed the labyrinth only seconds before Jack and Ben. Lauri and Gary needed directions from the staff to find their way out.

The holiday season began in earnest the following day. Lauri, Gary, and the kids were joining family members at her brother's home for Thanksgiving dinner. Lauri thought back to the prior Thanksgiving and the trauma of the clogged kitchen sink. So much had changed in the short span of a single year.

Lauri, ten months into her battle with pancreatic cancer and two months into her "chemo holiday", felt okay—not good, but okay. It was impossible, but the couple made every attempt to deflect their attention away from her cancer during this reprieve from treatment.

However, Lauri was haunted by her cancer. She often wondered what was going on inside her body. Lauri hadn't felt the cancer growing the first time. Would she know if it was growing again?

The family attended church before making the drive south. Lauri always had a strong faith in God, although, in the few years preceding her illness, she had strayed from a weekly attendance at services. This all changed after she got sick. The couple made every attempt to get to church at least once a week. With healing services on Wednesdays, most weeks they were there twice. Lauri felt a little hypocritical about her newfound passion for her faith.

LAURI
NOVEMBER 22, 2007 8:00 a.m. HAPPY THANKSGIVING
Hello Everyone,

I want to wish all of you a wonderful and Happy Thanksgiving. I have so very much to be thankful for this year...my improved health, my wonderful loving family and friends, and all of the people who have given me their love and support through the year. I am thankful for all of you.

I was at the hospital yesterday and they did another CAT scan and ran some lab work. I still have a fair amount of nausea. Dr. Benton will call me on Monday with the results. I am certain he will figure it out.

I will be in touch.

Have a Happy, Happy Thanksgiving.
All our love, Lauri, Gary and family

GARY
NOVEMBER 29, 2007 9:26 p.m. CAT SCAN RESULTS
Lauri had not been feeling well for a few days. A CAT scan was done. There has been a change from her prior scans with a new enlarged lymph node. While her original tumor couldn't be defined by CAT scans, most often as the tumor spreads, it can be seen on follow-up scans. We are meeting with Dr. Benton on Friday to consider options. It is likely he will restart chemotherapy, possibly with a new drug. We will know more after the appointment. Lauri will be attending the healing service on Wednesday night.
Gary

GARY
NOVEMBER 30, 2007 2:46 p.m. LAURI'S TREATMENT PLAN
Lauri and I met with Dr. Benton today. Her recent CAT scan shows recurrence of her cancer with an area of lymph node involvement near the liver, and an area of involvement around blood vessels and nerves near where the portion of her pancreas was removed. Her options were to go on a clinical trial with an investigational drug, or to go on 5fluorouracil, one of the chemo drugs used to treat pancreatic cancer. She chose 5fluorouracil. She received her first dose today. This is an IV infusion, like her previous med, although the infusion is longer, 2-3 hours. She will also be restarting her oral chemotherapy. The plan is a once a week IV infusion for three weeks followed by one week off. For those of you who may consider signing up for a chemo day, this will likely be an all day affair. Lauri told Dr. Benton she wanted to hit the cancer hard, harder than the first time. "I can handle it," she said. He is doing just that. The battle continues. Our thanks to everyone for your continuing support and prayers.
Gary

The return of Lauri's cancer devastated the couple and the family. Eleven months had past since her initial diagnosis. Her hopes for a cure were taken away by the cancer, just as it had taken almost everything else in her life. Relentless and greedy, the cancer didn't just want to kill her, it wanted to inflict maximum suffering every step of the way. The cancer showed no compassion for Lauri despite the unparalleled intimacy of their relationship. It was her own personal Grinch, bringing her the early gift of coal for Christmas; the second year in a row she had received such a "gift."

Gary, also overcome with negative emotions, had suspected it was only a matter of time before pancreatic cancer reentered their life by rearing its terminal and angry head. However, he had hoped for a merciful break, for Lauri's sake. He secretly wished that the "chemo holiday" would at least carry them through Christmas and the celebration of their first anniversary on January 1, 2008. Very few of their wishes were granted during the first year of their marriage.

Gary knew the couple would resurrect some inkling of hope and happiness, as they had done so many times before. He remembered back to the summer when Lauri had learned of a pancreatic cancer support group at the hospital. She had made some inquires and was contacted by the social worker in charge of the group. The social worker explained that the group began meeting six months earlier with a total of seven members. There were only two members still alive. Those two were away on vacation for a few weeks. Not naïve, but always hopeful, Lauri had recounted her findings to Gary that evening. "Hey, at least two of them are out there enjoying life. I want to be like them," she said.

Lauri now needed to fight to resurrect her prior optimism. She divided her strengths between battling her cancer and believing she had a chance to win that fight. Gary wondered how much strength she had left. He wondered that same about himself.

chapter 36

THE RETURN OF Lauri's cancer transformed the sparsely filled in date boxes of the December calendar into thirty-one days with only the rare vacant space. The battle had resumed, and everyday represented another twenty-four hours fighting for her life. Lauri's two-month Chemo Holiday failed to fully rejuvenate her body or her spirit as she struggled to mount the physical and emotional strength she needed. Lauri felt herself fading, and this thought scared her more than the cancer.

The family picture for December was taken eighteen months earlier by Gary's neighbor. As it was always difficult to get everyone together, Lauri had opted for a "Christmas in July" family photo, which she had used with the prior years holiday cards. The family, all dressed in light summer clothing, stood on the dock at the lake. The kids, begrudgingly, wore Christmas stocking caps.

Lauri smiled as she remembered the carefree summer. At the time, there was no indication of the challenges the family would face.

LAURI
DECEMBER 5, 2007 11:45 a.m. NEW CHEMO
Hi everyone,
My first chemo treatment hit me pretty hard. I have been dealing with a great deal of fatigue and exhaustion, however not as much nausea as before. So that is some good news.
Love you, Lauri

GARY

DECEMBER 16, 2007 10:29 p.m. THIS PAST WEEK

Lauri had a difficult time this past week with persistent nausea and fatigue. She did have a good day and evening on Saturday and we attended a Christmas party with friends. Lauri even was able to get some dancing in. Sunday was another rough day. She is slated for chemo again on Monday.

I am always amazed at her courage. I once read a definition of courage as "grace under fire." Lauri is a shining example of this definition.

Gary

LAURI

DECEMBER 23, 2007 1:00 p.m. MERRY CHRISTMAS AND HAPPY NEW YEAR

Hi Family and Friends,

Gary and I wish you and your families a happy and healthy Christmas and New Year! You have been so very supportive and loving throughout the past year. We thank you.

Sorry I haven't spoken to some of you. I appreciate the phone calls and messages and will try to get to back to you when I am up a little more. I have had a couple of down weeks, but am looking forward to having a week off from chemo and having some more strength and less nausea.

Happy holiday to all of you and we love you.

Lauri and Gary

The family spent a quiet but joyous Christmas morning at home. Lauri felt blessed to touch and be touched by her family. A warm hug was the only present she wanted.

She wore a thick red and white sweater with a pattern of reindeers prancing about the forest as snow fell from above. The festive scene was not mirrored on Lauri's face as she looked worn out. Her smile, at times, seemed artificial; an attempt to force some happiness back into their lives. Gary often noticed a glazed look in her eyes. He knew that the combination of cancer and all her medications had clouded her ability to think and respond. She was no longer the woman who had captured his heart. Perhaps, that woman was gone forever.

After the gifts were opened, Lauri rested on the couch, attempting to gain strength for the drive to meet family for dinner. "Gary, could you get me my meds? My nausea is back."

"Sure."

Gary went to the large cupboard next to the kitchen sink. The ample space was crowded with plastic amber colored bottles with white, safety protected, twist-off tops. Over the last eleven months, medication assumed such a dominant place in their life that it seemed like a new member of the family. It demanded its own place in the home, and it required the couple's undivided attention.

Lauri and Gary were also on a friendly, first name basis, with the local pharmacists. Tom and Steve always asked how Lauri was doing when she or Gary picked up her prescriptions.

Gary painstakingly organized her meds to avoid errors. All medication bottles were labeled with capital letters that were referenced on a laminated sheet hung on the inside of the cabinet door. The list included: A for Ativan, AN for Anzemet, B for Bactrim, C for Compazine, CA for Carafate, D for Dilaudid, DX for Dexamethasone, G for Glycolax, H for herbs, K for Keflex, KY for Kytril, M for Marinol, N for Naltrexone, O for Oxycodone, P for Pancreas, R for Raglan, S for Senna, T for Tarceva, Z for Zofran.

As the number of medications increased, the couple joked about running out of letters of the alphabet. The house became a mini pharmacy.

Tucked between the bottles and the side of the cupboard was a 3X5 card. Gary pulled it out. Scribbled in Lauri's handwriting was the following:

C-consumption of the body and soul
A-anxiety and fear
N-never ending nausea
C-chemotherapy
E-exhaustion
R-relief will come

Lauri's honesty and awareness took Gary's breath away. Now was not the time to reveal his discovery. Maybe, he never would. Gary began to understand the profound privacy associated with Lauri's battle with cancer. It was a concept that he struggled to define and respect. While he wanted to be with her every step of the way, there were places that only the cancer stricken could enter. Parts of Lauri's journey were traveled alone, an uninhabited path to walk, with no hand to hold.

chapter 37

GARY
DECEMBER 29, 2007 6:47 a.m. UPDATE
LAURI HAD CHEMO *on Friday and is having difficulty with continued nausea and fatigue. She and I know everyone is very concerned and would love to have the opportunity to talk to her directly. She literally doesn't have the energy to do this. She is very sorry for missing the healing service on Wednesday, as in addition to the spiritual support, it provides a welcome opportunity to reconnect with friends and family. As is often the case, it is impossible to predict when her fatigue and nausea progress to levels which make it impossible for her to travel. She wanted me to thank everyone for their continued support and understanding.*
Gary

The 2008 family calendar lay atop Lauri, who had fallen asleep on the couch. Gary sat in the den, able to watch her through the open door while he used the computer to catch up on bills and other necessities. His head shook as he reflected on the past year—their first year of marriage. For twelve months they'd struggled with illness and uncertainty. In his mind, despite all they had been through, the real challenges were yet to be faced.

He turned off the computer and walked over to his resting wife. Lauri had spent much of the past year either too sick to enjoy life, or, as a consequence of the ravages of cancer and the side effects of medication, asleep. She had little energy for anything else.

Gary gently lifted off the calendar and sat down on the floor beside the couch. He slowly leaned back so as not to disturb her much needed slumber. The family photo for January 2008 was a montage of baby pictures of the kids, all captured at about five years of age. Nick R was on the back of a pony, his face lit up by a smile as wide as the open prairie. Ben was poised on the edge of the pool, dripping wet, ready to execute another perfect dive. Paige was in a princess costume Lauri had made for Halloween, complete with a twinkling tiara. Nick C was in a basketball uniform, looking focused, the "rock" tucked under his arm. Jack wore sunglasses, his hair slicked back for effect as he strummed a kid-sized electric guitar.

The pictures reflected the joy and promise of youth; the earliest chapters in their individual book of life. Gary's mouth quivered as he looked toward Lauri. He wondered how many chapters were left in her story.

LAURI
JANUARY 4, 2008 3:47 a.m. HAPPY NEW YEAR
Hello Everyone,
Thanks for your New Years and the first wedding anniversary well wishes.
We had a quiet New Years. Next year I hope to plan something big and fun!
The last chemo caused more fatigue than nausea. Gary and I are working together with my meds trying to control the nausea.
Happy New Year to everyone. I miss you all and hope to see you soon.
Love you, Lauri XOXOXO

Lauri and Gary quietly sat in the front row of the church waiting for the others to arrive for the Wednesday night healing service. While not feeling well, Lauri had insisted they attend. The serenity disappeared with the subtlety of an explosion as the door at the top of the aisle burst open and the clatter of hard sole shoes with taps anchored to their heals resounded off the stone floor.

The couple turned and witnessed a young girl skipping toward the altar, her body bundled in winter clothing, a red and white knitted cap covering her head.

"Slow down Sweet pea," called out the women trailing the child through the door, her matching cap tucked under her arm.

The petite woman was followed by an average height well built man with a heavy coat slung over his shoulder. "Wait for me Amanda," he said.

Amanda skidded past Lauri and Gary. "Hi," she said, waving her hand as she turned to the left, heading toward the piano and instrument stands at the side of the altar.

"Sorry," the man said as he reached the front and then briskly walked in the direction of the little girl.

Gary stood as the woman reached the first row.

"I'm so sorry," she said.

"Don't be," Lauri said. "She's beautiful. A breath of fresh air."

"Today is a good day." The woman extended her right hand which Lauri took as she struggled to an upright position. "I'm Kim and that's Amanda and my husband Todd."

"I'm Lauri and this is Gary. Join us." Lauri and Gary slid in making room for three more.

"We came early," Kim said. "This is our first time at a healing service."

Not wanting to pry, Lauri and Gary remained silent.

"We came for Amanda."

Lauri, having noticed no hair showing below the edge of Amanda's cap, knew she and the little girl shared a fight for their lives. Amanda's slightly out of proportion pudgy facial features she also shared with Lauri—steroid medication side effects. "She looks good…she's responding well?" Lauri reached out and took Kim's hand.

"So far," Kim bowed her head. "The brain tumor has shrunk with the surgery, chemo, and steroids. This is the best she's felt in six months."

"That's promising," Gary said.

"There isn't much long term hope, according to the doctors. That is why we're here."

"Us too," Lauri said.

Kim pulled a tissue from her coat pocket and wiped her eyes. "She's only five years old."

Lauri extended both of her arms and Kim gently collapsed against her chest. They remained quite while Amanda, sitting on her father's lap, lightly touched the piano keys.

Kim eased back. "And you, Lauri?"

"I'm doing well today."

Kim's moistened eyes, weighted down by heavy dark circles, asked the question she hesitated to voice.

"Pancreatic cancer," Lauri said. As the words left her mouth, Lauri felt a wave of guilt pour over her body. That uncomfortable in your own skin feeling, as if she had gotten away with something—Lauri was forty-eight, Amanda only five. Kim didn't need to shoulder Lauri's burdens. Kim already had more than any person should have to carry.

"Would you like to pray together?" Lauri asked.

"I would love that." Kim turned toward Amanda and smiled. "That sounds great!"

Lauri and Gary lightly clapped their hands, which prompted Amanda to slide off her father's lap. She stood straight up, wrapped one arm in front of her waist and the other behind her back. Amanda took a much deserved bow for her playing, and in the hearts of the adults, for her bravery.

The chance meeting would provide support for the two families battling cancer. Lauri and Amanda fast became friends with "Sweet pea" preferring to sit on "Ms. Lauri's" lap during the prayer driven healing services. Lauri spent the time asking God to heal them both. If God had to choose, he should pick Amanda. However, if he had two miracles in his pocket, Lauri would like to get the other one.

GARY
JANUARY 20, 2008 11:30 p.m. CHEMO UPDATE

Lauri had chemo today. Our thanks to Tina for driving.

Lauri has been very fatigued over the last month; the post chemo days are the most difficult. With the kids home from school on break, they, along with Lauri's mom, have provided a daily presence in the home. Along with her increasing exhaustion, she continues to have episodes of nausea. She is also, not unexpectedly, starting to have some bouts of depression for which Dr. Benton prescribed medication. I am sure some of the blues relate to the isolation from friends and family caused by the increasing challenges of her illness.

It is hard to believe Lauri's illness started almost 13 months ago. It has been a learn-as-you go experience. We have been very fortunate to have the limitless support of family and friends.

Lauri and I have discussed the idea of inviting people up for the day to both spend some time with her and provide some assistance to her. I want to be clear that we are not talking medical care. I also want to be honest that Lauri, at this time, spends a fair amount of the day resting. I feel the direct contact with others may go a long way to elevating her spirits. We both feel that, at this time, we should limit this to one person at a time.

Gary

GARY

JANUARY 27, 2008 1:14 a.m. LAURI HOSPITALIZED

Lauri needed to be hospitalized for increasing pain, nausea and exhaustion. She should be in for a few days for medication adjustments and tests.

Gary

GARY

JANUARY 31, 2008 11:46 p.m. CAT SCAN RESULTS

The most recent CT scan results are not as good. The region of tumor involvement is not improved, and in one area, it may have mildly progressed after seven weeks of her new chemotherapy. This indicates that it is not having any positive effect on the cancer, and she won't benefit from continuing it. Dr. Benton feels Lauri is worn down and needs a few weeks off any additional chemo. There are some options for other chemo meds to consider. Lauri and I will be meeting with him in two weeks to discuss her options. Lauri, as always, wants to thank everyone for their support.

Gary

Thirty days into a new year, thirteen months of struggle, and the bad news now came in waves. The medical profession had no hope of a cure to offer. Their attempts at "comfort care" were constantly thwarted by Lauri's cancer. Dr. Benton was a driven but compassionate man who tactfully made Lauri aware that at any time, she was free to discontinue her treatments. It was her choice, and her choice alone, "When to say when." As Lauri's husband and best friend, Gary knew the time had come to dedicate more emphasis to her spiritual wellbeing.

When he was at home, and if Lauri was awake, Gary was at her side. If she had the energy, they went out and did whatever she wanted. If she was fatigued, they sat together in bed or on the couch watching movies or TV. They spent hours watching "chick flicks" and wedding shows. With all she had been through, Lauri had difficulty concentrating. These programs didn't require a sharp focus of either her mind or her eyes. The real pleasure was in the time they spent together.

Within a few weeks, it would be one year since Lauri began treatment for cancer; the battle of her life, and for her life. Sometimes, it seemed as though the time flew by at the speed of light with both Gary and Lauri unaware of the days that rolled into weeks and months. At other times, there was a minute by minute awareness of the grinding fight, which in one year, had taken several years off of both of their lives.

For many months, Gary struggled with the idea of creating a future for Lauri beyond the limits of earthly vision. He was striving to give her a tangible description of spiritual life after physical death; creating his view of what heaven would be like for her. He wanted Lauri to have faith in a spiritual future. If she wasn't granted the earthly miracle she sought, he wanted her to get that miracle in heaven.

However, after all the effort, he was uncertain of how to proceed. Would sharing his vision with Lauri give her comfort, as was his original goal? Would it in any way soften the reality of her impending death? Or, would it show her that he had lost all hope for her survival? The Latin phrase drilled into doctors during medical school echoed in his head, "Primum non nocere: First, do no harm." Lauri had suffered enough, and at the very least, Gary didn't want to compound her misery. This dilemma ate away at him while Lauri's cancer relentlessly devoured her body and spirit.

As they lay together at the end of another cherished day, Gary decided to act. In his heart, he knew that Lauri, above anyone else in his life, would embrace the intention in his heart if not the content in his mind. "How are you doing?"

Lauri knew Gary so well that she always accurately sensed when this simple phrase was inquiring about her physical or her emotional wellbeing. "I'm worried about how long I have left." Lauri voice was calm as she reached across Gary's body and gently took his hand, intertwining their fingers. "The cancer is growing. Nothing seems able to stop it. I don't have much energy left to fight."

Gary clenched his free hand and bit his lip. He paused to take in a deep breath. "I know. It's been a long battle. I'll do whatever you need or want."

"You have already been my miracle. I couldn't have made it this far without you." Lauri squeezed Gary's hand more tightly. "I need you to be there for my kids when I am gone. They'll need you…and you'll need them too."

Gary's lips quivered as he suppressed the tears that yearned to erupt to the surface. Lauri elevated her head and kissed his lips, sharing her calmness. She rested her head on his chest. "Tell me more about heaven and all that stuff you've been writing."

Gary was not at all surprised by Lauri's awareness. When he was not at Lauri's side, he was at the computer writing. When Lauri had asked what he was up to, he always said, "Just doing some things."

Gary relaxed his clenched fist and ran his hand through Lauri's hair. Their special connection was obvious, dating back to the very earliest phase of their relationship. "Well, I've been writing some stuff for you. I wanted you to believe in a future...to believe there is something beyond our earthly existence. I hope I did the right thing."

Lauri kissed Gary again, a deeper and longer kiss of love and commitment rather than strength and resilience. As their lips separated she said, "Do you think I'll get into heaven?"

Gary smiled while shaking his head. "If you don't, heaven must be empty."

"I'm so lucky to have you in my life. Read to me. I hope heaven is further off than we both fear."

Gary reached for the folder on the nightstand. He propped himself up against the headboard while Lauri nestled her head on a pillow resting against his chest. This would be the first night of many that Gary shared the most intimate details of his hopes and dreams for Lauri as she ventured into the great beyond. He was without the mortal power to prevent the inevitable. However, there was still time to partially sooth Lauri's fears prior to her spiritual transformation.

chapter 38

GARY SAT AT THE kitchen counter with medication bottles spread out in a large semicircle; each of the amber bottles with their white tops looked like the columns of a Roman temple. He'd assumed the Sunday evening ritual of organizing Lauri's next week of medication several months ago, as the complexity of the task progressed beyond her ability to concentrate. Three white plastic weekly medications containers, the seven individual compartments labeled with blue capital letters indicating the days of the week, were all snapped open before him. On the sides of each container, written in black felt marker, were the words: MORNING, AFTERNOON, EVENING. It took an hour to make sure the correct medication made it into the appropriate compartment of the right container.

The morning and evening doses were not a problem. Gary got Lauri her meds before he went to work and then before she went to bed. He called her everyday at 2 p.m. to check in and to remind her to take her afternoon pills.

Gary took the family calendar and filled in the known appointments for the month of February. He smiled as he remembered taking the photo Lauri had picked for this month. Lauri hated the cold, so she chose to occupy the winter months of the calendar with pictures that reminded her of warmer days. This shot was taken four years ago on visiting day at Paige's summer camp; Paige was fifteen years old and working as a counselor.

Lauri and Paige were locked in an embrace in front of the massive oak tree. The sun reflected off their faces as the stood cheek to cheek. At the time, Paige was only one inch shy of reaching Lauri's 5'9" frame. Lauri's little girl had grown up.

Lauri's illness caused an accelerated emotional maturity of the kids. They all called home more than normal with offers of help and support. Paige, who had been living away at college in Connecticut, transferred to a local college and moved back home. While Lauri initially resisted, Paige insisted, handling the task completely on her own. Lauri loved having her daughter at home while Paige needed to be at her mother's side.

GARY
FEBRUARY 4, 2008 11:12 p.m. AT HOME FLUIDS
We are starting at home fluids to help Lauri avoid episodes of dehydration. Lauri is starting to experience more pain, which we are treating. She is having some memory and communication issues. We did a brain MRI and it looks okay.

She wanted me to tell everyone that she thinks of all of you and hopes to find the strength to resume her previously active life.
Gary

LAURI
FEBRUARY 13, 2008 9:25 a.m. HELLO
Hi everyone.

Thanks for your continued support and encouragement. I am having a pretty good week. Seems like the nightly infusions and the steroids may be helping. If that's so, I will continue to get strong. I see Dr. Benton on Thursday. I am sure he will have some advice.

I am planning on attending the healing mass tonight. I would love to see any of you. If by chance anything comes up, I will email the change or Gary will. Thanks.

Gary took me to gamble yesterday. I won $500.00 on the slots!!!!! I was so excited. Took my winnings, we had lunch and came home. Now... what do I buy????????? We had fun.

Tomorrow is Valentine's Day.

I wish all of you, my special Valentines, a lovely, romantic, happy and special day. I love you.

Love, Lauri

GARY

FEBRUARY 14, 2008 6:14 p.m. APPOINTMENT WITH DR. BENTON

Lauri and I met with Dr. Benton today. Lauri is doing better. He feels her tumor is growing slowly, based on her progress so far. As she has already had the chemo agents, which are used as front line meds for pancreatic cancer, we will be moving on to other agents in the near future. The plan is to leave Lauri off chemo for several weeks and repeat her CAT scans to check for any more tumor growth. Dr. Benton feels Lauri isn't strong enough at this time to withstand additional chemo, as the agents she would be going to have even more severe side effects than the agents she has already been on.

She will remain on pain meds, as she continues to have pain.

We are reducing the at home IV infusions to 3 times per week to attempt to encourage her to take fluids on her own.

Gary

LAURI

MARCH 2, 2008 2:50 a.m. HELLO

Just wanted to send a little update. I haven't been feeling great pretty much all week. Saw Dr. Benton on Wednesday. We discussed our next plan of attack.

Gary and Dr. Benton decided to put me back on steroids so I can make my trip to Florida. I leave tomorrow (Sunday) and return on the 27th. Paige is joining us on the 20th. I will bring home some sunshine.

Thanks again for all your good wishes and prayers. You are all amazing people and you should know that. How you have responded to me has been a miracle and I know how truly blessed I am to have you all in my life continuing to pray and offer good wishes. Thank you.

Look forward to hearing from you.

Thanks again. I love you. Lauri

Gary marveled at Lauri's strength and resilience. She had been fighting pancreatic cancer for fourteen months. Despite all of the setbacks, she kept on battling. She made a five-day trip to

Florida, and was set to make at seven day religious pilgrimage half way around the world to Medjugorje. Gary was scared to death to let her go, but she was insistent. She wanted to go, she needed to go, and she was going—period. She would make the trip with her two brothers and her best friend.

The trip to Medjugorje was no small task for a healthy individual. There was a seventeen-hour plane ride followed by a three hour bus ride into the remote mountains of Eastern Europe. The shrine was known for miracles, and Lauri was determined to go after her own, rather than waiting for it to come to her.

Spirituality had displaced medical treatment as the primary focus of Lauri's attention. She was not yet willing to stop chemotherapy, but she was not naïve to the fact that her cancer was growing. Lauri knew that in spite of the best intentions of the medical profession, her cancer was like an anchor, constantly trying to pull her under. At this time, the best she could hope for from chemotherapy was to increase the slack on the chain that bound her to the darkest depths of her impending fate. She would forcefully drag that anchor to remote Bosnia in hopes of getting her miracle.

The concept of spirituality had always been a difficult one for Gary. Lauri's cancer caused him to constantly wrestle with the concepts of belief versus non-belief. He was amazed at the intellectual clarity and conviction required to either passionately believe or not believe in God.

To be an atheist and reject the concept of a supreme being, Gary thought you must then claim to know with certainty that humans are alone with no connection beyond their earthly existence. It seemed ironic that someone who dismisses the concept of God or a supreme being, must themselves claim to know all truths. Gary felt his knowledge was too incomplete to be a committed atheist.

On the flip side of the coin, it was equally difficult to unquestionably believe. How can one reconcile the concepts of good and evil relative to God? Life and death had nothing to do with fairness. It seemed to Gary that people's faith was a lot like water. It had a fluid component that took the shape of whatever container it was poured into. Namely, their faith changed shape depending on the circumstances in which they found themselves.

Gary was most comfortable being an agnostic, accepting that there were many issues, both natural and spiritual, which remain unexplained. Perhaps, his lack of conviction was why Lauri had wanted to make the trip with others who firmly believed in the power of the spirit. Gary fully understood. Lauri needed all energies focused on the belief in the healing power of God.

LAURI
APRIL 15, 2008 4:25 a.m. HELLO TO FAMILY AND FRIENDS
Well, today is the day. We leave for Medjugorje for one week. We are all feeling very secure, positive and hopeful. Our encouragement continues to be our strong equal force. Thanks to all of you for the support and love you continually send to all of us, especially me. We continue to receive numerous unending amounts of support, love and encouragement on a daily basis and from all sorts of folks. We are so thankful for everything you are all doing. We will remain positive and hopeful, and will return with all the good news we have been waiting so long to hear. God Bless all of you. You will remain in our prayers and hold a special place in each of our hearts. We will be in touch when we return. We will return with miracles!
Love you always.
Lauri xoxoxxoxoxo

LAURI
APRIL 24, 2008 8:27 a.m. HOME
Hi friends and family.
We are home safe, sound, healthy and peaceful from our trip to Medjugorje. We had a wonderful time. Can't wait to show some pictures.
My health held up good while I was away. I even got to climb a mountain!!!!!!
Unfortunately, my abdominal pain from the disease has increased. Sometimes it's almost unbearable. I saw Dr. Benton yesterday. He is talking about putting me back in the hospital for a few days to try and balance out the pain medicine so I can get relief. Thanks for your support.
Talk to you soon. Love you. Lauri

GARY

*APRIL 26, 2008 10:29 p.m. LAURI ADMITTED TO HOSPI-
TAL*

*Lauri is resting more comfortably tonight. She will likely be in the
hospital for about five days. She has been having increasing symptoms over
the last few weeks and battled through them to make the trip to Medjugorje.
She is very glad to have made the trip. I am relieved she is home.*

*Her CAT scan yesterday showed further spread of the cancer. With
pancreatic cancer, one of the most common areas for spread is in the posteri-
or part of the upper abdomen at the site of previous surgery. This is the area
where her cancer has been slowly growing despite her previous chemo. The
latest scan shows more rapid growth of the cancer. This area of the abdomen has a large number of nerves and blood vessels. The cancer, invading
and surrounding the nerves, is responsible for the pain. When the cancer
invades and surrounds the blood vessels, there are problems with blood
flow. Some of the cancer now involves the vein draining her left kidney. She
is going on blood thinners to attempt to improve the blood flow in this vein.
The doctors are also switching her pain meds to give her some relief.*

She wanted me to thank everyone for their support and prayers.
Gary

GARY

MAY 3, 2008 6:46 a.m. HOSPITAL UPDATE

*Lauri's pain control is improving on IV pain meds. She will be go-
ing home on a continuous IV pump infusion. She started a new round of
chemotherapy on Thursday. This is causing her nausea to increase. The
medical staff is trying a whole range of meds to try to get her nausea back to
a tolerable level. This has been difficult, and she will remain in the hospital
until this can be accomplished.*

*She is on twice a day injections to treat the clot in her left renal vein.
These injections will continue at home with myself and Paige giving them
to her.*
Gary

The hospital had become an unwelcome but integral part of the couple's life over the past seventeen months. Lauri was recognized and loved by many of the hospital staff.

Whenever she was admitted, Gary contacted Emily, Lauri's original nurse, who would drop by to check on her favorite patient. Emily would remove her three sets of prayer beads from their engraved wooden box. She would intertwine the beads between Lauri's hands and her own, while the two friends shared spiritual support. Emily's visits provided a rare moment of serenity to Lauri.

With this hospitalization, as with all others, Gary would drive to Boston after completing his work day in New Hampshire. He used the hour in the car to make "update" calls to family. Prior to her illness, it was rare for the couple to talk on the phone during the work day. Now, they talked several times a day whether Lauri was at home or in the hospital. It was something both of them needed.

Gary encountered Emily in the hall just outside Lauri's room. She gave him a big hug. As she sped down the corridor, the strands of her unrestrained long black hair separated as she gained speed. Her hair flared out looking like it was influenced by the effects of static electricity. Gary always felt there was something unique about Emily and the spiritual chemistry of her relationship with Lauri.

Gary entered Lauri's room and closed the door. Lauri's beautiful smile welcomed him as he approached her bed. Her spirit and warmth were treasured possessions that the cancer would never be able to take away. Gary returned Lauri's always-contagious smile and said, "I see they've got you hooked up to the pump."

Lauri half chuckled. "Yeah, this is my newest friend." She pointed to the morphine pump hanging from the large IV pole next to her bed. "It comes with me everywhere. They will be in later to train you on the smaller at-home version. Lucky you."

Gary bent and kissed Lauri. As he began to pull back, she reached up and wrapped her arms around his neck. "Hold me," she said. Gary helped Lauri sit up in bed and he sat beside her. The couple embraced as tears flowed from their eyes. They knew the final stages of Lauri's illness had arrived, and they were scared to death of being without each other. Lauri sobbed openly while Gary suffered in silence. He knew that as tough as life had been, times were going to get a lot tougher, both physically and emotionally. He would hold Lauri until the end, but now, it was painfully obvious, that the end was fast approaching.

After a long embrace, Lauri released her arms and Gary gently eased her back onto the bed. He wiped her eyes with some tissue from the nightstand. "Hey beautiful, anything special you want to do when we get you home? I'm off this weekend."

"Let's go to the lake and plant my spring flowers."

"That sounds great to me."

This would be the last spring they would spend together; it would be the final time they toiled in the garden during the season of renewal.

"Could you do me a favor and help me take a shower?"

"Sure. This should be a bit of a challenge with the pump. Let me get the okay from your nurse."

Gary briefly left the room, returning with fresh towels and clothing for Lauri, along with instructions from her nurse. With some careful maneuvering, Lauri was inside the shower with Gary standing outside the stall holding the pump and tubing. Unbeknownst to Lauri, the shower curtain was too short, and the water was cascading beneath it, drenching Gary's shoes. The humidity from the hot shower raised the temperature in the bathroom, causing Gary to perspire. The small dots of sweat on his shirt joined into larger geographic pools. The little remaining hair on his head was now moist and limp against his scalp. His glasses were completely fogged.

Lauri shut off the water and pulled back the curtain.

Gary handed her a towel. "Nice shower?"

Lauri looked at Gary and almost collapsed as she shook her head and chuckled. "Why didn't you tell me you were getting wet?"

"Because, you needed a shower and a good laugh. No need to thank me." Gary grinned. "Besides, I needed a shower too."

chapter 39

GARY

MAY 6, 2008, 8:04 p.m. LAURI AT HOME

LAURI IS ADJUSTING TO *the challenges of being attached to a continuous IV pump. It is a small device, placed in a shoulder or fanny pack, from which she gets a continuous infusion of pain medication. I taught Paige how to give Lauri her injections. I give Lauri her morning shot; Paige gives her the evening shot. Paige has been a fantastic help.*

Lauri is quite fatigued and is finding it difficult at times to get around. Lauri's mom has been a great help too. Lauri and I are discussing inviting people to come up and spend part of the day with her for companionship and some assistance (no shots involved). As I am sure all of you can imagine, it has been very hard for Lauri to give up her independence. This is one of the many things the cancer has taken from her.

Gary

GARY

MAY 16, 2008 11:35 p.m. LAURI HOSPITALIZED

Lauri is having a difficult time with her symptoms and was hospitalized today. Her type of slower growing pancreatic cancer comes with greater survival time than most patients with metastatic pancreatic cancer, but also tends to have symptoms that become harder and harder to manage. Her physicians have tried, and are continuing to try, any and all meds for nausea, with limited success. They have put her back on a high dose of steroids to attempt to control the nausea. She continues to battle, but is becoming increasing worn down, both physically and emotionally. We are keeping visits to the hospital to a minimum, by her request, as she doesn't feel up to many visitors. Lauri did want me to thank everyone for their unending support and prayers, and she hopes to be in contact with all of you soon.

Gary

GARY

MAY 19, 2008 7:31 a.m. LAURI COMING HOME

Lauri will be coming home this afternoon. She is still quite ill, but she really wants to get out of the hospital. I am off this week, which will allow her to come home in spite of her current condition.

Lauri's symptoms are becoming more and more difficult to control. While the meds make her drowsy, she is reaching the point where sleep is preferred over nausea. It is becoming increasingly important that we support her in any decisions she makes about the future course of her care. There are times in life when comfort and peace are the greatest gifts we can bestow on someone we love.

I will let everyone know when she is up for visits. We will likely be offering times for friends and family to come and spend some time with her and to assist her with her daily needs.

Gary

GARY

MAY 21, 2008 9:09 a.m. LAURI AT HOME

Lauri is happy to be home. Her pain is under good control. Her nausea, while still a challenge, is less severe than before being admitted. We are hoping to be up at the lake for the holiday weekend. It should lift her spirits. Some of the kids will be joining us.

Our thanks to all of you for your support. Lauri's challenges will progress, although the rate of progression is unknown.

Gary

Gary had the long Memorial Day weekend off, including the Friday leading into it. The couple spent Friday morning in Nashua planting the traditional beautiful array of pansies in the metal planters along the deck railing on both upper levels of their condo. This allowed Lauri to see the colorful blossoms from either the

main floor or her bedroom. Lauri, too weak to physically participate, directed Gary, who did the planting to her exact wishes.

She educated Gary as to their misnomer; pansies were not
"pansies." They were actually a quite hearty flower, resistant to the
predators and environmental insults that killed less virile flowering plants. Gary wished Lauri had been more of a pansy for both
of their sakes.

The openness of the convertible allowed the gentle summer
breeze to caress Lauri's skin during the afternoon drive to the
lake. The blazing sun beat down on her body, keeping her warm
and comfortable. The narrow crowded back seat overflowed with
bags, all strapped in to prevent an unplanned exit from the vehicle. Lauri's medical bag, her lifeline, filled with needles, syringes,
numerous medicine bottles, IV bags of narcotics and fluids, and
various other essentials, sat securely wedged between her feet.

Over the last seventeen months, Gary became an expert at-
home nurse. He gave Lauri shots, changed her IV infusions, adjusted her narcotics, cleared her chemo-port when it clogged, and
did whatever else was required to avoid any unnecessary trips to
the hospital. With her progressively failing health, Gary promised
Lauri he would do all he could to keep her at home, for as long as
she wanted.

The sun burned brightly all weekend at the lake with all five
of the kids arriving on Friday evening and staying through Monday. They each spent some quiet moments with Lauri, laughing
and reminiscing about the many happy times they shared. Time
was no longer something any of them could take for granted. The
mood was peaceful. Lauri, as she always did, led by example. Comfort was the staple of their time together, and Lauri made sure she
held the hands as well as the hearts of every family member.

Saturday morning, as the kids slept in, Lauri and Gary planted her flowers: red chrysanthemums, yellow daisies, mixed gladi-
olus, and assorted impatiens. She struggled to move around, at
times using her chair as a makeshift walker. Her previously frail
body was now larger than it had ever been, a side effect of chronic
steroid use. The steroids had become a necessity in recent months

to take some of the edge off of her symptoms. With the benefit, came a cost; considerable weight gain.

Lauri desperately wanted to do some of the planting herself. She feared this would be the last time her hands would work the soil on the banks of the lake she loved so much. At each planting site, Gary helped her to the ground. She knelt and ushered forth the energy to place the flowers in the hole Gary had dug. Together, they filled in the dirt, their hands patting the soil together. By the end of the morning, all the flowers were planted. For the remainder of the weekend, Lauri enjoyed the colorful fruits of her labor. She loved the beauty of nature.

After lunch, the family loaded into the boat and cruised the lake, retracing steps that dated back to Lauri's teenage years. Lauri had spent time on Lake Winnisquam every summer for the last thirty-five years. She entertained the family with funny stories from her childhood. She and her siblings had run wild on the lake during their adolescence.

In the late afternoon, they anchored at the north end of the lake in the loon sanctuary. The boat gently rocked to the rhythm of the wind and the waves. The occasional surreal and somewhat haunting call of the loons intermittently disturbed the peace and quiet. The group, in dire need of spiritual support, gained strength and guidance from the location and each other.

That evening, Lauri and Gary retired early. They had adjusted to a routine that involved a regimented series of tasks associated with Lauri's medical and personal needs. Before her shower, her IV tubing was detached from her chemo-port and the port was covered with plastic wrap and tape. Gary stood next to the shower door in case Lauri needed help. After showering, the port was flushed and her IV lines were reattached after appropriate adjustment of the controls on the morphine pump. Gary then helped Lauri into bed. As he laid her down, a somber look smoothed the smile wrinkles which had adorned her face for much of the day. She placed her right hand on Gary's face. "I wish I could stop being your patient, and go back to being your wife."

chapter 40

LAURI

MAY 26, 2008 9:22 p.m. HELLO

THANK YOU ALL FOR *the beautiful messages you have all posted. I get such a sense of peacefulness as I read them and remember back to some happy and funny times I have spent with my dear friends and family. Thanks for not forgetting me. I continue to work with my medical team and plan on beating this nasty illness. Your prayers and thoughts are the cement I need to build my support off of. Thanks again.*

Love and kisses. Lauri

GARY

JUNE 2, 2008 6:32 a.m. UPDATE

Lauri is doing okay. She still battles her nausea on a daily basis. We had home health/hospice come in and do an evaluation for thoughts on additional considerations for her nausea. They are discussing ideas with Dr. Benton, mainly an increase in the dose of some of the meds Lauri is already on. The down side is that the increase will make her more tired than she already is—a tough trade off.

We are meeting with Dr. Benton on Thursday to get her next dose of chemo, as long as her blood work allows.

Gary

GARY

JUNE 5, 2008 4:30 p.m. CHEMO UPDATE

Lauri had her second dose of her new chemotherapy agent (Mitomycin) today. Prior to the treatment, we met with Dr. Benton. Lauri's pain is under good control. Her nausea remains a challenge. We are increasing some of her current meds.

One of the ways to follow Lauri's cancer is with the cancer marker C19-9. In the past, her level of this marker was in the normal range. Her most recent level, drawn last week, showed an increase in the marker level above the normal range, another indication of the progression of her cancer. The plan is to recheck her CAT scan and C19-9 level in three weeks to see if this latest dose of chemo has any positive effect. Future treatment considerations will depend on her response to this chemo dose.

Thanks to everyone for their continuing support.

Gary

GARY

JUNE 9, 2008 7:24 a.m. CHEMO UPDATE

Lauri is having a difficult time with this latest round of chemotherapy. She has experienced an increase in her nausea. The combination of her symptoms, her cancer, and all of the meds, has kept her in bed most of the time since her treatment on Thursday.

Gary

Lauri leaned against Gary as they both sat on the couch watching TV. Gary's arms were wrapped around her. They spent much of the past eighteen months in this very position. The cancer had taken nearly all she had to give; her body exhausted, her emotions depleted. The staple of Lauri's viewing pleasure was once again on the screen, a wedding show.

"I feel like I'm now an expert on wedding issues," Gary said.

"That's the idea," Lauri said in a soft and weary voice. "Now you will be able to help Paige with hers."

Gary was stunned and unable to respond. They both knew, and now they both accepted that the battle was nearly over.

Lauri shifted her position so she could look into Gary's eyes. With no strain in her voice she said, "I want to stop the chemo…I just can't do it anymore."

Gary silently nodded. Lauri's head gently came to rest against his shoulder and they embraced. Gary bit his quivering lip and closed his eyes.

✳ ✳ ✳

At Dr. Benton's suggestion and with Lauri's blessing, Gary looked into hospice care. The cancer was progressing, and every option to make Lauri comfortable need to be investigated. Gary didn't feel Lauri's death was imminent, rather, he felt that hospice care could help with medication adjustments and give her a little better quality of life. Lauri's decision to stop chemotherapy represented a turning point; a difficult choice with consequences she accepted, recognition of her fate that others needed to respect.

GARY
JUNE 15, 2008 11:50 p.m. HOSPICE HOUSE
Lauri and I visited the hospice house today. It is a beautiful facility. Lauri was both pleased and impressed with the surroundings and staff. The choice of hospice care reflects a change in orientation with the emphasis on comfort and peace. Lauri will probably be admitted next week for some adjustments in her medications to attempt to better control her nausea. Her pain is under good control. She will come home after a short stay and be visited on a weekly basis by the hospice staff. Below is an email I sent to Dr. Benton and his nurse practitioner Susan. They both spent a great deal of time with us. I thought including it for all of you to read, would help explain Lauri's choice to transition to hospice care.

Dear Randall and Susan,
We greatly appreciate your assistance in facilitating Lauri's transition to hospice care. It was a tremendously difficult decision to make, fraught with many additional emotional concessions layered upon the ones we have already made. Given Lauri's worsening symptoms and cancer progression, she felt the time had come to favor personal comfort over further treatments. Someone once told me that the definition of courage is "grace under fire."

Lauri, in my eyes and by any definition, is one of the most courageous people I have ever known. In your chosen profession, I imagine individual profiles in courage are something you witness on a daily basis.

There are no words that can adequately express the gratitude we feel toward both of you for the level of care you provided. As a colleague in the medial profession, I often marveled at your ability to dispense expert care interwoven with genuine concern and compassion. You were both always there when we needed you, never once leaving us to feel that we were in this fight alone. While the outcome of the war may have been a foregone conclusion, you were constantly at our side, willing and able to fight the good fight, giving Lauri every imaginable opportunity to win as many battles as were humanly possible.

We now travel an alternate path, striving less for the benefit of time and more for needed and welcomed physical and spiritual peace. There are others who will shepherd us forward, and we will miss your presence at our side.

With our warmest regards and most heart felt appreciation,
Gary and Lauri

chapter 41

GARY

JUNE 22, 2008 4:42 p.m. LAURI ENTERING HOSPICE HOUSE

LAURI WILL BE *entering the community hospice house tomorrow. I will be with her all day and staying over with her the first night. I will put out frequent updates as to her progress. The first few days are anticipated to be difficult as she transitions from oral to IV anti-nausea meds. I will let everyone know when she tells me she is ready for visitors.*

Gary

GARY

JUNE 26, 2008 6:07 a.m. HOSPICE UPDATE

Lauri is improved as the new medications have done a better job with her nausea. It will take about a week to determine the full effect on controlling her symptoms. The staff is very experienced. The primary goal of hospice is to give patients the best quality of life possible. Lauri may be in hospice up to two weeks.

Thanks to everyone for their support.

Gary

Friends and family filled Lauri's room at hospice with cut flowers and live blooming plants. On Thursdays, volunteer gardeners, many of whom had a personal attachment to the facility, worked the manicured and serene grounds. As many other patients were inclined to do, Lauri donated the live plants and participated in picking the spots for the vibrant anonymous memorials. It was a chance to give back to those whom had given so much.

There was an eerie and profound emptiness in the condo as Gary sat on the deck with the sun inching above the rolling hills in the distance. This physical separation from Lauri felt different than the many hospital stays while she battled with cancer. Lauri's fight for a cure was over. She now struggled for comfort.

The pansies along the railing were fading from the summer's heat. He plucked a few of the remaining vibrant ones to give to Lauri when he stopped by the Hospice House on his way into work. Even pansies don't live forever.

After wrapping the pansies in moist paper towels surrounded by aluminum foil, Gary headed out of the kitchen. He paused at the pantry door. The family calendar hung on the inside, its squares blank since Lauri's decision to stop chemotherapy. Gary avoided the cupboard; he couldn't bear to look at the pictures.

Gary rarely felt sorry for himself over the past year and a half. There were things that needed to be done, so he did them. It seemed selfish to focus on the changes in his life, as his burdens were small in comparison to the crosses Lauri had to bear.

He spent the time of Lauri's illness shifting roles between concerned loved one, medical advisor, at home nurse, and most importantly, friend and confidant. Often, what Lauri needed most was a hand to hold. His hand was the one she reached for.

Gary wondered whose hand he would reach for. His loss was becoming intimate; close enough to cut him deeply. Who would stop his bleeding?

GARY
JUNE 30, 2008 10:35 p.m. UPDATE
The staff continues to adjust Lauri's medications. The early benefits of her new meds have subsided and they have increased the dose in hopes of a return to its positive effect on Lauri's nausea. A decision about using IV Versed will be made in the next few days. Lauri will likely be in hospice for at least 7-10 more days.

She sends her best to everyone and wants everyone to know she misses *you.*

Gary

GARY
JULY 2, 2008 8:03 a.m. UPDATE
Lauri had a difficult day yesterday. She has decided not to go with IV Versed at this time as it will increase her sedation and limit her ability to interact with family and friends. Lauri has lived with the nausea for 20 months. As always, she continues to fight for as much quality time as possible.

Gary

Lauri faded with each passing day. Gary felt the essence of her life slipping through his fingers. Gary and the hospice staff couldn't predict how much time she had left. When she was originally admitted, the plan was to adjust medications and send her home. Now, while her fate was clear and coming faster, the time frame remained blurred.

Lauri, intermittently still sharp, joked daily with visitors and staff. Alone with Gary, the walls were crumbling. He asked her several times if she just wanted to go home. Each time, she declined.

"Can we go to the lake today?" Lauri asked, her voice straining to sound enthusiastic.

"Sure," Gary said. "Anything you want."

"I need to see the water. It always makes me feel good."

"I know. Me too."

Gary assembled all of the necessary medical supplies. All trips, even short ones, now required a small overnight bag. The couple headed for the lake, top down, sun shining, and uneasiness blowing in the wind.

Lauri's infusion pump alarm pierced the silence as the convertible exited the highway. Gary felt Lauri's hand twitched as the noise awakened her.

"It's all right," he said. "We're almost there."

Within minutes, they pulled into the gravel driveway of the lake house. The crunch of stones beneath the tires drowned out the leaves rustling in the trees.

Gary helped Lauri into the bedroom. As she lay on the comforter and gazed at the water through the windows, Gary went through the procedure of re-accessing Lauri's port with a new needle and tubing while also re-adjusting her IV infusions. Lauri's cancer was relentless, refusing to give them even one day of reprieve from its constant menacing intrusion into their lives. It had won the fight, but that wasn't enough. The cancer wanted Lauri to suffer.

They tried to go out in the boat, but after only a few minutes on the water, Lauri became severely nauseated. After returning to the dock, they spent several hours reclining in adjacent lounge chairs, hand in hand.

"I need to go back now," Lauri said.

"Okay." Gary stood up and reached down, grasping both of Lauri's hands. He gently helped her up.

She leaned toward Gary, wrapping her arms around his neck and resting her head on his shoulder. Lauri squeezed him as tight as she could. "Thanks Gary. Thanks for being the love of my life."

✱ ✱ ✱

Gary continued to send out daily email updates. Whenever Lauri was alert, there was always a familiar face for her to look at. She had individual periods of time with each of the kids, a difficult but necessary time for them, and for her. Lauri told them how much she loved them and how proud of them she was. "I will always be with you," Lauri said.

GARY
JULY 6, 2008 9:02 a.m. LIMITING VISITS
Because of Lauri's worsening symptoms, for now, visits are limited to immediate family members. The staff at the hospice is doing everything possible to make Lauri comfortable, which is becoming more and more challenging. She appreciates your kind thoughts and prayers and hopes to be able to see all of you soon.

Gary

GARY

JULY 7, 2008 7:00 a.m. NEW MEDS

Lauri was switched to IV Versed yesterday morning to attempt to better control her symptoms. She has showed some positive response, with the side effect of increased sedation requiring constant supervision if she is not asleep. Her sleep is still very fragmented despite a dose of medication that would literally put most of us into a coma.

Gary

GARY

JULY 9, 2008 4:32 a.m. UPDATE

Lauri is resting more comfortably. The staff continues to increase her dose of medications as well as provide an equal amount of spiritual support. Lauri's parents spent the day with her, and the kids and I spent the evening. With the increased sedation, her ability to communicate has been significantly reduced. She is monitored and attended to on a 24-hour basis. Thanks to everyone for their continued support.

Gary

Gary sat at the bedside holding Lauri's hand. It was just after midnight; the last of the family, the five kids, had gone home. Over the past week, family members had taken turns sleeping on the brown fold out couch in Lauri's room. Gary understood that everyone needed time alone with her.

The dark stillness of the room contrasted the scattering of his emotions. When they met seven years ago, nervousness caused him to have difficulty finding words. Now, it was sorrow that kept him silent.

Gary wondered where to go from here. His life with Lauri—the Lauri he knew and loved—was over. Her body still held on, but not for long. If Lauri still recognized him, she no longer had the ability to show it. Her cancer had nearly taken it all; the only remaining sign of life was the beating of her heart.

Gary sighed and felt inner warmth as he thought about Lauri's best quality, her heart. She unselfishly shared it with everyone she ever met. When Lauri left a room, people felt a piece of their heart go with her. Gary bowed his head, closed his eyes, and wondered if he could survive with only half of a heart.

GARY

JULY 11, 2008 1:35 p.m. UPDATE

Lauri's condition has worsened. They are increasing her meds to keep her comfortable. She is unable to communicate but is at peace and resting comfortably. The staff feels the end is near.

This has been an ordeal for all of us, and there is some comfort in knowing that Lauri's suffering will soon be over. Our deepest thanks to everyone for their support and prayers.

Gary and Lauri

GARY

JULY 12, 2008 3:32 a.m. LAURI'S PASSING

Lauri passed away just after midnight. Her mother and I were at her side holding her tight as she made life's final journey. There are no words that can adequately express the sense of loss we all feel. Lauri and I want to thank everyone for their limitless efforts and well wishes bestowed upon us over the past twenty months. I will post arrangements as soon as they are finalized. Lauri did express a wish that in lieu of flowers, a donation be made either to support pancreatic cancer research to continue her battle, or to community hospice care where she spent the last weeks of her life receiving expert and compassionate care.

Gary

chapter 42

GARY FELT SOME relief, but it was bittersweet. If he had the power, he would never have kept Lauri alive and suffering only to prevent the profound loss that was now his to bear. It was a burden he would shoulder for the woman who meant the world to him. It was the only gift he had left to give.

He had been preparing for her death for some time...intellectually at least. His medical background grinded the terminal statistics of her cancer into him with the brutality of heavy grit sandpaper, removing each layer of hope he painted on the surface for Lauri's benefit, as well as his own. Had his eroding optimistic exterior held out as long as Lauri did? He hoped it had.

Now, optimism was an empty emotion, devoid of purpose, as reality had shattered the illusion.

Gary's emotional preparation for her passing was about as successful as bailing out a sinking boat with a pasta strainer—wasted effort. Death is not an event that can be prepared for, not really. The loss is only truly felt when it occurs, and that feeling slaps you as unexpected, no matter how many times you told yourself it was going to happen. The finality of the event is jolting; no matter how much cushioning you have surrounded yourself with. At that instant, we realize our loss can never be replaced; it can only be endured.

Six months before her passing, Lauri and Gary had scheduled two weeks of his vacation time to spend with family and friends at the lake. It was the first time in the last thirty years that he was able to get two weeks off back to back. Lauri died on the Friday leading into those two weeks off. Gary wondered if she planned it that way.

We all become somewhat haunted by the ghosts of the dying process. Our loved ones physical pain lives on in our own sensitive nerve endings; a phantom agony that we experience until time slowly dulls our perception. Their emotional suffering, along with our own, remains vivid; memories stay etched into our mind with the near permanence of chiseled granite.

As the days progressed toward Lauri's funeral, the depth of Gary's loss and loneliness settled in. He spent his quiet time composing Lauri's eulogy, which he delivered three days after her passing.

Lauri's Eulogy
While these are my words, the inspiration and content also comes from Lauri, Nick R, Nick C, Ben, Jack and Paige.

The term eulogy comes from the combination of the Greek words *eu* meaning good and the word *logos* meaning word. Thus eulogy means the good word, and I can't think of a more apt description of how Lauri lived her life than using the expression, The Good Word.

Many of us here today would not be at all surprised that Lauri wanted to have some input into today's gathering. She and I lived side by side, and hand in hand, for the twenty months of her battle with pancreatic cancer. She was unique in so many ways. To me, unique is an inadequate word to use to describe the essence of her being. In her battle, she never lost hope, but she also never lost perspective. During her fight with cancer, she and I had many discussions about death. There were many times we both thought she had little time left, so she made sure almost all preparations were in order. She also gave me a few suggestions about the eulogy.

First, she wanted the eulogy to serve a greater purpose than to just focus on her life. This is completely characteristic of Lauri's gift of bringing people together, without needing or wanting to be the center of attention. Second, she wanted the eulogy to have some humor. She loved to laugh, and while she knew there would be a lot of tears, she also wanted this to be the beginning of the healing process for all of us. In her life, there were many more laughs than tears, and she felt the eulogy should reflect the character of life as she tried to live it, and not focus on her untimely death. Finally, she wanted me to thank everyone for the limitless support she received from them, not only for the period of her illness, but for the entirety of her earthly presence.

Let me start with her final request and say thank you to everyone. I'll do my best on Lauri's other two requests, but I am sure she will forgive me if the eulogy turns out to include quite a bit about her, and doesn't incite as much laughter as she might have liked.

A common thread that runs through the fabric of humanity regardless of ethnic, social, religious or any other characterization of diversity is that at sometime in life we are all exposed to tragedy and loss. It is a universal commonality that neither recognizes nor respects any boundary, either physical or psychological.

The only saving grace associated with loss is that it is unmistakably and intimately related to gain. You cannot feel the black hole depths of unimaginable despair, unless you have also risen to the pinnacle of happiness and delight. It is an undeniable truism that unless you know light, you would not fear the darkness. The comfort of warmth embraces your body and soul because you have experienced the isolation of the cold. This is why losing a loved one is so gut wrenchingly painful. The loss pulls at every thread of your being, striving to unravel the entire tapestry of your existence. You feel as through you can't go on because you have lost the consistency of matter that binds you together.

However, what stitches you back together over time is recognition, and reflection on the gain, the good times you shared, and the joyful memories you created. By mentally resurrecting their smile, their soothing touch, the essence of their being, you use this positive and life giving energy to reconstruct and sustain your own life. You can see your loved ones spirit and form carried on by those closest to them. Maybe the mother and daughter share the same emerald twinkle in their eyes. Maybe the mother and sons share the same bold indomitable spirit. It is these inherited or acquired gems that span the generations, allowing us to re-experience a treasure from our past. It is either by the reality of ongoing life, or by the warmth and love we resurrect from memories, that we garner the strength to go on living. We don't heal by forgetting. We can only mend by remembering.

Lauri had an uncanny ability to cherish and appreciate the good times in life and the good qualities in others. This was a character gem she possessed and not even a terminal illness could tarnish its luster. She rarely shared her pain, either physical or emotional with others, always adorning her face with her sweet smile shining like a beacon of hope and happiness. She was so good at this that many people, including those in the medical profession, were fooled into thinking she was not as sick as she truly was. This was Lauri's way of lessening the burden on others.

Lauri told me to be receptive to the fact that she would be sending signs to all of us after her passing. She knew I was more than a little skeptical about this concept. I was at the funeral home on Friday with Lauri's brothers, her father, Nick R and Ben. We were placed in the only room in the large well-cooled facility that was above 80 degrees. You see, Lauri loved the heat. We went through the preparations and were at a point where I needed to pick an urn for her ashes, the only item she hadn't completed. Just after I made my choice, I was stricken with this intense cramp in my right thigh. It was one of those cramps that bolts you right up out of your chair and has you walking around trying to relieve the discomfort. The others gathered began suggesting other options for the urn, and we all agreed on the choice you see in front of the altar. Like Lauri, the urn is sleek with an understated but obvious beauty, both inside and out. Once we had made our decision, my cramp subsided. So you see, I have already received signs from Lauri, and I am sure there will be many more to come for all of us.

Beyond the signs we will receive, we need only to look around to be reminded of Lauri. She became a part of all of us who are gathered here today. Lauri had the ability to draw out the best that others have to offer. She is most beautifully represented in the traits and character she instilled in her children. The seeds of Lauri's positive approach to life are wide spread, and they will continue to germinate for eternity making life better for all of us. We had all hoped for a miracle to allow us to have more time with her. We had that miracle. That miracle was Lauri.

I would like to close with a poem written for Lauri by a poet friend of ours, Cristina Norcross. The title is:

Each Unspoken Word Lives On
(For Lauri)

Every broken curve and each unspoken word
has brought me to this point –
of scattering joy
like pebbles in the shallows,
while cresting waves suggest
there is more life in the distance.

I balance on this weathered piece of wood,
my arms outstretched.
Instead of empty air,
my hands search
and find
the tanned, fit arms of my children,
all offering a buoy of support.
I see myself being lifted to the sky.

A white expanse of clouds,
like drifting cotton,
provides respite for my weary head,
and I sink into this plush repose.

In another life I am strong and well.
I am running on the shore,
stopping only to pocket a soft-edged, square
of polished, green sea glass.
I am filling my arms with a thousand hugs –
as many as I can bundle close against my chest,
like bouquets of tall irises.
The fresh perfume glides through my hair like fingers,
replenishing my spirit.

In this other life,
I am complete,
and you are all with me.
This newness of my soul will come back again,
to see the same sun that appears outside your window.

That purple iris you see in a garden,
on a card,
or gracefully falling to the ground in a film,
will be my song to your soul.
I will sing the refrain over and over
until you hear my heart,
and know,
that it beats with you every day.

✳ ✳ ✳

Gary returned to the gravesite as the sun was setting. Lauri's urn was safely interred beneath the engraved granite marker the couple had pick out two months before. The only inscription missing was the date beneath Gary's name; the day he would make his final journey.

The location was of Lauri's choosing, a wide-open space bathed in bright and life giving sunshine. Lauri ashes rested only a stone's throw from Helen's site, her beloved Grandmother.

A storm of emotions swirled in and around Gary. One of his greatest motivations to live was no longer an intimate part of his life. Thoughts of Lauri were now devoid of the present tense. Only her memory was left to hold his hand and comfort his heart. He thought back to the heaven he had envisioned for Lauri. Gary looked to the sky, secure in the belief that his beautiful angel was finally at peace.

chapter 43

THE STRUGGLE OF THE past twenty months, while clearly etched in her mind, lacked the pain and sorrow that had dominated her prior feelings. Lauri experienced the deepest sense of both physical and emotional comfort, which calmed and soothed her to the core. She knew she had passed away, although there was a total absence of negative emotion as she pondered and accepted her mortality. Lauri felt at peace with the concept of her passing, and peace was an emotion in scarce supply in the recent past.

Thoughts and visions of family and friends flooded her mind with the power of the Niagara River cascading over the falls. Prior to her passing, this torrent of emotion would have evoked a proportionate flow of tears. She had cried more since her diagnosis of pancreatic cancer than in all the prior years of her life, sometimes because of the pain, often because of the persistent nausea, but most often over the desperate feelings of loss.

Lauri felt cancer was the cruelest of adversaries. It was a mighty blade with a razor sharp edge, which in one stroke sliced away any hope of a future. With the return cut, the cancer used the opposite steel edge to destroy the present. The depth of despair over the feelings of missing out on so many future events in the lives of her children and other family members was devastating enough. This cruelty was compounded by the cancer robbing her of the energy and capacity to experience a reasonable life between diagnosis and her final fate. There was so much she had wanted to do, but the cancer prevented her. Now, in her renewed state of a spiritual being, these thoughts were mere intellectual reflections that were devoid of their prior emotional brutality.

Lauri, acutely aware of her surroundings, felt no sense of an earthly existence. She relaxed in a quiet place illuminated with bright but gentle sunlight. She felt the comfortable sensation of sitting in a beach chair at the water's edge with the familiar surroundings of Lake Winnisquam. She saw her family's cottage and remembered the joys of her childhood spending carefree summers at the lake with family and friends. Lauri also pictured the modern home her father subsequently built where she brought her children to frolic in the warm sunshine and calm water. She felt the flower print summer dress caressing her skin, the sunglasses resting on her nose, the summer broad brim hat shielding the rays from her face, and the gentle breeze rustling through her hair—thick shinning hair. *I like that.* Lauri, perfectly attired for the prevailing weather, couldn't remember ever being more comfortable.

Lauri felt the presence of an individual next to her. She knew his name was James, but she didn't know how she knew it. He wasn't someone from her past.

James reminded Lauri of her English grandfather. His green cardigan sweater was tightly buttoned up the front and his pants were thick brown corduroy. His thinning mixture of grey and brown hair was slightly tussled, as if he had been out in a gentle wind. Oval, metal rim glasses were perched on the bridge of his nose. He sat in a high backed brown leather chair nestled in the corner of his mahogany paneled study; his right hand firmly wrapped around a brandy snifter. Lauri appreciated the aroma of the liquor wafting through the air mixed with the smoky scent of the crackling fire in the hearth.

Lauri was confused but not disturbed by the difference in their surroundings. Their mutual contentment seemed more important than a similarity of their environments.

"Hello Lauri. You already know my name is James."

"Yes, but how do I know? Do I know you?"

James smiled. It was a colossal grin that brought immediate and profound soothing warmth to Lauri. The leather gently squeaked as James shifted in his chair. "Remember the Chinese proverb, 'A journey of a thousand miles begins with a single step.' Lauri, this is your first baby step."

A tight smile graced Lauri's face and her brow slightly furrowed. "I'm in heaven?"

"Yes, oh yes. How could *you* be anywhere else?" James' expression was a subtle mixture of awareness and delight. "It's the funniest thing, everybody asks that question."

James grasped his chair and shifted it forward, bringing him close enough to touch Lauri. She heard and felt the vibration of the legs rubbing against the hardwood floor. James leaned toward Lauri, resting his elbows on the smooth padded armrests of his favorite Queen Anne chair. "I am your spirit guide. I will walk with you on your path from an earthly to a heavenly existence."

"Really?...Really!"

"Yes Lauri, really."

"If you don't mind me asking." Lauri shifted in her chair. "I mean, I'm not trying to be disrespectful."

"Go ahead, ask me." James face was as comforting as Lauri's favorite afghan.

"Okay. Why you?" Lauri said. "Why are you my spirit guide?"

"Not an easy question to answer as it is a choice that neither you nor I get to make." James paused for a moment. "The simplest answer is that you felt safe asking the question. Your first spirit guide must be someone you can trust and someone you feel free to exchange ideas with. Sometimes it is a family member, sometimes not. At times, it is someone you know. At other times, not." James brought his left hand up under his chin. "I hoped that helped."

Lauri smiled. "It did. Thanks. Where do we go from here?"

James explained that Lauri had the freedom and unlimited ability to continue experiencing life by using her memories as the foundation to construct her future. She had the power, within the vast spaces of her mind, to transport herself anywhere she wanted to go. You might say, "The world was now her oyster," although the motto was inappropriate for someone not fond of seafood. Lauri was reminded of the comments Gary recited to their children to motivate them, as his mother had recited to him: "To think is to create" and "What you can believe, you can achieve." They quickly became her anthem for the journey ahead.

There was no anxiety or fear. Even more puzzling was the complete lack of any negative thoughts or feelings.

Lauri's mind became a whorl wind of questions. Where specifically were they? How did she get there? Could she see what was going on in the lives of her loved ones who were still alive? Each thought propagated another, and in the blink of an eye, the corners of her mind were overpopulated with thought provoking inquisitions.

"Lauri," James said, "I know this is a bit overwhelming. In time, you will settle into your new surroundings." James explained that she would become comfortable navigating a path of discovery, fulfillment, and contentment. The physical illness and the emotional trauma that confounded her pursuit of happiness on Earth no longer existed. Lauri, now at peace, could bask in the warmth of the sun for eternity.

James took her hand. His rough, dry weathered skin sharply contrasted the soft smooth delicate texture of her own. Her hand, as well as her entire being, was enveloped with deepest sense of security, reminding her of holding Gary's hand with the attendant calming effect it had on her. When she and Gary grasped hands, Lauri always felt a transfer of energy, and, she was sure Gary felt it too. Lauri half expected to hear the utterance, "Hey Baby."

Lauri knew James would be at her side as she transitioned into her unfamiliar state of a spiritual being. While foreign to her, she was not worried. James instructed Lauri to let her thoughts wander through the experiences of her past, much like an unhurried soothing stroll through a meadow of blooming wild flowers with the sun warming her neck and a gentle breeze cooling her face.

"Think of places you loved," James said.

Lauri thoughts were coaxed into her past. She felt the comfort of resting back in a green Adirondack style chair and gazing out over the water of Lake Winnisquam. The twinkling of the sun reflecting off each gentle wave moving across from one side of the lake to the other. The smell of barbeque was in the air and she envisioned her father standing at the grill with an oversized kitchen towel tucked in the front of his shorts to prevent splatter from hitting his pants. By the end of the day, while the upper portion of his pants were clean, the lower half of his shirt was splattered with a cornucopia of grease spots from the food items he prepared. He so enjoyed having family for a visit.

Lauri reclined a few feet above the water, on the deck at the end of the long dock. The thirty-five foot straight portion of dock, along with the deck at the end, formed an exaggerated L configuration. The large rectangular deck afforded ample room for several people to sit together, joyously sharing conversation while suspended above the tranquil blue water.

Many memories were locked up on the shore and in the waters of Lake Winnisquam. Lauri's family shared a long history with the fourth largest lake in New Hampshire. They began enjoying its pleasures long before Lauri Ann was even an emerald twinkle in the eye of her English and Irish parents.

Lauri and Gary purchased the property she cherished so dearly after her first course of chemotherapy. She believed the lure of the lakeshore would be a magnet to attract their children and their subsequent families to joyful gatherings, as it had during her lifetime. She bravely articulated to Gary her belief that it would also help keep the family together after she was gone. The couple, faced with the ominous battle against Lauri's cancer, was constantly balancing optimism against realism.

Lauri had wanted to proceed quickly with the purchase. It was apparent to Gary that she was compelled to own the home. They had planned to buy it in a few years, prior to her becoming ill. However, the cancer prompted an accelerated, and at times, a wonton pursuit of life with the afflicted striving to condense their future into a regrettably shortened period of time.

Now, time was no longer an issue. It ceased to define the future. Sorrow, fear, and longing were also no longer relevant. Lauri's new reality of a spiritually centered, gravity free existence was taking root.

Lauri's mind carried her back to the lake. She sensed the warmth of the day and felt the frosted glass in her hand filled with a cool drink. She felt the condensation of the glass bathing the inner surface of her fingers. She had so loved coming to the lake, and she was surprised and pleased that the lake had "followed" her to heaven.

The mind is a powerful thing. To think really is to create.

❊ ❊ ❊

Lauri again appreciated James' presence. He now wore a mid-length tan field jacket and a gray cap. He walked with a stiff upright posture with his right arm extended, his gloved hand firmly grasping a leather leash. Extending his bondage to its fullest measure was a jovial brown and white beagle. The hound intermittently pulled to the right and yapped at the snow piled up on the side of the road, and then tugged to the left, splashing up mud on his owners' favorite brown walking boots.

Looks like the dog is taking James for a walk, Lauri thought.

Spence, a feisty but lovable canine companion, demanded focused attention. If James wasn't vigilant, he surely would be horizontal and sullied. James was often bemused as to who was leading whom during this interplay. Despite the inherent challenge, walking the country roads of England with Spence had been one of the most pleasurable parts of his time on Earth. James, like Lauri, was glad that the most cherished parts of his earthly life had joined him in the life beyond.

The sensory clarity of her current environment slightly stunned and disoriented Lauri. As she watched James and Spence, their experience both belonged to them, and to Lauri. She could see, hear, and feel what was going on: Spence's intermittent snapping bark, the splashing sound of James' boots hitting the puddles, the spray of turbid water moistening the dog's paws and his companion's pant legs, the unsteadiness of James' footing. Finally, and most profoundly, Lauri felt the heartwarming personal joy and contentment felt by both James and Spence.

Simultaneously, and with the same transparency, Lauri was surrounded by her own authentic visual, auditory, and emotional stimuli. At times, it seemed like a cocoon, a sharply defined experience for her alone. However, she now knew it was the exact opposite of an enclosure. In reality, her new reality, the pleasures of life are supremely vivid, and to be enjoyed by everyone. Not only could she experience the goodness of life through her own activities, she could glean equal happiness from the pleasures that others experience. It reminded Lauri of the quintessential joy a parent feels when their child experiences pleasure. The purely unselfish act of feeling good, just because someone else is happy.

"Lauri," James said, "how are you doing?"

"I'm a little confused. Take us talking like this. I see you and Spence, and you are nowhere near me. Yet, I feel as though I'm right there with you. We can talk just like we were right next to each other."

"Great isn't it?" James stopped along the road as Spence nuzzled the snow bank for a presumed hidden treasure, his tail wagging with the ferocity of a turbine engine. "It takes some getting used too. The physical concepts of space and time don't apply here...in heaven."

"An ethereal experience I guess," Lauri said, with a gaping grin on her face. "Gary taught me that word, ethereal. It means heavenly, airy, like floating on the clouds. It was on one of those word-a-day calendars. Santa put one of them in Gary's stocking every Christmas."

James returned the smile and he sensed the warmth that Lauri felt as she talk about Gary. James rested his hand on Lauri's shoulder. "Isn't it nice to remember Gary and feel only the goodness?"

Lauri closed her eyes. Visions of the pleasures that she and Gary shared danced in her head, an exquisite ballet filled with joy, grace, and love. "Yes," Lauri said, drawing in a deep rejuvenating breath as her heart pounded and her body fluttered with butterflies. "Yes, it is."

chapter 44

A CALMNESS AND serenity surrounded Lauri. Her early steps along the transition from a terrestrial to a spiritual way of life were complete. *Way of life,* she thought, *that's strange. I'm dead, and yet I live. If I could feel pain in heaven, these thoughts would give me a killer of a headache.* Lauri laughed at her own cleverness. *It is good to laugh again, really good.*

James had told her she could create her future from her past, that her memories and wishes would enable her to experience all that she feared she was going to miss. He told her to concentrate on an unfinished part of her life that she had left behind, a part of her future she believed was lost.

Lauri thought back to the times, the many times, she had pleaded for more time. Once she was diagnosed with pancreatic cancer, time, and how little she might have, frequently dominated her thoughts. She remembered the devastation and the extreme fatigue, both physical and emotional. Thoughts of death constantly weaved their way in and out of her mind's attempt to remain optimistic. Thoughts of longevity were linked to a time frame: short or long. She had always prayed for a cure, hoping for that one miracle of total relief and rebirth. That miracle never came. If not a cure, at least enough time to see her children through more of their milestones. Almost all of those were denied. The last milestone she got to see, two months before her death, was Nick C's graduation from college. She was so sick she couldn't attend the ceremony. At least she got to watch the DVD and attend the party.

Lauri focused on what would have been the next milestone, Ben's college graduation. She knew in her heart he would graduate. He was only a year away from the glorious and well-deserved recognition when she passed away.

Now was Lauri's chance. She closed her eyes, allowing visions of Ben to swirl in her head. She envisioned the young boy who loved to dress up in a suit and tie. Lauri could hear herself tell him how "sharp" he looked. This always made Ben beam with pride. She remembered how he loved to play in the family pool. By the time she literally pulled him from the water, his fingers looked like ten wrinkled prunes. All of their years together represented a book filled with laughs and love. *It's time,* Lauri thought, *time to write the next chapter.*

❋ ❋ ❋

"Mom...Mom," Ben yells as he runs out the entry door of his college dorm. He spent his final night on campus, probably unable to sleep in anticipation of the big day.

It is a beautiful, sunny, late spring morning, a perfect day to transition into adulthood. Ben sprints toward me and his strong legs carry him effortlessly across the spotty mixture of grassy green patches and barren brown spots that separate the red brick building from the crowded parking lot. Vehicles jostle for a place to park with spaces being quickly snatched up by families and friends of the Class of 2009.

I beam with pride as Gary turns off the engine of our metallic blue convertible. I stand up inside the car, left hand gripping the metal casing at the top of the front windshield, my right hand waving with excitement. As Ben approaches, my thoughts are carried back to the frail beginnings of my second son, now a mature man in body and spirit.

I remember the weak body he was initially given, his immune system compromised. His physical challenges were great. At times, his survival was uncertain. Ben's immune system needed support; he required numerous injections of gamma globulins, supplements to correct his immune deficiency. The nurses held my defenseless child down as the doctor forcefully injected Ben's underdeveloped thighs, one…and then the other. Ben hardly required the restraint as he never even whimpered—an early and telling sign of the strength and drive that would carry him to accomplishments I only dreamed of.

Just like his siblings, Ben and I spent evenings together as "study buddies" during the formative years of his education. I helped Ben master reading, writing and arithmetic; he enlightened me about R + D…resilience and determination.

Words are inadequate to capture the depth of emotion I now feel. However, tears of joy will have to do, and the waters flow down my face.

"Crying already, Mom." Ben slaps his hands down on the hood of the car. The loud smack of skin on metal barely precedes the jolting reverberation of the entire car.

"Hey Ben," Gary said, killing the ignition, causing a second, less severe shudder, to travel through our bodies. "We are both really proud of you."

"Thanks." Ben slides around the front end, moving up next to the open passenger window.

I bend down, turning my cheek toward my son, now a grown man. Ben dutifully plants a kiss on my face. I spin toward him, tightly wrapping both of my arms around his neck, nearly pulling him into the car. I press my face against his, feeling like I never want to let go.

"Okay, Mom, I need to get ready."

I release my love grip. Ben eases back from the car. "Hold still a minute." I unsnap the clasp on my tan leather clutch, pulling out a tissue. "There's some lipstick on your face." Ben tilts his head to the left and I wipe the red smear from his skin. I feel a deep and familiar warmth inside as I think about the many times I have wiped away dirt, and even a few tears, from his gentle face, a face now rough with the stubble of early manhood. *How fast they grow up.*

"All done, Mom?"

"Yes, Benjamin."

"Where is everyone else?" Ben scans the parking lot entrance for any familiar vehicles.

"On their way," Gary said, opening the car door. "They'll be here soon."

"I saved seats for everybody—spread over a couple of rows—all the grads were scrambling for spots. I hope I got enough."

Gary comes around the back of the car extending his hand. He and Ben shake hands; the solidness of their grip mirroring the permanence of the bond they have built over the years. Gary became a fixture in Ben's life, a consequence of Gary willingly providing space in his life for stepchildren, and my children allowing, and wanting, Gary to be a supportive and influential part of their lives. My relationship with Nick C and Jack followed a parallel heartwarming path. We built a family, one brick of triumph cemented to one brick of tribulation, a human fortress to protect the precious love we now all share.

"Don't worry, Ben." Gary slaps him on the back. "I'm sure we'll all find seats. Anyway, I'll be running around with the camera."

Ben chuckles. "Yeah, Gary, I know how much you love to take pictures."

Gary opens my door, reaching for my hand, and helping me out of the car. I nearly stumble as my tan pumps are unsteady on the rough asphalt. I release Gary's hand and carefully step toward Ben. "Give me a real hug," I said, nearly falling into his arms.

"Steady, Mom." Ben engulfs me, pressing my body against his own. Our faces touch, cheek to cheek.

"Where did the little boy go that I used to carry," I said, with a smile, my eyes welling up for a second time.

"I'm still here, Mom, but now I can carry you."

✳ ✳ ✳

The graduates are all seated; a sea of black and white caps and gowns looking like a disjointed ebony and ivory tile floor, or a mutant zebra with jagged stripes. Scrawled in capitol letters on the top of many caps, easily visible by their contrasting color, are combinations of letters: TMAD (thanks mom and dad), JOMY-P (just one more year—please), GS-TG (grad school—thank God), and on Ben's and many other criminal justice majors—FLE (future law enforcement.)

The rumble of the large crowd settles to a white noise hum as the ceremony begins. The speeches are followed by polite applause as the breeze produces crackles in the amplified sound system, making it difficult to decipher all the words being spoken. No matter, the joy is more the experience than the final transfer of wisdom and motivation. The most boisterous eruptions of the student body are reserved for the episodes of beach balls being batted about. The colorful balls are confiscated by staff members when they stray beyond the protective black and white clad sentries. A colossal communal "BOO" is heard when each childhood toy is deflated. The end of fun and games is on the mind of every graduate.

The robed seniors stand in succession and approach the stage. They walk, one by one, stepping across the bridge that spans the canyon separating dependence from independence. The scrolled parchment they receive is a tangible declaration of the one-way odyssey they have just traveled. In theory, they are now responsible adults. However, we parents know there will always be room under our protective wing when they need shelter.

As Ben's name is called, his personal contingent of family and friends bellow forth with pride and approval.

"Way to go Ben!" Paige screams.

"Ben, Ben, Ben," Nick R, Nick C, and Jack chant, fists thrusting into the air.

The grandparents, aunts, uncles, and cousins clap.

Gary holds my hand as I stand in silent awe of my little boy, now a strong and capable man, poised to meet the challenges before him. Memories of the twenty-two years of his life provide a kaleidoscope of emotions, a shifting array of colorful events along the path that brought him to this stage of life. I fear letting go and I fear holding on. A parent's cross to bear for their cherished offspring; you must teach them to fly, and then you must set them free from the nest.

Ben pauses before stepping down from the stage and turns toward the mass of people. He finds me in the crowd, our eyes transfixed on each other. "I love you, Mom," he mouths.

I choke on my reply. "I love you, too."

✳ ✳ ✳

The sensation is indescribable. Lauri felt that a treasure previously lost had been rediscovered, with all the attendant emotions of appreciation, joy and love. A comforting air of contentment and pride enveloped Lauri. It is a reassuring feeling, like the weight of heavy blankets pressing your body against a mattress when you are drifting off to sleep.

One of the devastating voids created by her early passing was filled. She witnessed Ben's graduation and shared the intimate emotions of mother and child. Lauri's joyful tears were real and heartfelt; wept from her own eyes and wiped from her own cheeks. It was her own child she embraced, never again having to let go.

Lauri knew James' guiding hand and supportive heart had skillfully steered her through uncharted waters. Now her future was both real and attainable. She saw James and Spence cresting a gentle hill along the spruce lined countryside road. They slowly disappeared beyond the incline.

chapter 45

LAURI KNEW JAMES would return to her side whenever she needed him. He was a gentle yet focused guiding light that provided both direction and illumination for the inaugural stage of her eternal journey. Their interactions provided a window through which Lauri could gaze to witness some of the favorite and most comforting times from James' past, his reflective times in his study and his invigorating walks with his faithful four legged companion Spence. These were cherished signposts from his earthly existence, memories to sustain his eternal lifetime. Lauri's thoughts now drifted to one of her favorite places.

She resurrected the view enjoyed from their condo in Nashua. Their hilltop location provided unobstructed eastward views of the lush rolling hills. Every clear morning, the sunrise brightened their entire home.

Lauri loved the warmth and light provided by the direct exposure to the sun. The deck, or the couch facing the wide floor to ceiling windows partitioning the living room from the deck, had been her sanctuary during the months battling cancer. At times, it seemed to take the strength of Hercules for her to struggle to a vertical position and move around the home. Either of her preferred perches had been a welcome relief to console her ravaged body and soul.

The iridescent sun climbing across the sky to begin a new day had always captivated Lauri. She, like the rest of nature, was sustained by the life-giving rays. She remembered relaxing in the patio chair and admiring the full bloom in the pansy filled flower boxes that adorned the railing on their deck. She lovingly planted and nurtured them every spring.

Lauri conjured up visions of hot aromatic coffee with chocolate pastries and could taste the delectable mixture of the blended flavors. This was truly a treat, as for unknown reasons, after her diagnosis and subsequent chemotherapy, she no longer could tolerate many of her favorite foods and beverages. How unfair it seemed that even the simple pleasures of life were confiscated by her cancer.

Lauri remembered hoping and striving for a healthier and more active life despite the challenges imposed by her illness. She would preface a goal with the statement, "WHEN I GET BETTER." She would be able to spend more time with the family, "WHEN I GET BETTER." She could reconnect with friends, "WHEN I GET BETTER." She would occupy her free time with volunteer work to attempt to repay the kindness afford her during her struggle with cancer, "WHEN I GET BETTER." The frequency of this utterance increased as her condition had worsened. It was as if she were grasping for healing by sheer repetition, much like anyone attempting to master an unfamiliar task. "WHEN I GET BETTER" had been Lauri's mantra.

Lauri finally was better. In fact, she was grand. As she passed away, so went the bodily disfigurement and limitations caused by her cancer. Her body and mind were again her own, not longer restricted by the demon that took her earthly existence.

❊ ❊ ❊

Lauri felt the evolving presence of a companion, much as she had originally sensed James' arrival. Lauri knew in an instant that she was being joined by Doris, Gary's mother.

Their fingers intertwined and the connection was immediate and dramatic, person to person, soul to soul. There was none of the slightly awkward physical separation she felt with James. *A new experience*, Lauri thought. *I like this.*

Lauri and Doris walked along the ocean cliff path of Carpinteria, California. It was a location Doris loved and knew well, a beautiful stroll Lauri had taken only once with Gary, holding his hand and heart at the time.

The path meandered along the cliff edge, the ocean a one hundred foot vertical drop, straight down. A mixture of native bushes, scrubs and blooming wildflowers covered the plateau, the air thick with the scent of natures' bounty. Below, the blue waves of the Pacific Ocean were transformed into billowing white foam as they crashed over the jagged rocks, sending a refreshing salty onshore breeze up the cliffs. As the waves receded, the green moss surrounding the trapped pools of water shimmered in the mid-day sun.

Lauri and Doris walked in silence until they reached a weathered wooden bench. Doris motioned with her hand; the couple sat down. "This is my favorite spot," Doris said.

"I know. It was Gary's, too."

Lauri felt the weight of Doris' hand in her own. This touch blossomed into an extended warm embrace that soothed them both. Tears of joy and remembrance trickled down their faces. Like all of the interactions in her new environment, the character of their encounter played with Lauri's senses. She was slowly adjusting to the uniqueness of spiritual life after physical death.

Lauri felt at home, the warmth and comfort born of a familiar attachment. That link was in the form of a mother's child who was also a wife's husband. Lauri and Doris shared Gary in life, and in death.

At this spot in the path, the cliffs were less sheer with a more gradual descent to the shoreline. This provided an open view of the narrow beach. Below was the seal rookery; a small patch of sand nestled between the rocks where the mother harbor seals reared their pups. The sand was covered with a patchwork of the dark brown backs of the adults and light tan bellies of the young.

"How are you settling in?" Doris asked.

"I'm trying to go with the flow." Lauri gave a subtle chuckle. "My interaction with you is so different than with James—more direct—more life like."

Doris smiled. "Your experience in heaven will take many forms—all comforting, all revealing, but all somewhat unique."

Lauri marveled at Doris' appearance: full rosy cheeks, thick dark hair, and able to hold a conversation without gasping for air. It was an unfamiliar site for Lauri's eyes. Lauri thought, *It would be nice if Gary knew how good his mother is doing.*

Lauri had only met Doris twice before she passed away after a protracted battled with emphysema. During both of Lauri's visits with Gary to California, Doris struggled to talk. Her smoking had destroyed her lungs to the point where she could barley breathe. She carried around oxygen in a small tank, the tubing extending up to her nose. Every few seconds, a rhythmic puff of sound signaled the delivery of life sustaining oxygen to her ravaged lungs and withered body, her 5'4" frame supporting far less than one hundred pounds.

Doris had died three years before Lauri...on September 8th, Lauri's birthday. This strange coincidence had always bothered Lauri. Gary had tried to soften Lauri's concerns by saying, "It connects the two most important women in my life. We will celebrate your birth and my mothers' life, both on the same day." It was a nice gesture, but for Lauri, the happiness and the sorrow of the day would forever be linked.

In heaven, there was no sorrow. Lauri and Doris were healthy, happy, and enjoying each other's company.

Doris reached into the pocket of her unzipped white windbreaker and pulled out a photo. "I always keep this with me." She handed it to Lauri.

The photo was of Gary, age eight at the time, and his three siblings, sister seven, and brothers age ten and twelve. They were all standing on the bumper of a beat up VW Beetle with all the families worldly belongings strapped to the roof. All the kids were in shorts, wore dark sunglasses, and held ice cream cones in their hands.

"It's precious."

"We were in Arizona at the time," Doris said. "Only one state away from California."

"Gary told me some of this story. I can't believe you had the guts to move all the way across the country."

"Best choice I ever made." Doris looked toward the ocean, reflecting on the decision that changed the life of her entire family. "As I always told my children, 'The door to opportunity is marked PUSH.'"

After two failed marriages and with no support other than generated by her own two hands, Doris, age twenty-eight at the time, decided to escape New York and move her young family to California. She stuffed the kids in the car, tied the suitcases to the roof, and planned to drive west until she reached salt water. And, that is exactly what she did.

Lauri and Doris shared the common history of single parent hard working moms who each raised a troop of well behaved, successful, and well adjusted children. The two moms were woven from the same swatch of cloth.

The sacrifice of the individual for the greater good of the group was essential in a single parent home. The two had in common a firm but fair approach to parenting, which was necessitated by their dual roles as mother and father to their respective broods. They also both embraced the philosophy that you get more with sugar than with a stick, and thus, unconditional love was the principle method of rearing their young. However, both wielded appropriate weapons of persuasion when the circumstances required.

Doris had often joked that the follies of her children might be indicative of their genetic link to her. With each of their missteps, and there were many as her teenage children were at times nauseatingly normal, she sternly reprimanded the offender. While growing up in Southern California was fraught with landmines of self-destruction, no mercy was shown when the offense warranted it. Doris often mused that her children had a long way to go before they could compete with her past failures. Gary, when he was older, affectionately suggested to his mother that the shortcomings of her children were more reflective of a missing link, rather than a genetic one.

"Let's walk some more," Doris said, springing to her feet. "I can't get enough of it now that I am able."

"I would love too." Lauri stood up. She extended her hand with the photo. "Why do you carry this particular picture?"

Doris took the treasure and returned it to her pocket. "It reminds me of all the things we are capable of...all of the possibilities to experience life when we put our mind to it."

Lauri reached for Gary's mother's hand as they continued along the cliff, the muffled barks of the seals fading in the distance. "Can you tell me about Gary as a child? There is so much I would like to know."

Doris grinned. "That is one of the many pleasures of heaven; learning new things about loved ones, sharing the joys of life. In time, I will. And, you'll have to tell me more about your life together."

"It's a deal!" Lauri's skin tingled as goose bumps erupted.

"Now, it is time for me to go." Doris turned toward Lauri, grasping both of her hands. "There are many more mysteries yet to unfold."

Lauri rested her head on Doris' shoulder.

"Lauri, I want you to think about Paige. Think about continuing your life together with no limits, only possibilities."

chapter 46

MY HEART FLUTTERS with anticipation despite the seemingly bland repetition of the moment to an outside observer. With each presentation, I marvel at the creation beneath the covering. I am seated on an ornate, stark white, antique English love seat, positioned against the only teal colored painted wall in the spacious octagonal bridal gown viewing room. The remaining walls are covered with beveled edge floor to ceiling mirrors. I sit patiently, hands neatly folded on my lap waiting for Paige's entrance—possibly the hundredth rendition of our roles as mother-of-the-bride and bride-to-be, duly charged with choosing the matrimonial garment. Over the last two months, I feel as though I have viewed more wedding gowns then the royal servants to the six wives of Henry VIII. No matter, with each presentation, my heart skips a beat.

Plans for the wedding have consumed our lives, mostly joyful consumption. A rift now and again between mother and daughter is expected. I dream about wedding gowns: Brocade, Crepe, French Satin, Shantung, Silk Duchess, and many more, a myriad of styles and fabrics, colors only white or ivory. Today is the day, Paige and I have decided. It is out of necessity as the wedding is only two months away. Today we pick the dress she will glide down the aisle in, her brothers each taking an arm, escorting her to my side as I stand proudly as her matron-of-honor.

I had only gently protested her choice, believing it more appropriate for her to choose a close girlfriend, someone she giggled her way through life with. Paige remained steadfast and determined her wish be fulfilled. "You are my Mom. You have always been, and will always be, my best friend."

No argument from me as she lovingly cradled my soul with her desire.

"What do you think, Mom?" Paige says, as she emerges from behind the angled mirrored false wall that swung open at the hands of the attendant. Behind the wall I see rack after rack of gowns, longingly draped over hangers, desperately waiting to jettison their wallflower role.

"You look beautiful…this may be the one." I know I have used this line several times before. "Wait a minute. Haven't we seen this one already?"

Paige smiles demurely. "Yes." She spins around, the lower lace gently drifting away from her legs, reaching for her outstretched hands. She comes to a graceful stop. "We almost picked this one six weeks ago." She laughs and spins again. "Now it is the one. Do you think so, too?"

"Most definitely." I reach up, placing my slightly trembling hands against my cheeks, attempting to contain my emotion. "You look stunning. No one will be able to take their eyes off of you."

I stand up, pause in wonder, then walk over to the woman who will always be my little girl. Paige's eyes twinkle with hope and anticipation, her mind swirling with thoughts of the threshold she is about to cross. I look to the mirrors seeing a thousand reflections of her outward radiance and inner beauty. *It is time,* I think, *time for my last baby sparrow to leave the nest; time to build a nest of her own.*

I place my hands on Paige's face. She tips her head down as I pull her toward me, her head coming to rest on my shoulder, a mother's shoulder that has absorbed tears of sorrow and tears of joy. The tears we shed today are a blend of feelings, recognition of the past and the future, a shared understanding that time never stands still.

✳ ✳ ✳

"Mom…Mom! I'm never gonna make it!" Paige screams, with a flood of panic in her voice. It is a surge of fear I have heard many times over the last twenty-eight years, to say nothing of the last twenty-four hours.

"You're going to be fine—me, I'm not so sure of. I'm more worried the matron-of-honor won't make it down the aisle before the bride."

"I need help with all these buttons." Paige sighs. "Who picked this dress anyway? Didn't we notice them all? What were you thinking?"

"Paige, please take a breath. Your face is turning blue." I slide behind the bride-to-be and begin fastening the forty-four buttons, neck to waist. "I was thinking you would look beautiful walking down the isle in this dress, and you will." I fasten every button, each one a subtle rose formed out of delicate silk. The ornamental flowers match the open blossoms that adorn her shoulder length veil.

"Thanks, Mom—really. I know I'm out of control. I'm sweating up a storm…do I look like I'm sweating?"

"Slow down, Dolly. You're not sweating, you're glistening."

"Thanks a lot. I'm not sweating like a boy pig, I'm glistening like a girl pig! Swine is swine, Mom. What's that line about lipstick on a pig?" Paige throws her hands into the air. "Can we just skip the ceremony and have a party?" Paige lowers her arms and gently brushes the folds in her gown. "Just kidding, Mom, but this whole thing is driving me crazy."

"I know, honey. We'll blast the air conditioning in the car. It will cool you right down. For now, let's sit you by the fan. Other than your veil, you're done. You look angelic."

"Mom, you're the best."

I position the glistening, not sweating, bride near the fan so the breeze doesn't wreak havoc with her perfectly styled hair, a precisely twisted classic French Crown braid with two looped accents. Her best friends from camp worked their magic on her golden locks just a few hours ago. Paige sat perched on a dark mahogany stool while her three girlfriends circled around her like court maidens primping their queen. They pulled out strands of her long fine hair, first combining, then stretching, tightening, twisting, intertwining, and tucking them together. After forming the perfect crown, they crafted two delicate accent loops that draped across the back of her bare neck. I shed tears of remembrance as I watched them, recalling the many family days at camp when they all pranced around with matching taut hairdos. Eleven years at camp gave Paige many things to carry with her for the rest of her life, including a whole flock of "sisters."

❊❊❊

The deep tones of the organ reverberate throughout the brightly lit church with the afternoon sunshine piercing the stained glass windows creating defined, heavenly streams of illumination. I couldn't have dreamed of a more perfect day or setting. We are all tucked in an alcove at the back of the church. Nick C and Jack just finished seating the last guests. The seats burgeon with family and friends.

We stand in a tight circle, holding hands. I am across from Paige, mesmerized by her aura and grace. On either side of her, standing guard as they have done for her entire life, are Nick R and Ben. The next links in our human chain are Nick C and Jack. Gary and I complete our family ring, an everlasting and unbreakable bond of souls. We bow our heads in reverence, humbled by the sheer magnitude of the moment. After a shared whispered prayer, we are ready to proceed.

"It's time, Paige," I say. We all release our grasp.

Jack and Nick C move toward Paige, each hugging her and kissing her cheek. They move to the back of the center aisle.

Gary reaches out, grasping both of the bride's hands. His eyes are moistened with the love that has grown between them. Paige is the only daughter he will ever have. "You look beautiful." He kisses her forehead. Gary eases to the side, opening the path between mother and child, both gowned in satin and united for eternity. Gary joins Nick C and Jack in the procession line.

I step forward, my face nearly touching the unveiled features of a woman with whom I literally, and joyously, share life. We reflect a union that only parent and child share. Our bond is absolute and resolute. Nick R and Ben fold in next to Paige and me.

They represent the two other purely unconditional loves of my life. We share a silent embrace.

I lean back, looking at my three children. A contented and proud smile adorns my face. I internalize the fleeting yearning to return them to childhood; a maternal desire to go back in time and shelter them under my protective wing. In unison, they smile at me, expressions of comfort and appreciation. I give them each a hug and a kiss, the last remnants of innocence, as my baby is moments away from her sacred right of passage.

"You are all amazing," I said, reaching up with an embroidered silk handkerchief to dab my tears. The royal floral design was hand sewn by my own mother and Paige carries a matching heirloom—something blue. "I love you all so much."

"I love you too, Mom," they all respond.

I touch my right hand to my lips, blowing them a final kiss. I join Gary, Nick C and Jack.

"Are you all right?" Gary asked, taking my left hand.

"I'm fine." I turn and kiss his face.

"Ready to go, Mom?" Jack said.

"You look great, Mom," Nick C adds.

The intimacy with which Nick C and Jack acknowledge me warms my heart.

The church falls silent and the procession begins. Gary, Nick C and Jack deliver me to my place of honor. They sit in the front row. I look to the back of the church. Nick R and Ben each support one of their sister's arms. Paige's hands are cradled around an arrangement of white roses and purple irises, which are centered at her waist. The bouquet slightly trembles.

The church resounds with the first notes of *Here Comes the Bride*. The reverberating tones of the organ are momentarily dampened by the thundering vibration of all those gathered, standing as one.

Paige and I make eye contact. Through her veil, I see a gleaming smile. A knowing and loving smile creases my own lips. We connect at a distance, a transfer of emotion we will always share, no matter our physical separation. The bouquet now rests calmly in my daughter's hands, her body and soul at peace. My three children walk toward me. I feel the deepest sense of comfort knowing that wherever life leads, my children will always be able to find me.

✳ ✳ ✳

I stand to Paige's left, my knees slightly trembling, my hands still, and my heart racing with excitement. The bride and I exchange glances during the ceremony, subtle smiles of recognition. The mother and daughter connections are airy and lighthearted as well as heavy and heartfelt. I do my best to restrain the gush of joyful tears that are yearning to stream from my eyes. I don't want dark streaks of mascara to mar my face and tarnish the upcoming photos. *Still waters run deep*, I think, I hope, as I struggle to suppress a waterfall of emotion.

Paige is the picture of poise and grace. She calmly hands me her bouquet, which I pass to the bridesmaid next to me. I remove the wedding bands from my right ring finger and pass the gold emblems of unending love to my daughter, hoping they are lifelong attachments to the fingers they are about to adorn. I roll my left thumb over my own wedding set, feeling the cool metal and savoring the warm permanent comfort they emit. Life can be uncertain; we all know that. Perhaps that is why Paige insisted I hold the rings. "I know I can count on you, Mom," she had said, "the best man—too risky." A bump in the road is avoided as Paige and Brian share their vows and exchange the symbolic tokens of their love.

The couple turns and I delicately shift Paige's train to the side, opening her path to a new life. It seems appropriate that I am the one to clear the first obstacle she faces as a wife. For all the years of her life, I have been the hand in her back pushing her forward and the shoulder to rest her head upon. Now I must share, or more accurately, relinquish this role. The bride and groom are announced and I feel a momentary shock of awareness and maternal lament as I hear my daughter's name, Paige, attached to a new and unfamiliar last name. The truest reflection of my own flesh and blood now belongs to another: to have and to hold, to honor and to cherish, for as long as they both shall live.

chapter 47

DURING HER TWENTY months battling pancreatic cancer, Lauri frequently pondered issues of spirituality. This conflict of the mind and spirit added to the mental anguish associated with her disease. It seemed ironic to her that at the time of greatest personal need and risk, she both more intensely questioned the existence of a spiritual power, while at the same time more passionately looked for spiritual support and intervention. It was the yin and yang of her belief system.

Lauri knew it was exceedingly rare for someone to turn away from spirituality at their time of greatest need. She also knew it was common for those who lacked belief to grasp for divine intervention at their time of greatest peril. The adage that, "Everyone finds God in a foxhole," often rang true.

Lauri's spiritual conflicts went far beyond, "why me." She had suffered, and when she prayed for the suffering to cease, it continued. When she finally accepted that being healed was not going to happen, she prayed to be taken. Still, nothing happened. In the end, it was not that she was comfortable with death; it was that she was so uncomfortable with life. The fear of the unknown was overshadowed by the pain and suffering of the known. It wasn't that she embraced death; it was that she hated life, and death was the only alternative. Lauri wondered why God wasn't doing anything. She felt God had abandoned her twice; first when she wanted to live, and then, when she wanted to die.

At the end, Lauri's will to fight was released along with her fear of the journey ahead. She believed that at the very least, the suffering would finally end. She had hoped that her physical end of life would coincide with a new and healthy spiritual beginning. That wish, her final one, had come true.

❊ ❊ ❊

While acclimating to her renewed body and mind as a spiritual being, Lauri continued to reflect on the mysteries of life. Her recent memories, formed in the context of her fateful battle with cancer, represented cherished times with family and friends. Despite her illness at the time, they were still fond recollections that warranted an additional photo in the album. There were far too many things the cancer had taken from her. Lauri would never relinquish the love and fellowship she shared with everyone who filled her life, during the fight for her life.

Lauri's spiritual journey continued as she again was joined by James, this time as a much younger man. He stood on a barren windswept plain with dust swirling around his legs, his denim pants partially covering his dirty black cowboy boots. The sleeves of his tattered olive colored rugged cotton shirt were rolled up. His broad brim felt cattleman's hat had a brown leather band, which was anchored by a kangaroo emblem centered at the front.

James reached up, pulled his hat from his head and smacked it on his thighs. This produced a billowing dust cloud that hovered in front of his body.

A broad smile overtook his face as his eyes made contact with Lauri's. "I loved my time in Australia," he said. "Probably as much as you loved your time at that lake."

Lauri felt comfort both from James' return as well as from her memories of family and the lake. Water and Lauri were like catsup and french fries; they were just meant to be together. "Nice to see you, James." Lauri paused, thinking about the unique pleasures and freedoms her spiritual life provided: new friends and loved ones who guided her forward, renewed health and vitality, and the quintessential joy of experiencing renewed life after physical death—Ben's graduation and Paige's wedding. Lauri's "education" on spiritual life had been exciting and enlightening thus far with each revelation producing a new set of questions.

"What are you doing in Australia?" Lauri asked.

James extended his right arm and flung his hat away from his body. The hat floated in the air like a Frisbee as it headed west. "I'm going back to Ayers Rock, that big block of stone in the distance. When I was young, my parents were missionaries in the Outback. We traveled to the rock for peace and spiritual rejuvenation."

James explained that Ayers Rock represented the largest monolith in the world. Namely, it is the largest block of solid stone that can be found on the Earth. The walking path around the base of the rock is a 5.6 mile journey from start to finish. Ayers Rock has spiritual significance to the local inhabitants. While gigantic, it is a tiny example of the wonder of the natural world; one of the many jewels to be admired, which reflected the connection between heaven and earth. In the evening, the massive rock developed an orange iridescent glow, reminiscent of the setting sun.

During his family's time in Australia, they took pilgrimages to the rock. It was a sanctuary that fostered escape from the troubles of everyday existence and enabled the family to reflect on the many blessings in their life. The family interacted free from the distractions and turmoil of the modern world. James' father brought along a modern version of the world's oldest wind instrument, the didgeridoo. It represented a natural wood trumpet-like instrument made from a eucalyptus tree branch that had been hollowed out by termites. The mouthpiece was made of beeswax. The low tones of the didgeridoo reverberated off of the colossal stone and echoed a spiritual connection to their past, their present, and their future.

"James?" Lauri asked. "I'm confused about spirituality and the role God plays on Earth."

"Aren't we all," James replied with a broad smile. "Your spiritual journey doesn't end with physical death, it continues. Over time, through interaction with others and by your own experiences, you will develop your own understanding of the mysteries of the spiritual and terrestrial worlds."

James motioned to the large rock. "It's amazing how humans have always believed in something beyond their earthly existence. Whether that belief involved one God or many Gods, whether they worshiped at the base of a natural structure or inside a magnificent cathedral, whether that spirituality solved their problems or just made them easier to bear, that belief has always, and will always exist."

"I know what you mean." Lauri was soothed by her memories, thoughts that surrounded her with the security and warmth of the quilt her friends had given her. "Sometimes we are comforted by a large congregation singing a hymn, sometimes by a single nurse and a set of three prayer beads."

Lauri was eager to continue her interaction with James. There were so many questions that lingered in her mind. Lauri felt like she did when she neared the end of a novel. With each turn of the page, she approached resolution of the story with the emotions of excitement and apprehension. Would it end as she expected? Would she be comforted or disappointed? Would the tears by joyous or sorrowful? Only time would tell.

chapter 48

LAURI REFLECTED ON her spiritual existence and all the possibilities it presented. Her Earthly existence was a beginning, not an ending. Her life existed as a perpetual canvas upon which new experiences could be layered upon the old, fresh paint to portray continued life. Her journey of gradual enlightenment wasn't without questions, but it was free of pain and worry, emotions all too common before her passing.

Lauri envisioned herself as a child at the lake, soothed by the rocking of the waves as she embraced the innocence of youth. Sitting on the rock retaining wall, her bare feet dangled in the cool water, her limbs jostled by the wakes of the motorboats scurrying about. The jubilant screams and chatter coming from the families on the water was tenderly muffled as it reached the shore.

As an adult, despite her attempts to look on the bright side as much as possible, it was sometimes difficult to adopt such a blissful carefree attitude. Lauri loved to laugh, and when times were challenging for herself or others, she tried to find some way to lighten the load with humor. "Let me give you a tip," Lauri would say. "Don't eat yellow snow." This jovial warning always got a laugh.

Now, Lauri's state of grace as a spiritual being reminded her of the relaxed days of her youth at the lake. Her spiritual guide, James, brought a sense of calmness, much like being at the lake did.

"Looks like you had a great childhood," James said, still surrounded by clouds of dust in the desolate Outback of Australia.

"Most definitely." Lauri shimmied up from a sitting to a standing position, the remnants of the lake water running down her legs and pooling on the top of the rock wall. As she took a step, a temporary silhouetted footprint outlined her dainty foot and five slightly curled toes. "James?"

"Yes, Lauri."

"Do you see me as I feel, or as I am? I mean, in my mind right now I am eight-years-old with a long braded blonde ponytail. I have the wisdom of an adult and the energy of a child, everyone's wish." Lauri reached down with her right hand and brushed the few grains of sand off the tops of her feet. She tilted her head up and the blazing rays of the sun made her hair shimmer. "How do you see me? As the adult I was when I died, or as I feel right now: four feet three inches tall, skinny as a rail, able to run from sun-up to sundown, and constantly craving ice cream and chocolate. "Well," Lauri cast a sly innocent smile in James' direction, "the last item could really refer to any age."

James and Lauri chuckled.

"The simple answer…" James folded his arms across his chest, "is that I see you as you want to be seen. Our spiritual life isn't restricted by earthly constraints."

Lauri's thoughts shifted toward more adult concerns and she felt her body transform to match her ideas. It was an odd sensation that her body tended to adjust to her way of thinking. *This is going to take some getting used too.* She rested on a white lounge chair at the end of the dock with her torso inclined so she could gaze out over the tranquil water. The sun had nearly settled beyond the horizon. The sky was ablaze with jagged crimson streams of light darting between mammoth grayish clouds.

Lauri reached out and took James' hand. Despite the gritty texture of his skin caused by the grains of dust and dirt, Lauri felt only peace and comfort in his sandpaper grip, a freedom that allowed her to discuss anything she wanted.

"Why is my interaction with you so different than with Doris?" Lauri asked. "She and I were completely together. With you, there is a separation—we are connected on an emotional level, but on a physical level, you and I mostly exist in different locations."

"That is because you and Doris were actually connected on Earth. You shared experiences, and that closeness followed you to heaven. As you and I get better acquainted, our physical separation will disappear."

Lauri's slightly furrowed brow relaxed. One of her many questions was answered. "I will like that."

"So will I."

Lauri leaned forward; starring at nature's displayed on the horizon. It was a lot like life, she thought. From one perspective, it appeared peaceful and serene, from another perspective, it appeared turbulent and scary—same event, vastly different interpretation.

"James," Lauri said, "I find myself spending a lot of time thinking about good and evil. Thinking about why evil exists and trying to understand why things happen, particularly bad things. How does all of this relate to God and spirituality?"

James gently squeezed Lauri's smooth delicate hand in his own. Their ability to hold hands was really more a reflection of an emotional closeness rather than a merging of their physical worlds as James remained in Australia and Lauri reclined at the lake. "Lauri, the concepts of good and evil are difficult enough on their own." James stepped toward a large rock conspicuously settled in the middle of the barren plain. "Trying to reconcile good and evil relative to anyone's or everyone's concept of God and spirituality will certainly take some time."

"Another words," Lauri winked at James, "enough philosophy for today."

"To coin a saying of yours'," James pulled a red bandana from the pocket of his jeans and made an exaggerated swipe across his forehead, "Most definitely."

chapter 49

ANOTHER SUNNY AND warm day in heaven, Lauri thought, *just like Gary promised*. Lauri was back at the lake house, and she assumed she would be spending a good portion of eternity there. *How lucky am I.*

She sat on the steps of the porch, staring out at the absolutely flat surface of the water; a sheet of glass, perfect for waterskiing. The break of day calm was the only good reason she and her brother's could find to rise early in the morning during the summers they spent on Lake Winnisquam. Her father would oblige by firing up the ski boat and giving them each a few spins around lake before he headed into work. The would often dry off, return to bed, and then wake up for a second time the same day, this time around noon. *What a life.*

Lauri rose to her feet and walked toward the dock. The dew on the grass moistened the sides and top of her blue canvas sneakers. The hem of her yellow flower print dress fluttered in the gentle breeze. As she walked out on the wooden dock, she left a trail of wet shoeprints from the sandy shore to the flagpole at the end of the thirty-five foot span. She remembered her father's morning ritual of raising "old glory."

Sitting in the cushioned chair next to the flag flapping in the wind brought back memories of the many times family or friends gathered at this very spot to share stories or solve problems. Lauri thoughts turned to her earlier discussion with James, and she felt his return.

"Life and death are tough to figure out," Lauri said. "Often, more questions than answers. It is hard to know what to believe."

James settled down onto a large boulder. He lifted his right leg and rested his heel half way up the rock on a chiseled outcropping. He leaned slightly forward. "Understanding, acceptance, and belief are independent but often intertwined emotions," he said. "How we feel about something or someone is not static, it is influenced by the circumstances we encounter over time. Quite literally, our view of life is shaped by life itself." James paused but Lauri remained silent. "Take for instance how your views of God and spirituality were influenced and challenged by your cancer."

Lauri shifted in her chair. Her cancer had shaken every foundation she had, including the cornerstones of her faith. "James," a forced thin smile creased her lips, "I struggled with my faith because of the cancer. I felt abandoned by God." Lauri bowed her head. "I felt guilty for having those feelings."

James turned toward Lauri, reaching for her hand. Lauri raised her fallen brow. He looked into her eyes with penetrating warmth that cradled her soul. "I know," he said. "We all experience conflicts of faith many times during our earthly life. Faith, by its very nature, involves struggle and reconciliation. If having faith were easy, everyone would embrace the concept."

"Most definitely." Lauri's features relaxed and she became the picture of serenity. She truly enjoyed her time with James. She felt comfortable sharing her thoughts and questions. "What about all the evil on Earth? Why does it happen and why is it allowed to happen?"

James pushed off the rock and stood in the soft dirt. As he slowly walked about, miniature brown dust clouds circled his worn cowboy boots. Despite his movement and apparent separation, Lauri still felt his rough hand cradling her own.

James looked at the glowing structure of Ayers Rock. "The evil acts people commit on Earth relate to our own human flaws. By our nature, we exclude people from our life that we don't understand or that we feel threatened by. Differences in the way humans look, act and think, is a catalyst for heated debate and deadly

interaction. Unfamiliar ways breed contempt and distrust with resultant aggression, either in thought or action." James paused and
the dust cloud ascended to his knees. "Sorry, it sounds like I'm
giving a lecture."

"Don't be. I'm enjoying our discussion. I think I would like to
walk as well." Lauri sprung to her feet with the easy of a child. *It's
so nice to be healthy,* she thought. Lauri glided along the dock and
past the house to the street. She headed up the shaded road, the
sun blocked by mature pine trees. The silence of the moment was
punctuated by the rhythmic crunching of pinecones and needles
beneath her feet. With Lauri wrapped in the lush abundance of
the New Hampshire forest and James in the bleak barren cocoon
of the Australian desert, their exchange continued.

Lauri considered all the conflicts that seemed to dominate
human interaction on Earth; fights between individuals and wars
between groups. It seemed ironic that often the deadliest interactions were waged over differences in religious beliefs. Did our own
human imperfections, which made us exclude other ways of thinking and acting, cause us to place such little value on the lives of
others? Is what makes us human, also what makes us inhumane?
This is a tough pill to swallow, Lauri thought, *and where was that honey
when you needed it?*

Lauri and James both saw a connection between her illness
and society's woes. Lauri had been internally invaded by cancer
cells; society was externally attacked by cancerous humans. You
can have cancer, or you can be cancer. People suffer and succumb
to internal cancer; humanity is destroyed by external cancer. Either way, death is the result.

"James...why doesn't God step in to save us—to protect us
either from disease or from ourselves?"

The corners of James' mouth curled up while his lips remained
together. He gently shook his head from side to side. "You're not
wasting any time trying to unravel the philosophical mysteries that
have confused humans for all of history. Why don't you tell me
what you think."

Throughout her illness, Lauri had pondered this very issue many times. She shared her thoughts with James about spiritual intervention on Earth. She believed there was spiritual guidance, support, and influence, but not a direct physical cause and effect relationship. Human faults and imperfections, along with their resultant behaviors, no matter how heinous, were neither allowed nor prohibited by spiritual powers. Human suffering, no matter the cause, could not be prevented by spiritual intervention.

If you believed direct intervention was possible, you were left to explain why it didn't occur. Your only conclusion would be that the potential recipient of this intervention, either a given individual or all of mankind, was unworthy. Finally, if the spiritual power was willing to withhold intervention, than how all loving and understanding could that spirit be. In the end, in Lauri's mind, there were significant limits to spiritual intervention. Perhaps, all that is negative on Earth reflects those limits. God is good, and where God cannot intervene, bad things happen. Maybe it was as simple as that.

Lauri's thoughts now focused on the positive impact of spirituality on humanity. She saw the goodness of mankind as an outward expression of an inward grace that gushed forth for the benefit of all. From the simplest act of one neighbor helping another, to the global expression of world wide humanitarian efforts, human beings were unselfishly driven to heal the wounds of others in need.

Lauri believed that at the core of this goodness was the maternal bond. There was no stronger or more protective instinct than that between a mother and her child. Come hell or high water, a mother would sacrifice anything, including her own life, to save her offspring. It is this uncompromising commitment to the welfare of others that is the greatest earthly expression of divine influence.

chapter 50

LAURI'S HEAVENLY EXPERIENCE had answered some questions, but more importantly, it opened many doors, passageways to a renewed life that was real, not just dreams that she and Gary had shared. Lauri cherished all the happy memories from her earthly existence. They were the guiding hand that led her forward to new and rewarding experiences.

The thatched cabana on the white powder beach of the tropical island shielded Lauri from the direct sunlight. She never got tired of the perpetual warmth she enjoyed in heaven. The fragrance of the ocean excited her senses; the humidified salinity gently scratched her face. The waves rhythmically rolled up upon the sand converting it from alabaster to muted brown. Flickers of sunlight danced off the scattered pebbles and shells. The sky was awash with pinkish puffy clouds, transformed from their cotton white by the sun settling over the horizon. Lauri's thoughts drifted like the ocean currents, her memories filled with the love and laughter she shared with family and friends.

She thought about meeting Gary in 2001, in the midst of the technology revolution. No wonder they first made contact electronically, over the Internet. Lauri had submitted a picture of herself at Nick R's high school graduation, his long and reassuring arm around his mother's shoulder. No subtlety here Gary had thought—family first and foremost—an immediately shared conviction for the not yet introduced couple.

They dated intermittently over the first few months with their attachment growing in increments, rather than by leaps and bounds. There were many plans cancelled by the accepted needs and unwelcome follies of their children.

Memories of her family flooded her mind. *Heaven is a bit like unlimited access to a vault of home movies*, she thought. Lauri remembered the cross stitch she made in 1988 which first hung in her own home, and then, in the family room she and Gary shared as husband and wife.

OUR HOUSE RULES

IF YOU SLEEP ON IT—- MAKE IT UP
IF YOU WEAR IT—- HANG IT UP
IF YOU EAT OUT OF IT—- WASH IT
IF YOU TURN IT ON—- TURN IT OFF
IF YOU STEP ON IT—- WIPE IT UP
IF YOU BORROW IT—- RETURN IT
IF IT RINGS—- ANSWER IT
IF YOU OPEN IT—- CLOSE IT
IF YOU USE IT—- PUT IT AWAY
IF IT'S WET—- HANG IT TO DRY
IF YOU EMPTY IT—- REFILL IT
FLUSH – FLUSH – FLUSH
IF IT HOWLS—- FEED IT
IF IT CRIES—- LOVE IT

LAURI 1988

Lauri's thoughts extended further back in time to her own childhood. The memories surrounded her with the warmth and security of her grandmother's hand-sewn quilt. These reflections on the past were sheer pleasure, an opportunity to relive all of the good times of her past, and a chance to stimulate future experiences.

The inviting features of Nanny's kitchen took shape in Lauri's mind: the oak kitchen table nestled in the corner covered with a flower print lace cloth, three precisely placed chairs adorned with embroidered seat cushions and back rests, the deep rectangular sink where Lauri was bathed as an infant, and the familiar smell of gingerbread cookies.

A large window dominated one wall, allowing direct penetrating sunlight to brighten the room. Lauri and Nanny both loved the sunshine. The tight quarters allowed for physical as well as emotional closeness. Lauri frequently reduced the space even further by forgoing her own chair to occupy the preferred seat of comfort, Nanny's lap.

An honored and frequent visitor, Lauri spent many weekends with Nanny and Papa, (Helen and Arthur). She enjoyed the full and undivided attention of her grandparents, away from the competition to be noticed when she was at home with her parents and siblings. Returning home from work on Fridays, Arthur was greeted by his wife, who asked, "What are we going to do for the evening?" Before he could respond, Lauri jumped out from behind the couch and exclaimed, "Play with me, silly." This routine played itself out every weekend Lauri was over.

As expected and desired, Nanny and Lauri were joined at the hip, roaming the surroundings completing household chores to Nanny's exacting standards. Tightly tucked hospital corners were mandatory on the beds in the two-story Colonial.

Every afternoon, grandmother, granddaughter, and Lauri's favorite doll, Emma, shared a cup of tea, as was the English tradition.

Helen was a slightly built, no nonsense, strong willed, powerhouse of a woman who was never hesitant to speak her mind, and Lauri loved her beyond words.

Lauri cut her proverbial homemaker teeth on the two-burner white gas stove which was conveniently positioned on the wall adjacent to the window. A large maple tree dominated the back yard and the cooks admired all its natural glory. As the temperatures plummeted, the leaves became awash with vibrant color, satisfying even the most discriminating leaf peeper.

Lauri and Nanny stood cheek to cheek, Lauri elevated to Helen's height by standing on a chair. They wore matching hand stitched aprons while they stirred Helen's homemade creations. Helen prided herself on preparing delicious meals for her husband, who promptly turned the key of the front door at six p.m. Only once did Lauri not heed Nanny's warning about the danger of the flame, which resulted in the familiar refrain, "IF YOU PLAY WITH FIRE, YOU WILL GET BURNED."

Lauri was too young to appreciate the broader definition of the phrase. That meaning would become apparent later in life. Despite her initial anger, Nanny lovingly bathed the injured finger in butter to ease the pain.

Arthur, a straight-laced proper man who traced his roots back to the early English colonies, mowed the lawn in a tightly buttoned collared shirt and tie. He refused to relinquish his formality even for such a common task, regardless of the oppressive heat and humidity in the dog days of summer.

Every evening, the trio sat at the dining room table for ice cream. Nanny prepared hot fudge sundaes with a mountain of whipped cream covered in jimmies. Lauri couldn't wait to start the excavation.

At bedtime, Arthur entered his bedroom. Lauri began pushing him out of the room saying, "No no, Papa. I am sleeping with Nanny. You must go to the guest room." Lauri bubbled with pride as she won the prize of sharing her Nanny's bed.

Lauri and Nanny, hand in hand, retired in their room. With Lauri perched on a hand painted stool, they stood next to each other at the sink brushing their teeth. They knelt together at the side of the bed saying their prayers, and then snuggled together as they fell asleep. Nailed to the wall above Nanny's nightstand was a poem she wrote.

LAURI IS A SUNBEAM DANCING
IN OUR LIVES ON CLOUDY DAYS,
WITH A MANNER ENTRANCING
AT HER INNOCENT BLUE GAZE.
WITH HER GOLDEN TRESSES CAPTURED
IN A SAUCY PONY TAIL,
SHE SKIPS ON HER WAY, ENRAPTURED

BY THE BLUE HILLS AND THE DALE.
LAURI IS A JOYFUL REASON
TO BE LIVING AND AWARE
THAT IN WINTERS' DREARY SEASON
THERE IS SUMMER EVERYWHERE.
ALWAYS IN A SHADOWED SKYWAY,
I CAN GLIMPSE A BIT OF GOLD,
JUST AS LONG AS GOING MY WAY
THERE IS LAURI, THREE YEARS OLD

NANNY

The bond between grandmother and granddaughter flourished. Nanny was a constant in Lauri's life. Gary and Lauri visited her in the one-bedroom senior apartment that she occupied during her twilight years. She lived to be ninety-four, and when people commented about her ripe old age, she wasn't sure whether they meant she was sweetened to perfection, or rotten to the core. Always sharp tongued, Helen provided a steady stream of humor, even when she wasn't trying to be funny. Helen's passing left a void in the lives of the entire family. For Lauri, it took a piece of her heart.

chapter 51

EARTH AND HEAVEN were fused, the quintessential melding of music and lyrics to blossom forth perfect and perpetual harmony. Lauri achieved a state of grace. She felt the supreme comfort of knowing she could watch over her family for eternity. Now at peace, her destiny remained as an unfinished book, which her imagination would fill with an endless array of chapters overflowing with love and positive emotion. Her memories and dreams were her escort. Life would proceed in any and all directions she chose. Visions of family and friends would forever blossom with the joy and beauty of flowers coming into bud during a perpetual spring.

Lauri mentally took pen in hand and composed more of her future into the present. She envisioned her life at the lake with her family grown in age and number. Lauri heard her family's voice calling out and she felt familiar hands pulling her forward.

✳ ✳ ✳

"Grammy? Grammy, where are you?" my grandson Luke yells as he runs around the corner of the house. "Oh, there you are." He stops suddenly, almost falling forward from his exuberant momentum. "What are you doing, Grammy?" Luke tips his head to the side. His smile is wide as a canyon. Although, the center of the canyon wall is missing two large white rocks, incisors I think they are called. His father, Nick R, much to my dismay, taught him to shoot water a county mile through that gap. Luke is so proud of his newest talent.

"Weeding my beautiful flowers," I said, as I effortlessly stand up. My blonde hair—the gray washed away yesterday at the salon—lightly dances around in the early morning summer breeze. July is always the windiest month on Lake Winnisquam. Our home, nestled in a subtle cove on the Northeast side of the lake, always has a soothing on-shore breeze.

The morning dew, mixed with the rich soil from the flower-bed, covers the soft alabaster skin on my knees with dark muddy patches. Streams of turbid water slither down my shins and race toward my ankles.

Luke laughs and points at my legs. "Grammy, you're all dirty." His interrupted white picket fence of a smile gleams brightly in the morning sun.

I reach down with my gloved right hand, sweeping my index finger across my left knee, retrieving a tainted morsel of mother natures' bounty. I dab a spot of dirt on Luke's nose, covering a few of the ocean of freckles that dot his face. "Now we're both dirty, little man."

We burst into infectious laughter. Luke wraps his long skinny arms around my waist, pressing the side of his head against my bony hip. "I love you, Grammy."

I pull off my soiled green rubber gardening gloves, tossing them on the grass. Cupping both of my hands around my oldest grandchild's head, I intertwine my fingers in his short light brown hair. *Has it really been seven years since the glorious day of his birth?* Bending, I kiss the top of his head. "I love you, too."

Holding Luke reminds me of my early years as a parent, never wanting to let go of my own children. Gary and I have talked many times about that unique bond of shared flesh and emotion only achieved between parent and child. Gary called it the "eternity bond." It is an attachment that knows no earthly bounds, stretching beyond physical barriers and time constraints. The life of the parent, both figuratively and literally, becomes secondary to the needs and survival of their offspring.

"Hey, Mom," Nick R says as he comes around the side of the house, his left shoulder brushing against the tan vinyl siding.

Firmly cradled in his right arm is my four-year-old granddaughter, Ann—Annie to the family. She is hitched all the way up his right side with her long bare legs dangling free and intermittently tapping against her father's side. Annie's arms are securely locked around my son's neck. Her smooth curved chin rests on top of her daddy's head. Her long blonde hair cascades in front of his face like many strings of beads in a doorway. Nick peers through the broken curtain.

"Be careful up there, Pumpkin," I shout.

Annie releases her arms and waves them wildly above her head. Annie's flailing causes her body to separate from her father's grasp. "Grammy," she yells as she loses her balance. Annie's head and torso swing out perpendicular to her hips, which are still firmly corralled by her father's right arm. Her golden locks spread out in a starburst pattern.

"Oh no!" I gasp.

In one quick fluid motion, my son swings his left arm around, bundling it beneath Annie's upper body, catching his fallen little angel in his strong supportive arms. "Gotcha," he says, with a wide grin.

He swings Annie around, her legs clasped around his waist. Her body rotates in a circle, like a human merry-go-round, her hair flaring out from her scalp. After several rotations with Annie gleefully screaming, the circular motion stops and Annie flexes up from the waist in one quick snapping motion, once again locking her arms around her father's neck.

"Thanks Daddy," Annie said. "Again. Again!"

"Annie my girl, you are a handful," my son says. "We'll do it again, later."

Annie smiles and kisses her father's cheek.

"Nick!" I said. "You two nearly gave me a heart attack." I release my arms from around Luke, grab his left hand, and pull him toward his father and sister.

"Great flop, Annie," Luke yells.

"What about your dad's catch?" I said.

"Yeah, my catch." Nick R wraps his muscled arms around his daughter's body in hopes of preventing another gymnastic display.

Luke releases my now sweaty palm. He throws both of his hands into the air as he jumps up. "Great catch, Dad. My turn."

"Annie, you must be careful." I reach out for my granddaughter with both hands. "One broken bone in the family is enough for this summer." (David, Nick C's six-year-old, sports a florescent orange fiberglass cast on his right wrist, a mishap from two weeks ago involving a miscalculation during a back flip off the dock. He was under the supervision of his grandfather. I remember hearing Gary say, "Go for it. You can do it." It was obvious that Gary felt worse than our grandson. At least David had his own personal radiologist to diagnosis the fracture. "Minor buckle type fracture," Gary had said, relief evident in his voice.)

Annie squirms out of her father's arms and settles into my own. She lunges her face toward mine, barely halting before our noses crash together. "Hi Grammy," she shrills, in a voice with the tone of fingernails on a chalkboard. She smacks me a kiss, lips on lips. Annie pulls her face back and rests her dainty hands on my shoulders. "Can we go swimming?"

"Sure, Pumpkin. Let me clean up and we'll change."

"Yippee!" Annie throws both hands into the air.

I grab my energetic granddaughter before we have another acrobatic adventure. I am not as adept as her father at compensating for her quick moves and gravity's unforgiving effect on a body not made for free flight.

With Annie in my arms, her fingers sifting through my hair, we stroll toward the covered porch and the side entrance to our home. My father built this home to take full advantage of its western exposure with an endless bank of windows facing the water.

Annie's sundress drifts effortlessly in the air. There is a meadow's worth of purple irises spread over the yellow cotton fabric. I am reminded of years past when I carried Paige for hours on end, never wanting our bodies to separate. Now it's my grandchildren I clutch tightly, a new generation of linked souls sharing life, love, and playful days at the lake.

✳ ✳ ✳

Annie nearly runs through the screen door as she bursts from the kitchen onto the porch, like a rocket lifting off the launching pad. The door smacks the side of the house, and with equal speed and force, returns to the latch with a loud cracking reverberation. My only granddaughter, energy personified, is cute as a button in her one piece bright red swimsuit, her bottom, half tanned and half pale, exposed for the entire world to see as she runs toward our gray wooden dock.

"Hurry Grammy," she yells.

"Coming, Pumpkin." I carry two pink beach towels, a matching set bought for me by my daughter-in-law, Sally, Annie's mother. She pulled the weekend shift in the intensive care unit. Annie loves to sleep in her mother's nursing scrubs. Sally will join the family for dinner after work.

"Now wait till I get there before you jump in the water," I yell to Annie, hoping my voice travels faster than her spindled legs. *It's lucky I'm still a good swimmer.* The virtue of patience has not yet been bestowed upon my fearless granddaughter. I hurry along the three-foot high granite retaining wall at the water's edge. Annie's bare feet slap the weathered wooden slats of the dock. A fresh coat of paint is already on the end-of-the-season, long honey-do list tacked up in the shed. The out-building is also in need of a facelift.

Gary and I had a busy spring. It prevented us from completing all the upkeep items for the lake house. We both semi-retired last year. We sold the condo in Nashua and moved up to the lake full-time. Life is full of surprises, "curve balls" as Gary calls them. He nearly struck out last fall, a moderate heart attack. "No big deal," he told the kids. "A minor hiccup. Don't worry."

Everyone did worry, even Gary. Now, nine months later, he is in the best shape of his life. He always told me that hope and fear were the two greatest motivators in life. I am sure both emotions played a part in his realigned priorities: less work, healthier lifestyle, and more time with family.

I reach the end of the dock, setting the beach towels on the white plastic lounge chair. "Annie, let's cover your body with sun block. We don't want you to burn."

Annie stands at the end of the dock, her tiny toes curled over the edge of the wood, perched and ready to jump into the four feet deep clear turquoise water. "Hurry Grammy, I want to swim out to Luke and Grandpa."

Gary is standing neck deep in the lake, holding an eight foot long blue plastic kayak. Grandfather and grandson are a good horseshoe's throw away; the gentle slope of the lakeshore enables us to walk far out into the water. Luke is using the kayak as a diving platform and Annie wants to get in on the fun.

I lavishly apply sun block to her skin, momentarily converting it from lightly tanned to stark white as I rub in the lotion. Her skin is warm and smooth. I feel the reflected heat of the sun on the surface of my fingers. I resist the urge to wrap my arms around her, engulfing her essence in mine. She is literally itching to get in the water. A small patch of blistering poison ivy adorns her left ankle, now a dusty pink from dried calamine.

"Okay, Pumpkin, let me get in first." I jump into the cool water and quickly turn back to the dock, anticipating my granddaughter catapulting toward me. Much to my surprise, she waits for my cue. I ease away from the dock, extending both arms back toward Annie. "Jump." My words are crossed in mid-air by Annie, her arms and legs in a disjointed ballet of movement. She splashes down just in front of me, spraying glistening droplets of water in all directions. I scoop my hands under her arms, pulling her out from under the water and up against my chest. Her hair is matted against her scalp.

"Let me go, Grammy." Annie's arms and legs churn as she remains anchored to me. I push her toward open water, releasing the youngest precious gosling of my flock. I follow behind in her wake, her hands and feet pounding the water into submission. I think, *God help those who block her path to future accomplishments.*

We reach the kayak. Annie propels herself up out of the water in one fluid motion looking like a dolphin performing at a water park. She stops next to her brother, almost knocking him into the lake.

"Watch it, Annie," Luke warns.

"Sorry." Annie slides away from him by pushing forcefully on the edge of the kayak. It tips backwards and sends her brother head over heels into the water.

"Nice move, Annie," Gary said. "You might want to get away before he comes up and grabs you."

Annie slithers into the water as her brother emerges from the depths, looking for revenge. Annie paddles toward me in search of safe harbor.

"Annie!" Luke screams with water spraying from his mouth as his head pops out of the lake. He curls both of his tanned arms over the top of the kayak. "I'm gonna get you."

"Easy Luke," I said. "It was an accident."

Annie wraps her arms around my neck, her legs still in motion creating white bubbles on the surface of the water—her own personal motorboat.

"Come on, Luke," Gary said. "Let's take the kayak around the lake."

Luke smiles, distracted. "Okay, I'll get the paddles." Luke dips under the kayak, emerging on the opposite side, only a few feet from Annie and me. He peers at his sister, sending a laser-guided jet of water through the gap in his front teeth—a direct hit on Annie's forehead. "Take that," Luke said, water dribbling out the corners of his mouth.

Annie wails and her tears mix with the lake water running over her face. I tuck her against my neck, the combined mixture now moistening my shoulder, her scarecrow-like body convulsing against mine. "It's okay, Pumpkin. Let's go back to the dock and dry off." I look at Luke, furrowing my brow. "Young man, tell her you're sorry or it's out of the water."

Luke turns toward Grandpa who tilts his head to the right. A gust of wind almost knocks the Red Sox baseball cap off his head.

"Go on, Luke. You know Grammy means business. I wouldn't cross her." Gary sends me a wink beneath the bill of the home team.

Luke turns back to me. The muscles on his face tighten, pulling his brown eyebrows nearly together. "Okay. I'm sorry...Can I still go out with Grandpa on the kayak?"

"Sure." I turn toward the shore and make my way back to the dock. Looking back over my shoulder, I see Gary scooping Luke up out of the water. My grandson climbs up on his Grandpa's shoulders. *All is forgiven*, I think. *More water under the bridge.*

✳ ✳ ✳

"Daddy, Daddy, Luke spit on me," Annie said as she wiggles in my arms.

"What?" Nick R drops the sports page in his lap and pulls off his black plastic sunglasses. He starts to push out of the lounge chair, his face flush with an expression I recognize, "Where is that brother of yours? Just wait till I get my hands on him!"

I gently drop Annie into her father's arms, preventing my protective son from gaining momentum in the direction of the lake. I rest my left hand on his shoulder. "All is well, Nick, Luke apologized. There were shots fired from both sides of the sibling battlefield."

Nick looks into the glaring sun, still able to see Luke and Grandpa paddling the kayak. They head west, toward a shallow section of the lake that separates the shore from a small island. Only non-motorized watercraft can pass over the sandbar that is covered with less than two feet of water. Kids, and adults alike, love to walk out to the island. It's a real thrill to "walk on water."

"Let them go," I said. "Gary loves being out there with the kids, you know that. And Luke loves being with his Grandpa. Let it go. Besides, I am going to braid Annie's hair. Huh Pumpkin?"

"Yippee!" Annie slides out of her father's arms and runs up to me, grabbing my leg. "Mommy loves my hair twisted."

"See? She's fine. Enjoy the paper."

"Thanks, Mom." Nick R takes a long pull on his bottle of beer. He replaces his sunglasses and relaxes back in the chair.

There is a new sly smile on my son's face, one I remember from when I was frustrated as the parent of young children. I wink at Nick, wondering if he's thinking: *Maybe the Grandparents would like to keep the kids for a few weeks this summer. Wouldn't that be nice!* I'll talk to Gary before I offer, already knowing he would love the company.

"Annie," I said, "let's get the beads and the rubber bands. We'll set you on a stool next to Daddy."

"Okay." She releases my leg, having already forgotten about her brother and his makeshift weapon, courtesy of his missing front teeth. "Come on, Grammy," Annie said, as she slightly flexes her knees, pulls her arms in tight against her body, and shakes her bottom back and forth, "twist me."

Nick and I burst out laughing.

❊ ❊ ❊

Through the large kitchen window, I see Luke and Gary easing the kayak up against the metal support posts of the dock. Luke jumps into the water to grab the tie-line, securing the white nylon rope through the aluminum eyelet on the bow. Gary is next into the water, performing the same maneuver at the stern. As Gary wades toward the shore, Luke jumps up on his back. As they walk toward the house, Luke reaches forward, pulling off his Grandpa's baseball cap and placing it on his own head. Luke, and his six-year old cousin, David, have a stash of Grandpa's baseball caps in their makeshift fort in the storage room above the garage. The boys always sleep on air mattresses amongst the boxes they've arranged to form the walls of their fortress. The sign on the door warns, NO GIRLS.

"Helping Grammy?" Gary asks, as he approaches the window, pressing his nose against the screen.

Annie giggles from her perch standing on a chair next to me at the sink, holding the next brown potato for me to peel. "You look funny, Grandpa." She reaches out and touches the potato to the deformed smoky wire mesh.

"Ouch," Gary said, playfully recoiling. This incites more giggles and a few wiggles from our granddaughter.

I steady Annie and the chair. "You boys clean up for dinner. Everyone else will be here soon."

"Grammy, is Dman coming?" Luke asked.

"Dman will be here, Lman," I said. (My grand boys, Luke and David, call each other Lman and Dman, their superhero adopted names. The comic books have Superman, Batman and Spiderman. Our family has Lman and Dman. The cousins have become so attached to the names that I'm convinced the monikers may someday show up on a legal document such as a diploma or license. I laugh every time I think about it.)

Luke and Grandpa move toward the side door of the house. "Dry off first," I yell.

"Here, Grammy." Annie hands me the next potato to peel. I hear crack, crack, crack, as her beaded strings of hair settle back down upon her head. Enjoying the noise, Annie flips her head back and forth, making island music with her Caribbean style hairdo.

✲ ✲ ✲

I place the last item on the crowded table, the large bowl of potato salad Annie helped me make just one hour ago. We tossed in the trash the few slippery mayonnaise covered pieces that flew from the bowl as Annie wildly stirred the mixture.

"Oops," she said, with each errant blending. For several minutes, there was a chorus of plop, as the piece hit the sea green kitchen tile floor, followed by "oops." I finally cradled her hand in mine, both of us gripping the wooden spoon, completing the task before we needed to peal another bag of Idaho's finest.

I take my seat opposite Gary, lifting Annie into my lap. She wiggles as she settles in, her beads rubbing against my chest. I kiss her reddened cheek, wishing I had applied more sunscreen earlier that morning. I look around the table, absorbing the warmth and permanence of the gathered generations. It is the simplest pleasures of life that hold the greatest meaning.

"Everyone join hands," I said. "Paige, please say grace."

Annie and I reach to my left, grasping her father's hand. Around the table the circle of connection is joined: Nick R to his wife Sally, Sally to their son Luke, Luke to the casted hand of his cousin David (Lman to Dman), David to his father Nick C, Nick C to his father Gary, Gary to Nick C's wife Brenda, Brenda to Jack, Jack to his wife Julie, Julie to Paige's husband Brian, Brian to Paige, and Paige to me and Annie. A longing is felt deep in my core as Ben is missing from the table. He will fly in tomorrow from Arizona. Tomorrow night at dinner, our family will be complete, an unbroken rosary of love. I can't wait.

Paige begins, "Thank you lord for that which we are about to receive. We are blessed beyond words. Please shepherd us forward so we may share our many gifts with those less fortunate than ourselves. Amen."

A chorus of amen's is rapidly followed by the clanging of decorative bowls and treasured family heirloom platters as the bounty is dispersed around the table.

"Uncle Nick, please pass me a burger," Luke said.

Nick C hands his nephew a juicy grilled disk of charbroiled meat on a lightly toasted bun. "Here you go, Lman."

"Uncle Nick," David pointed to the steaming corn on the cob, "please."

Nick R takes his nephew's plate, adds a piece of corn and a dollop of butter. "Here you go, Dman."

A guest at our gathering might be puzzled by this exchange, but our family adjusted many years ago to having two Nick's at the table. My grandsons are never confused. To them, it is either Uncle Nick or Dad, simple as that.

I sit quietly, listening to the exchanges as I cut Annie's and my steak into bit sized pieces. Paige is a physician assistant in a pediatrician's office. Sally is an intensive care nurse. They and Gary share common bonds. They often discuss the latest issues of medical treatments. Jack, Nick C, Brenda, and Nick R, are all in business related fields. If the quartet is not discussing the latest fluctuations in the markets, the trio of boys is bantering about the consequences of the most recent acquisitions by the Red Sox or the Patriots. Brian and Julie are teachers, High School History and Forth Grade English. I chuckle while thinking, *never a dull moment.*

The minutes rapidly flow by, along with the boisterous dialogue. Before I know it, we are pushing away from the table, full of food and fellowship. Gary and I are followed into the kitchen by the girls—sans Annie—who is nestled in her father's arms on the black leather couch with her uncles. Lman and Dman are lying on the floor. All eyes are fixed on the TV—Red Sox and Yankees—Saturday night battle of a three game weekend series. Go Sox's. The entourage of loyal fans will cheer for the next three hours. Jack will call his stepbrother Ben in Arizona several times on his cell phone to discuss controversial calls.

"All right, ladies," Gary says, "you know the routine."

We are all well aware of Gary's aversion to the dishwasher. He commands the spot in front of the sink, churning out spotless items, which are quickly snatched up and dried by me. The next generation places them into the appropriate gray laminate cupboard. The legion of support makes short work of the soiled wares.

Gary joins the spectators in the living room. Julie, Sally and Brenda sit out on the porch, looking west, enjoying the last hour of daylight, anticipating the brilliance of the setting sun against the soon to be blazing maroon horizon. Paige and I go for our traditional after dinner walk, along the deserted railroad tracks just up the street from our home.

I hook my arm in hers, my pink sweater caressing her light blue pullover sweatshirt. She momentarily rests her head on my shoulder as we step along the gravel embankment next to the railroad ties, the faint remnant smell of tar wafting about. The overgrown foliage along the trail is dense. Leaves of every shade of green are visible to our eyes, our pupils dilating in response to the waning daylight. The full moon is cresting the treetops, the only blue moon of the summer, destined to illuminate our way as the sun relinquishes its dominance of the sky. I feel at peace; nature and nurture, mother and daughter.

We walk silently for some time, not needing words to convey our emotions. The only sound is the rhythmic crunch of the gravel beneath our shoes. I sense Paige has something to say, but I let this moment blossom under her guidance.

I pause at the bend in the tracks. She releases my arm and steps in front of me, grasping both of my hands. A radiant smile adorns her face, illuminated by the gentle reflected light of the moon. "Mom, I'm going to have a baby."

"Oh Dolly, I'm so happy." I pull Paige against me, tears streaming down my face. I feel subtle whimpers of happiness rustle between our bodies. A new life is growing in my daughter's body, just as she grew within mine. Life begets life, from mother to daughter and daughter to child. We have a connection of strength and tranquility, a bond achieved by the shared miracles of creating and sustaining life, the wonder and rewards of motherhood.

"Mom." Paige eases her body back from mine, our hands still holding on tight. "I want to wait until tomorrow to tell everyone. I want Ben to be here."

"Okay." I wink. "Your secret's safe with me...and Gary."

"I know." Paige winks back and smiles. "There's no way you'll be able to keep this from him until tomorrow."

"He'll see it in my eyes the moment I walk back in the house. We can go inside through the screened porch off the master bedroom so I don't ruin the surprise. You tell everyone I needed a little rest."

"Sure." Paige leans toward me and kisses my face. "I love you."

"I love you, too."

✳ ✳ ✳

Propped up in bed with three pillows between my back and the dark maple headboard, I aimlessly thumb through a magazine. The light from the ornate lamp on my nightstand glares off the shinny pages. I am bubbling with excitement, waiting for the final out of the ball game and Gary's signature exit refrain from the family evening, "Last one in bed gets the lights."

A colossal cheer shakes the wall. I look up at the bedroom TV, picture on, sound muted. The Red Sox pitcher is in the air, his legs wrapped around the catcher's waist—a win for the Red Sox over the Yankees. All is well in Beantown.

The doorknob turns ever so slightly. "It's okay," I said. "I'm still up."

The door swings open sending a light breeze through the room. "I thought you might be sleeping." Gary closes the door behind him. I hear the snap of metal as the door latches. He starts to walk past the bed, then pauses, looking down at me with a comforting smile. "Hey, Baby." He reaches out with his left hand, placing his roughened palm against my cheek. "You okay?"

I reach out with both arms, clasping my hands behind his neck. The lavender lotion on my hands almost causes my fingers to slip apart. I pull Gary firmly toward me. He pretends to be off balance, cushioning his fall onto the bed by placing his arms down on top of the flower print comforter. He rolls onto his back and I slide up on top of him. I tip my face down, kissing his lips. The heat of the day comes off his auburn face. I pull back, propping my elbows on his chest, my hair draping down on either side of my face.

A sly closed lip grin brightens Gary face and his forehead crinkles as his eyebrows move up. "You and Paige have a nice walk?"

"Most definitely."

"Anything new?"

I enjoy this little game. Gary can tell I am about to explode, and yet he wants me to savor every moment. I can't hold it in any longer, my heart pounding with joy. "Paige is going to have a baby." My eyes fill with tears of happiness and anticipation; another life to nurture and marvel, the next miracle gift. "My baby is going to be a mother." I collapse onto Gary's body. He encases me in his supportive arms.

Gary slowly rolls to the side and I curl in tight next to him, our bodies merging with an imperceptible physical or emotional separation. Moonlight streams through the windows casting a soothing glow about the room. He will hold me in his arms until I drift off to sleep, a reassuring routine in good times and bad. It is a comfort and peace unlike any I have ever known. Fate brought us together, we share a common destiny. There is a new life growing in our family, a vessel to receive our light, and a future beacon to guide the path of others.

chapter 52

LAURI RELAXED IN THE eternal warmth of heaven, her body bathed by endless sunshine. Her soothing and enlightening spiritual quest had begun to unfold, using her memories to create a future. Life happily continued with permanent bonds to family and friends, bridging the terrestrial and the spiritual worlds. Lauri knew she would experience the joys of life alongside her family, never missing a beat of their collective hearts. They too would feel her constant presence. Love is the emotion that gives life, and sustains it.

Lauri thought about all the crossroads we encounter as we go through life. There are so many decisions that are like being on a one-way street; you are never able to go back. We are locked into a journey of compromise. We move forward carrying the consequences of our past with us.

Heaven was different. There were no one-way streets. Along with her memories, Lauri could now use her dreams to create new experiences she hadn't lived on Earth. A chance to walk new paths not previously traveled, a new twist or turn in life.

Lauri was excited to experience new aspects of her life based on alternative choices. She wondered how her life would have been different if: she'd gone to college, moved away from family, had more children, met Gary earlier in life...never gotten cancer. As someone once told her, "It's not the ups and downs of life that drive you crazy, it's all the 'what ifs' along the way."

Lauri smiled thinking how nice it would be for those whose lives on Earth had been filled with sadness and regret. Now, they would have a second chance to experience a happier life.

Lauri's terrestrial and spiritual lives were now perfectly blended. The visions she and Gary shared about the afterlife during her battle with pancreatic cancer had come true, just as he promised. At the time, Lauri knew Gary was attempting to calm her fears and give her hope. The heartfelt generosity of that gift reflected the depth of the love they shared. That gift however was incomplete. When faced with death, we all struggle with the uncertainty of the unknown. It is only by making the transition from a physical being to a spiritual soul that the true miracles of our hopes and beliefs become real. We live again, sustained by the rejuvenating breath of eternal life.

EPILOGUE

Amanda envisioned sitting at the miniature dining room set her father had built three years ago for her fourth birthday. It was time for afternoon tea and she prepared to serve her guests, a true menagerie of lifelong close friends and her favorite set of four legged companions. There was Fluffy the rabbit, Whiskers the cat and Buster the dog. This was the first party, for as long as she could remember, without an intravenous line getting tangled in her attempts to be the perfect hostess, just like her mommy had taught her. The excited guests had their own teacup and saucer and a plate of fresh assorted cookies. To Amanda's left was an unoccupied place setting for any unexpected guests. "Always be prepared," her mom used to say.

Gone was the suffering from with the malignant brain tumor with which Amanda had attempted to cohabitate. The cancer had tired of sharing her little body, and took it for its own. Cancer endlessly strived for inhabitation rather than cohabitation. The last year of her life barely allowed her to attend half of second grade. Amanda remembered the endless needle sticks followed by the congratulatory sticker placed on her arm as a badge of honor, acknowledging her bravery to endure the unending violations. Gone were the long car rides home after her chemotherapy; her father driving and Amanda stretched out in the back seat with her head half in her mother's comforting lap and half in the ever present bucket.

Amanda had been able to feel her mother's body tense in frightened anticipation, knowing her brave little angel would again be convulsing as if her body was attempting to expel the cancer by exorcism. If only that had been true. Amanda's mother experienced her own grinding emotional death as she witnessed the cancer abduct her baby girl. She would willingly, and without the slightest hesitation, have substituted her own death for the demise of her only child. When an adult is stricken with cancer it is unfair. Inhumane is inadequate to describe a child with cancer.

Amanda sensed an adult in her presence and their form slowly materialized in the unoccupied chair. The female guest, like Amanda, was smartly dressed in her Sunday finest and wore a spring bonnet matching her own. Amanda recognized the woman's features. She was tall and slender with a warm and gentle face and a twinkle in her eyes. Amanda immediately felt the deepest sense of comfort in the presence of her unexpected companion.

The gathering was all the rave on the second grade party circuit. It was a tough invitation to come by. There were many hopefuls left on the shelf awaiting their next opportunity to share the cherished table of honor. All the guests were polite and courteous. The conversation was decidedly one sided as Amanda loved to talk, a trait she shared with her mom.

As the gathering neared its end, Amanda thanked everyone for coming. She escorted Fluffy, Whiskers and Buster back to their respective homes scattered around her room. She felt a warm embrace as an arm stretch across her back, reminiscent of her mother's habit of pulling her near as they crossed the street together. Amanda felt the same all-consuming love and security of her own mother's touch.

Amanda tilted her head up as her body was wrapped in a familiar embrace. A smile of recognition and serenity graced her face. "Hi, Ms. Lauri."

Lauri's hand stroked the beautiful thick curled brunette locks that cascaded down to Amanda's shoulders which now rested against Lauri's hips. "Hi Sweet-pea."

The brilliant sun streaking through the window made Amanda's eyes sparkle. "Can we go for ice cream, Ms. Lauri?"

"Most definitely." Lauri knelt down, her nose almost touching Amanda's. "Of course, we will cover it with jimmies."

"Oh goodie!" Amanda's eyes widened. "Jimmies are my favorite...Mom's too." Amanda rested her head on Lauri's shoulder. "Can Mommy come?"

Lauri's arms surrounded Amanda's perfectly healthy body. "Of course she can." Lauri reached up and gently lifted Amanda's head from her shoulder. Lauri looked into Amanda's eyes with soothing warmth and unwavering confidence. "Your Mommy will come to you whenever you think of her." Lauri placed her hands on Amanda's cheeks. "She and I will be with you forever."

Amanda tilted her head to the side and a faint smile creased her lips. "Promise?"

"Yes, Sweet-pea. Promise."

Made in the USA
Middletown, DE
13 February 2015